**Volume 19**

# Organizational Behavior II
Managerial & Social Psychology, Human Resource Accounting, Leadership, Diversity, Skills, Sensemaking, Organizational Development

**Business Administration
Reading Lists and Course Outlines**

Compiled by Richard Schwindt, *Simon Fraser University*
September 1995

## NOTE TO THE USER

This is the fourth compilation of the Business Administration series of reading lists and course outlines. It is gratifying that acceptance of the series has warranted a new, completely revised set of materials. It is also gratifying that the request for contributions to this series was met with the strongest response ever. As a result, the collection is substantially larger than the 1990 version.

The intention is to disseminate quickly and efficiently information on what is currently being taught, and how it is being taught in leading business schools. It is recognized that there is a trade-off between rapid diffusion and polished appearance. The former has been emphasized. I hope that users of these volumes will agree, recognizing that nearly all of the outlines and syllabi pertain to courses given within the last year.

These volumes will be useful to both individual teachers and curriculum committees when revising existing courses and creating new ones. They will also be helpful for librarians responsible for acquisitions in the business area. But, as before, there is a less modest goal. Between publication in academic journals and integration into mainstream textbooks, scholarly research passes through the transition stage of classroom exposure. Hopefully, these volumes will facilitate that transition.

## ACKNOWLEDGEMENTS

I thank my colleagues, Graeme Coetzer, Irene Gordon, John Herzog and Bert Schoner, for compilation assistance in their respective areas of expertise.

Richard Schwindt, *Simon Fraser University*

---

© Eno River Press, Inc. 1995. All rights reserved. No part of this publication may be reproduced, stored in a retrieval system, or transmitted, in any form or by any means, electronic, mechanical, photocopying, recording or otherwise, without the prior permission of Eno River Press.

Eno River Press
115 Stoneridge Drive
Chapel Hill, North Carolina 27514-9737
U.S.A.
Fax & Phone: (919) 967-8246

ISBN for Volume 19: 0-88024-179-9
ISBN Eno River Press for this series: 0-88024-159-4
Library of Congress Catalog Number: 95-061171

# VOLUME 19

## ORGANIZATIONAL BEHAVIOR II
MANAGERIAL & SOCIAL PSYCHOLOGY, HUMAN RESOURCE ACCOUNTING, LEADERSHIP, DIVERSITY, SKILLS, SENSEMAKING, ORGANIZATIONAL DEVELOPMENT

Tom Allen, *Massachusetts Institute of Technology*
**Managerial Psychology** ............................................................................... 5

William Bigoness, Tom Bateman and Ben Rosen, *University of North Carolina*
**Management Competencies** ...................................................................... 13

Lorna Catford, *Stanford University*
**Personal Creativity in Business** ................................................................. 32

John L. Colley, Jr. and Robert Fair, *University of Virginia*
**Reading Seminars in Management** ........................................................... 48

Eric Flamholtz, *University of California - Los Angeles*
**Management of Human Resources** ........................................................... 63

Mary Gentile, *Harvard University*
**Differences that Work: Managerial Effectiveness through Diversity** ....... 107

Alexander Horniman, *University of Virginia*
**Managerial Psychology** .............................................................................. 122

Herminia Ibarra, *Harvard University*
**LEAD** ......................................................................................................... 125

Toby Kahr, *Duke University*
**Power and Influence in Organizations** ..................................................... 129

James March, *Stanford University*
**Organizational Leadership** ....................................................................... 135

Debra Meyerson, Jerry Porras, David Bradford and Jim Thompson, *Stanford University*
**Learning to Lead** ....................................................................................... 141

Debra Meyerson, *Stanford University*
**The Organization of Women and Men** .................................................... 155

Larry Moore, *University of British Columbia*
  **Organizational Change and Development** ................................................. 160

Charles B. Perrow, *Yale University*
  **Organizations and Society** ........................................................................ 164

Robert J. Robinson, *Harvard University*
  **Social Behavior in Organizations** .............................................................. 169

Mitch Rothstein, *University of Western Ontario*
  **Career Management** ................................................................................. 175

Kathleen Sutcliffe, *University of Minnesota*
  **Sensemaking in Organizations** ................................................................. 189

Kathleen Sutcliffe, *University of Minnesota*
  **Organizations and the Management of Change** ......................................... 195

Ross Webber, *University of Pennsylvania*
  **The Individual in the Organization** ........................................................... 200

Karl Weick, *University of Michigan*
  **Social Psychology of Organizing** .............................................................. 212

Rod White, Mary Crossan and Harry Lane, *University of Western Ontario*
  **Renewing Organizations** .......................................................................... 225

Marvin Zonis, *University of Chicago*
  **Theories of Leadership** ............................................................................ 236

Prof. Tom Allen

# MANAGERIAL PSYCHOLOGY LABORATORY
## (15.301)

### Course Requirements

I. <u>Term Project</u> (Two copies due **May 18**)
The term project will be performed in groups of four students. The group should choose a problem at MIT which can be attacked using behavioral science research methods. Shop around for a group, office or committee that is in need of data. Arrange a time for a group meeting with your TA during the week of February 21-24 to discuss your choice of topic. <u>Two copies</u> of the final draft of the project paper are due by noon on <u>May 18</u>. **LATE PROJECTS WILL BE PENALIZED SEVERELY IN GRADING.**

II. <u>Research Proposal</u> (**March 13**)
<u>Each member</u> of your group is required to do this assignment alone. After your group has decided on a project topic, each member is expected to conduct background (library) research. Look through published materials and find other studies which have addressed similar questions. Note what hypotheses, experimental designs, population samples, types of analysis, and results previous researchers have documented. This process will give you ideas for formulating and refining hypotheses for your group's project.

Next synthesize the information obtained and integrate it into a well formulated research proposal (as detailed by the handout distributed in recitation). A research proposal is a paper which explains and justifies how and why you are pursuing the particular piece of inquiry you intend to undertake. The purpose of the proposal is twofold:
(1) a proposal forces the author to think seriously about the topic;
(2) the proposal provides others with a brief but coherent understanding of the research endeavor.

III. <u>Homework</u>
There will be two short very assignments due in recitation. They are designed to develop your understanding of methodological and statistical tools and concepts.

IV. <u>Two Quizzes</u> (**March 20** and May 18)
There will be two in-class quizzes which will cover the lecture readings and discussions (not recitation related material).

| RELATIVE CONTRIBUTIONS TOWARD COURSE GRADE | |
|---|---|
| Research Proposal (Individual) | 10% |
| Midterm Quiz (Individual) | 20% |
| Final Quiz (Individual) | 25% |
| Term Project (Group) | 30% |
| Homework, Peer Evaluations, Recitation Attendance/Participation | 15% |

# MANAGERIAL PSYCHOLOGY
## Lecture Assignments
**15.301/15.310**　　　　　　　　　　　　　　　　　　　　**Spring 1995**

February 8　　**Introduction and Group Formation**
At the end of class, students will be helped to meet and form groups for the term project.
Buerschaper, Donahue, Gray, Marceau, Marmah, and Wong, **15.301 Handbook,** pp. 1-9. (Available through MIT Graphics in the basement of E52, the Sloan Building)

February 13　　**Overview of Organizations**
Steers & Black, Chapters 1 & 2.
**Attitudes and Attitude Change**
Steers & Black, Chapter 3.
Leavitt et al., Chapter 3, Mark Snyder, *Self-fulfilling stereotypes*
Leavitt et. al.,Chapter 3, Robert Cialdini, *Commitment and consistency*

February 15　　**Problem Solving & Decision-Making**
Steers & Black, Chapter 4 and Chapter 14, pp 472 - 495.
Leavitt et. al., John Hayes, *Cognitive processes in creative acts*
**Motivation**
Steers & Black, Chapters 5 & 6.
Leavitt et al., Chapter 1, David Nadler & Edward Lawler, *Motivation: A diagnostic approach*
Leavitt et al., Chapter 1, Barry Staw, *Intrinsic and extrinsic motivation*

February 21　　**Group Norms and Conformity I** *(Please note that this is a Tuesday.)*
Steers & Black, Chapter 8.
Leavitt et. al.,Chapter 3, Elliot Aronson, *The rationalizing animal*

February 22　　**Group Norms and Conformity II**
Leavitt et. al., Edgar Schein, *Management development as a process of influence*
Leavitt et. al., Irving Janis, *Groupthink*
Leavitt et. al., Kenwyn Smith, *An intergroup perspective on individual behavior*

| | |
|---|---|
| February 27 | **Group Decision Making I**<br>Steers & Black, Chapter 14, pp. 495 - 519. |
| March 1 | **Group Decision Making II**<br>Leavitt et. al., Chapter 7, Harold Leavitt, *Suppose we took groups seriously*<br>Leavitt et. al., Chapter 9, John Kotter, *What effective general managers really do*. |
| March 6 | **Leadership I**<br>Steers & Black, Chapter 12 |
| March 8 | **Leadership II**<br>Leavitt et. al, Chapter 5, Edgar Schein, *The role of the founder in creating an organizational culture*<br>Leavitt et. al., Chapter 4, Dafna Izraeli and Todd Jick, *The art of saying no* |
| March 13 | **(15.301 Only) Individual Research Proposal Due** |
| March 13 | **Leadership III**<br>Steers & Black, Chapter 15<br>Leavitt et. al., Chapter 6, Gerald Salancik and Jeffrey Pfeffer, *Who gets power -- and how they hold on to it*<br>Leavitt et. al., Chapter 6, Michael Moch and Anne Huff, *Power enactment through language and ritual* |
| March 15 | **Career Development I**<br>Steers & Black, Chapter 7 |
| March 20 | **Midterm Quiz** |
| March 22 | **No Course XV Classes** |
| March 27 - 31 | **Spring Break** |
| April 3 | **Career Development II**<br>Steers & Black, Chapter 18<br>Leavitt & al., Chapter 10, Richard Pascale, *Fitting new employees into the company culture* |

| | |
|---|---|
| April 5 | **Career Development III**<br>Katz, Ralph *Organizational socialization*, in **Managing Professionals in Innovative Organizations** (On Reserve in Dewey Library) |
| April 10 | **Organization Structure & Design**<br>Steers & Black, Chapter 10. |
| April 12 | **Organization Structure & Design**<br>Steers & Black, Chapters 10 & 11. |
| April 17 | **Holiday** |
| April 19 | **Communication in Organizations I**<br>Leavitt et al., Chapter 9, Robert Kaplan, Trade routes: *manager's networks of relationships*<br>Leavitt et. al., Henry Mintzberg, Chapter 9, *Managerial work: Analysis from observation* |
| April 24 | **Communication in Organizations II**<br>Steers & Black, Chapter 13<br>Allen, Ch. 7, *Structuring Organizational Communication Networks 1: The Influence of Formal and Informal Organization* (On Reserve in Dewey Library) |
| April 26 | **Matrix Organizations I**<br>Allen & Katz, *The locus of influence in the R&D matrix* (On Reserve in Dewey Library) |
| May 1 | **Matrix Organizations II**<br>Allen, *Organizational structure, information technology and R&D Productivity* (OnReserve in Dewey Library) |
| May 3 | **Architecture and Communication I**<br>Allen, Chapter 8, *Structuring Organizational Communication Networks 2: The Influence of Architecture on Communication* (On Reserve in Dewey Library.) |
| May 8 | **Architecture and Communication II**<br>Readings to be assigned. |
| May 10 | **Final Quiz** |

May 15    **Changing Organizations I**
Leavitt et. al., John Kotter and Leonard Schlesinger, Chapter 11, *Choosing strategies for change*
Leavitt et. al., James Quinn, Chapter 11, *Managing strategies incrementally*
Leavitt et. al., Eric Flamnholtz, Chapter 11, *Managing the stages of organizational growth*

May 17    **Changing Organizations II**
Steers & Black, Chapter 19
Leavitt et. al., Harold Leavitt, William Dill and Henry Eyring, *Strategies for survival:*
Leavitt et. al., David Boje and Terence Wolfe, *Transorganizational development*

May 18    **15.301 Final Project Due.**

# MANAGERIAL PSYCHOLOGY LABORATORY
## Recitation/Lab Section Schedule

**15.301**  **Spring 1995**

| Week: | Content/Reading/*Assignment Due* |
|---|---|
| 1. FEB 6-8 | **No Recitations** |
| 2. FEB 13-15 | Introduction to class/project requirements and an overview of research. Type of research problems, problem statements and hypothesis<br>Readings:<br>    Judd, Smith & Kidder, Ch. 14, Applied and Evaluation Research<br>    Judd, Smith & Kidder, Ch. 1, Acquiring Social Knowledge<br>    Judd, Smith & Kidder, Ch. 2, Examining Social Relations Research |
| 3. FEB 20-22 | **No Recitations**, BUT each group MUST schedule a meeting with their TA to discuss their chosen research topic. |
| 4. FEB 27-MAR 1 | Issues in Research Methods: Variables, measurement, reliability, validity<br>Readings:<br>    Judd, Smith & Kidder, Ch. 3, Measurement,<br>    Judd, Smith & Kidder, Ch. 4, Randomized Experiments<br>    Judd, Smith & Kidder, Ch. 5, Quasi-Experimental Designs, pp. 100-117,<br>***Recitation Homework: Nomological Net*** |
| 5. MAR 6-8 | Questionnaire Design: Layout, writing questions, problems to avoid, pretesting<br>Readings:<br>    Judd, Smith & Kidder, Ch. 10, Questionnaires and Interviews: Overview<br>    Judd, Smith & Kidder, Ch. 11, Questionnaires, Interviews: Asking Ques. |
| 6. MAR 13-15 | Introduction to Statistics: Sampling, frequency distribution, descriptive statistics<br>Reading:<br>    Judd, Smith & Kidder, Ch. 15, Coding Data and Describing Distributions,<br><br>***Individual research proposals due Wednesday, March 13*** |
| 7. MAR 20-22 | **No Recitations**<br><br>**Quiz #1 March 20**, Question and Answer session TBA |
| 8. MAR 27-29 | Spring Break, No Recitations |
| 9. APR 3-5 | Inferential Statistics: Sampling Distributions, differences between means, etc.<br>Reading:<br>    Judd, Smith & Kidder, Ch. 9, Practical Sampling,<br><br>***COUHES form due in recitation*** |

10. APR 10-12    Handling Nominal and Ordinal Data: Analysis of cross tabulations, chi square.
    Readings:
    Judd, Smith & Kidder, Ch. 16 Describing Relationships between Variables, pp. 373-379.
    Judd, Smith & Kidder, Ch. 17, Controlling for Third Variables pp. 408-413.

11. APR 17-19    Patriot's Day, No Recitations

12. APR 24-26    Correlation & Regression
    Readings:
    Judd, Smith & Kidder, Ch. 16, Describing Relationships between Variables, pp. 380-407.
    Judd, Smith & Kidder, Ch. 17, Controlling for Third Variables, pp. 414-424

    **Recitation Homework: Statistics**

13. MAY 1-3    Report Preparation: Providing guidelines for final report writing
    Reading:
    Judd, Smith & Kidder, Ch. 19, Writing the Research Report

14. MAY 8-10    No Recitations

    **Quiz #2 May 10, Question and Answer session TBA**

15. May 15-17    Project Presentations, Peer Evaluations, Recitation Feedback

    **2 copies of Final Project report due May 18.**

# BA 251-Management Competencies

## Fall, 1994

| Instructors: | Sections | Office (phone) |
|---|---|---|
| Professor Tom Bateman | Sections A,D | 314 Old Carroll (2-3128) |
| Professor Bill Bigoness | Sections B,E | 310 Old Carroll (2-3144) |
| Professor Ben Rosen | Sections C,F | 313 Old Carroll (2-3166) |

### Introduction and Course Objectives

Welcome to Management Competencies. The focus of the course is on helping you gain insights into your managerial strengths and areas for additional development, build a personal development plan, and improve your ability to manage and lead yourself and others.

Classes are small to provide for plenty of discussion, interaction, and feedback. We will use self-diagnostic instruments, cases, and other approaches designed to help build your management competencies. You will have opportunities to develop and practice your managerial skills in special management development workshops (September 2 and October 7), in your study groups, working on projects for other classes and in the Kenan-Flagler business simulation. The goal is for each MBA student to develop the managerial and leadership skills necessary in today's business environment.

### Course Materials

1. Covey, S.R. *The 7 Habits of Highly Effective People* Simon & Schuster, 1989.

2. Byham, W. and Cox, J. *Zapp: The Lightning of Empowerment* Fawcett Books, 1988.

3. Hill, Linda *Becoming a Manager*, Harvard Business School Press, 1992

4. *Collection of cases and readings.* Available from MBA Entrepreneurship Club

Course Evaluation:

Course evaluation is based on three components: a personal development plan, class contribution, and a team-based final exam.

The personal development plan is a five-page written plan describing 1) the results of your Covey Seven Habits Profile analysis; 2) a personal mission statement; 3) a set of specific self-improvement goals, and 4) an action plan for attaining your personal goals. Guidelines for preparing the personal development plan are attached to the syllabus.

Course contribution includes in-class participation and any and all additional activities that contribute to making the course a valuable learning experience for your classmates. It refers broadly to being an active, contributing "good citizen" of the course. This component could include any number of contributions such as in-class contribution, overall commitment and involvement, and helping your colleagues outside of class.

The grade for course contribution will derive 50% from my evaluation, which will include consideration of your personal assessment of your contribution. The other 50% will derive from peer evaluations.

The following weights will be used in determining final grades:

| | |
|---|---|
| Personal Development Plan | 33.3% |
| Class Contribution | 33.3% |
| Class presentations | 33.3% |

Important Dates:

| | |
|---|---|
| Covey workshop | Sept. 2 (a Friday!) Carolina Inn--University Ballrooms |
| Personal development plan due | Sept. 23 |
| Team-building workshop | Oct. 7 (a Friday!) New Carroll Classrooms |
| Presentations from Becoming a Manager | Sept 19 and Oct 3 |

## Course Policies

1. Classes begin at scheduled times. Please be prompt. Important administrative announcements will be made at the beginning of class. Also, it is very disruptive to have class members walk in when class is in session.

2. Everyone is expected to attend every class and contribute to the learning experience. Norms for the MBA program include preparation before class (thoroughly reading materials and reflecting on study questions) and substantive participation in class. Students and faculty share the responsibility for creating a positive learning environment.

3. Class discussions of cases will likely reveal a variety of perspectives. Attempt to be a "critical evaluator" when you listen to others. Be open to others' opinions and approaches to resolving managerial problems. Support positions of others based on your analysis and managerial experiences. Challenge ideas with which you disagree. Work hard to help the class reconcile differing opinions and reach closure.

4. At the request of the MBA Program Office and the UNC Judicial Program, your attention is called to the UNC Honor Code. For purposes of this class, all individual written work must reflect your personal analysis and presentation. This is not to preclude discussions within your study groups, but the work submitted must be your own. More specifically, discussions with former class members about written assignments is considered a violation of the UNC Honor Code.

Date:        Monday, August 29, 1994; #1

Topic:       Self-Management I

Objectives:
1. To discuss the management style of a general manager, and the competencies needed to be successful.

2. To discuss the importance of self-awareness in managing one's self, and others.

3. To discuss our mutual expectations for the course.

Assignment:
1. Learning by the Case Method
2. Case: Warner-Cable (A)
3. Covey: <u>7 Habits of Highly Successful People</u>, (pp15-62)

Study Questions:
1. Is Bruce McKinnon a good manager? Why/why not?

2. Would you want to work for him?

3. What additional "habits" does McKinnon need to be an effective manager?

4. If you were Gray, what would you say to, or do about, McKinnon?

Date:             Wednesday, August 31, 1994; #2

Topic:            Self-Management II.

Objectives:
1. To learn to think proactively
2. To examine how to take personal responsibility for change
3. To begin thinking about a personal developmental plan for strengthening managerial competencies

Assignment:

1. Stephen Covey: __7 Habits__  Habits 1 and 2

2. What ever happened to the take charge manager

Study Questions:

1. Among the habits described by Covey, which do you especially wish to develop?

2. Identify a situation, which you recently have experienced or anticipate experiencing soon, and describe a reactive response you exhibited or probably would exhibit. Then, describe a proactive response. What might be the different consequences for the two approaches?

3. Why are managers so susceptible to "flavor of the month" ideas? Have you seen this in your previous work experience?

4. What does it take to manage "pragmatically"?

5. How can you apply the ideas presented in "Whatever happened to the take charge manager" to your experiences in the MBA program and particularly to the readings in Management Competencies?

Friday, September 2, 1994

Topic: **Covey Workshop ....Carolina Inn University Ballrooms**

Objectives:

1. To learn about our strengths and weaknesses from the feedback of others with whom we have worked closely.

2. To begin building a personal development plan

3. To identify a coach who will provide support and feedback on our progress.

Representatives from the Covey Institute will distribute Seven Habits Profiles to each student. They will guide students in the interpretation of their personal feedback and provide a structure for building a personal development plan.

Wednesday, September 7, 1994; #3

Topic: Stress and Time Management

Objectives:

1. To identify major MBA stressors.
2. To examine a variety of coping mechanisms to reduce stress.
3. To learn time management skills that will help reduce stress.

Assignment:

1. Covey: <u>7 Habits</u> . .Habit 3
2. Burnout Questionnaire

Study Questions:

1. Make a list of the major causes of stress in your life.
2. What are the mental and physical consequences of operating under high levels of stress?
3. Make a list of your major time killers.
4. What is meant by the "Type A" personality? Are you a Type A?
5. Based on your own experiences, what are the least and most effective ways to cope with stress?

Date:       Monday, September 12, 1994    #4

Topic:      Career Management

Objectives:
1. To examine the changing relationship between organizations and managers.
2. To consider different definitions of career success.
3. To consider the price of career success.
4. To identify principles of effective career management.

Assignment:

1. Toward a career resilient work force

2. Case: Jane Moore--An Executive Woman's Career Story

Study Questions:

1. How has the "contract" between managers and their organizations changed during the past decade?

2. Given the new work relationship, what does it take to manage your own career?

3. What is your personal definition of career success? How will your definition fit with organizational expectations?

4. What special obstacles did Jane Moore face as a woman in a predominantly male corporate culture? Do minority employees face similar or different obstacles in white male cultures.

5. What were some of the defining moments and important events that helped Jane Moore achieve rapid career progress? What did she do right?

6. What is your reaction to Jane Moore's balance between her professional and personal life? Is it possible to achievement-oriented managers to have a personal life? How?

Date:             Wednesday, September 14, 1993; #5

Topic:            Power, Politics and Influence

Objectives:
   1. To discuss the (in)effectiveness of a manager's response to potential organizational change
   2. To discuss tactics that may more effectively influence top management
   3. To consider tactics for managing "up"

Assignment:
   1. Case: Donna Dubinsky and Apple Computer (A)
   2. Gabarro: Managing your boss.

Study Questions:
   1. Initially, was Donna Dubinsky managing her career well? Why/why not?
   2. How and why did things unravel? What should she have done differently?
   3. What additional "habits" does Dubinsky need to be an effective manager?
   4. An important part of career management is managing relations with your boss. Outline a brief orientation for newcomers on the dos and don'ts of managing your boss.

Date:        Monday, September 19, 1994   #6

Topic:       Becoming a Manager:  Group Presentations

Objectives:

1. To learn from new managers about their greatest challenges.

2. To convey all the important points of an important management book in a unique way.

3. To give you an experience making a presentation to your new colleagues.

Assignment

Your study team will be assigned one chapter from <u>Becoming a Manager</u>.  It is your team's responsibility to design and deliver to the class a 20 minute presentation on the material.  Your overriding objective is to help your classmates learn.  The best presentations will be creative, informative, and professional.  Here are some guidelines for your presentation:

1. Start and finish on time

2. Have both one-way and two-way communication.  In other words, a portion of the time should be spent conveying information, and a portion spent interacting with the class.

3. Have a one page handout with key learning points.

4. Be innovative.

Date:     Wednesday, September 21, 1994; #7

Topic:    Managing Conflict

Objectives:

1. To discuss five styles for managing conflict, and the circumstances in which each are the most effective.

2. To discuss which of these five styles of managing conflict characterize <u>you</u>, and the implications of this for you as a manager and study group member.

Assignment:

1. Case: Sturdivant Electric

2. Conflict management self-assessment instrument Complete and score the conflict style self assessment. In class, we will discuss how to interpret your score.

3. Covey: Paradigm of Interdependence and Habit #4 (pp.185-234).

Study Questions:

1. Think of personal experiences depicting any three of the six paradigms of human interaction (Covey pg. 206) and describe the consequences.

2. What factors led up to the conflict between Eden and Abrams in the Sturdivant Electric Case?

3. What are the consequences of leaving the conflict unresolved for Abrams? Eden? Sturdivant Electric?

4. Assume that you are in Harris Johnson's position at Sturdivant Electric. Develop an action plan for how and when you might intervene to resolve the conflict between Eden and Abrams?

Date:     Monday September 26, 1994; #8

Topic:    Communication

Objectives:

1. To discuss characteristics of giving feedback that are effective and ineffective.

2. To discuss characteristics of receiving feedback that are effective and ineffective.

Assignment:

1. Case: Bob Knowlton

2. Argyris: Teaching Smart People How to Learn

3. Covey: <u>7 Habits</u> . Habit 5  (pp 235-260)

Study Questions:

1. What are the major communications problems illustrated in the Bob Knowlton Case? Who is responsible for each problem?

2. What is your prediction of how Bob Knowlton responds to the situation in the weeks following Fester's presentation?

3. You're smart and, generally, successful. According to Argyris, what is likely to impede your ability to learn?

4. What <u>specific</u> actions can you take to enhance your chance of learning in the classroom? In your study group? In your next job?

Date: Wednesday, September 28, 1994; #9

Topic: Managers and Leaders

Objectives:
1. To examine the role requirements for effective managers.
2. To compare the roles of managers and leaders.

Assignment:
1. Kotter: What Leaders Really Do
2. Zalesnik: Managers and leaders, how they differ
3. Case: Fred Henderson
4. Case: Renn Zaphoropolious

Study Questions:
1. Think of someone you believe is/was a great manager. Is this person also a great leader? Why/why not?
2. Think of someone you believe is/was a great leader. Is this person also a great manager? Why/why not?
3. How do managers differ from leaders? <u>Should</u> they differ?
4. Compare Fred Henderson and Renn Zaphoropolious in terms of effective managerial skills and effective leadership skills. Cite specific examples from the cases where each demonstrated managerial competencies and leadership qualities. Who would you prefer to work with--and why?

Date: Monday, October 3, 1994  #10

Topic: Becoming a Manager: Group Presentations

Objectives: Refer to the information for Monday, September 19 for guidelines on making group presentations.

Date:       Wednesday, October 5, 1994; #11

Topic:      Delegating Power, and Empowering Employees

Objectives:
1. To examine the relationship between delegation and empowerment
2. To identify current corporate efforts to empower employees
3. To consider the benefits and costs of empowerment

Assignment:
1. <u>ZAPP</u> (first half)
2. MacGregor
3. Case: Nigel Andrews and General Electric Plastics

Study Questions:
1. What factors sap a sense of empowerment and what factors enhance empowerment?
2. What changes in management style must the typical manager make to Zapp or empower employees?
3. What do you like or dislike about MacGregor's management style?
4. How does MacGregor spend his time?
5. What are MacGregor's strategies for developing subordinates and building teamwork?
6. Is the workout program (described in the Nigel Andrews case) a bold move for G.E.? Why or why not?
7. What is your assessment of how Nigel Andrews has implemented workout up to this point?
8. What should Nigel Andrews do about the September session?
9. What if a key customer wants to visit on Wednesday?
10. Who is ultimately responsible under the G.E. Workout Program?

Date:           Friday, October 7, 1994

Topic:          **Team Building Workshop...Carroll Hall Classrooms**

Objectives:

    1. To examine the conditions under which groups make better decisions than individuals.

    2. To provide each study group with an opportunity to examine its effectiveness

    3. To develop a mission statement and action plan for improving study group effectiveness

Assignment:

    1. Covey Habit 6...Synergize

Students will work in their study groups during the workshop. Simulations, diagnostic questionnaires and group exercises will help each study group examine its overall effectiveness, the contributions of each member, and a plan for improving teamwork, cooperation, and support.

Date:         Monday, October 10, 1994; #12

Topic:        Managing Groups and Teams

Objectives:
1. To develop group management skills
2. To learn how to build self-managing work teams

Assignment:
1. ZAPP (second half)
2. Stayer: Learning to Let My Workers Lead Themselves
3. The team performance model

Study Questions:

1. What can a manager do to build self-managing work teams?

2. Why did Ralph Stayer decide to let his workers lead themselves? Why did Stayer wait so long?

3. From your reading of "The team performance model" at what stage is your study group? What are the issues that must be resolved to advance?

4. Have you ever experienced Stage 6 in the Model-- high performance? Describe the situation, the factors that contributed to high performance, and the accomplishments of the group.

Date:     Wednesday, October 12, 1994; #13

Topic:    Putting the Competencies Together: Managing Change

Objectives:

1. To discuss the competencies needed to successfully manage change.

2. To examine an attempt at a major change in an organization

Assignment:

1. Kotter and Schlesinger: Choosing Strategies for Change

2. Case: Peter Browning and Continental White Cap

3. Covey Habit 7 (pp. 287-307).

Study Questions:

1. Based on your own experiences, which of the strategies for change described by Kotter and Schlesinger are most effective? Which strategies are most difficult for middle managers to implement?

2. What was Peter Browning's predicament at White Cap?

3. What should his change objectives and timetable be?

4. What should he do with White, Larson, Stark, and Green? Be prepared to role play your approach and tactics.

5. What qualities are most needed to become a successful change agent?

## Guidelines for Writing A Personal Development Plan

The purpose of the personal development plan is for each student to craft a document that is _personally_ meaningful and useful. Your personal mission statement and areas targeted for improvement should be important and meaningful to you. They are your personal choices. Do not worry about using the Covey jargon or conforming to some type of preordained prototype paper.

Here are the criteria that will be used to distinguish good papers from the less-good papers.

1. **Thoughtfulness:** In most cases, we will be able to distinguish those who take the assignment to heart and give it their best shot from those who do not.

2. **Comprehensiveness:** It is important that you include all four elements of the personal development plan: 1) the results of your Covey Seven Habits Profile analysis; 2) a personal mission statement; 3) a set of specific self-improvement goals, and 4) an action plan for attaining your personal goals. An eloquent five page mission statement, without much of an action plan; or a detailed action plan without targeted goals will not be a strong paper.

3. **Quality:** Take time to do a high quality job with each component of the paper. You have resources at your disposal to help you do a good job. As examples, Covey Habit 2 will help you write your mission statement, the action planning guide handed out at the workshop will help you complete a concrete action plan, and you can call upon others to help you interpret your profile and brainstorm action steps. Use your creativity to find valid ways to monitor your progress.

4. **Logical Flow and Consistency:** Your mission statement, profile analysis, areas targeted for improvement, and strategies for tracking improvement should all be consistent.

5. **Miscellaneous**
   Number of targeted areas--The guidebook suggests targeting three areas for improvement. This is a good number, although two or four might be okay. To target only one goal might be too limited (if the goal is a narrow one) or too vague (if the goal is a grandiose one) to be useful; to target half a dozen goals might be too disjointed. Three, we believe makes for a useful exercise and a more easily organized paper.
   Linking goals to Covey Habits--The three target areas may well be three of Covey's dimensions, but they don't need to be. You may target particular roles or other personal traits and habits. If they don't coincide with Covey's dimensions, at least look through the items on the Covey Profile and see if some of them are specific indicators of the things you have chosen to target.

Profile analysis--Do not describe your mean score on each of the dimensions. Think about the data, get a feel for key strengths and areas in need of development, consider discrepancies, and so on. Look for intriguing, personally useful information--not just a statistical report.

Make this a personally meaningful assignment. Create a personal development plan that you will want to revisit during your time in the MBA program and beyond. Good luck!

Graduate School of Business  
STANFORD UNIVERSITY  
Mondays, 3.20-6.50. Spring, 1995

Dr. Lorna Catford  
Office: L276  
Teaching Assistant: Tony Anderson

## B.341
## PERSONAL CREATIVITY IN BUSINESS
## SYLLABUS

> "As a result of our training as well as of our experience most of us are disposed to approach any problem with as analytical an attitude as we can muster. We would be ill-advised to do anything else, yet paradoxically, efficient, economical and analytical perception is sometimes the enemy of creative insight."
>
> — Donald MacKinnon,  
> "Creativity: A Multi-Faceted Phenomenon"  
> Discussion at the Nobel Conference

> "We do not try to teach them creativity or risk-taking. If their attitudes haven't been formed by now, there's not much we can do."
>
> — Dean R. N. Rosett  
> Graduate School of Business  
> University of Chicago

> "Is it true that we haven't been teaching creativity enough? Probably, but who knows how to do that? No one."
>
> — Associate Dean J. F. Lubin  
> Wharton School

> "Through teaching the course [we] have gained the invaluable conviction that an ever-present creative source is available to each one of us, and we have watched our students gain that same conviction as they prove it in their daily business lives."
>
> — Rochelle Myers & Michael Ray  
> Graduate School of Business  
> Stanford University

> "A business is only as creative as the individuals who comprise it. Therefore creativity in business stems from creativity in one's Self."
>
> — Lorna Catford  
> Graduate School of Business  
> Stanford University

> "When you come right down to it, all you have is your Self. Your Self is a sun with a thousand rays in your belly. It is because I carry the sun in my belly that I can accomplish something from time to time."
>
> — Pablo Picasso

## I  PURPOSE

This seminar recognizes that true creativity in business results from the contagious energy of inspired and creative individuals. This is the "sun with a thousand rays in your belly" described by Picasso on the front page. Thus the course is designed to open participants to the creativity within themselves so that each person's business life can be a "work of art." This is not a marketing course, a course on managing creative organizations, or even a course on creative problem solving. While improved organizational performance and problem solving are results of this course, do NOT expect simply to gather techniques here. Be prepared for some introspection and attention to your innate personal creativity. If the purpose of the course does not suit you, or you want a light course, this one is not for you; return this syllabus immediately and drop the course. In any case, read the first section of readings in the Syllabus Packet before making a decision to stay.

## II  OVERALL SCHEDULE

We meet on Mondays for three and a half hours.* You are expected to attend all nine meetings, and each student will also schedule a 20-minute individual meeting with the instructor, and one with the teaching assistant. During the last hour of some classes, outside speakers will share their personal experiences and applications of creativity in various areas of business. In addition, the course is organized like a journey, starting with the *preparation*, continuing with a *quest* for expanded self-knowledge, and culminating in the *return* where this knowledge is applied to the business context, and you give presentations.

  * PLEASE NOTE: The first meeting is Wednesday April 5, and attendance is **required**.

## III  COURSE THEME

The course theme is presented in the form of a pair of questions for you to reflect on and develop in your final project. The questions are:

### "Who is my *Self*?  What is my *Work*?"

The capital "S" on Self and the capital "W" on Work are used advisedly. We are talking about your higher Self, your complete potential — that which allows you to be fully creative in all parts of your life. We are talking about your life's Work, that which gives your life meaning, satisfaction, and a driving sense of purpose.

These seemingly innocent questions, if answered with attention to your inner depths, not off the top of your head, can yield profound insight and direction for the next step of your journey - post MBA. Your answer will be based upon your experience and observations from the class, the Live-Withs and other assignments, your journal, your weekly papers, and your reading.

While you will have the opportunity to explore these questions (and other course material) with your colleagues in a small study-group, you will be responding as an individual. This is not a group dynamics course. Rather the emphasis is on exploring your inner creative life and its application to the business world. Thus, the assignments are intended to provide a structure within which you are encouraged to make your own personal explorations.

## IV  COURSE REQUIREMENTS

### A.  REQUIRED MATERIALS

*Creativity in Business*, Michael Ray and Rochelle Myers. New York: Doubleday, 1986
*The Path of the Everyday Hero*, Lorna Catford and Michael Ray. New York: Tarcher, 1991
Materials fee: $20
Blank bound Journal, 8.5 x 11 inches
Set of colored marking pens, pencils or crayons
> (Please bring your journal and colors to class each session.)

### B.  COURSE STRUCTURE

We have found that developing your own creativity and certainly exploring your own *Self* and bringing it out in the world in your *Work* is not always easy. It is, however, an exciting challenge. Therefore your "creative journey" through the quarter consists of three parts, to ease you into knowing the answers to the two core questions.

The first meeting, **The Preparation**, introduces you to the major themes of the course. It identifies essential tools for exploring your creativity (*Faith in Your Own Creativity, Absence of Judgment, Precise Observation,* and *Penetrating Questions*), and allows you to provide an initial answer to the two questions.

The next seven weeks, **The Quest**, constitute an in depth exploration of how these tools can be applied to develop greater knowledge of your distinctive *Self* and your *Work*. During the first three of these weeks, you will use one of the four essential tools each week to uncover hidden nooks and crannies of your personal creativity, and will also explore books of your choosing (Use the bibliography or find your own.). At the end of this time you will write a brief synopsis of your reaction to one book. During the next four weeks you will use the four tools again, this time for deeper probing on the nature of your *Self* and your *Work*, with an eye to using what you learn to move towards a richer answer to the two questions. During this time we will also address some challenges confronting those who seeks a meaningful life. These challenges are: *living with purpose, dealing with stress, achieving personal and professional balance,* and *finding true prosperity*.

The last week, **The Return**, is a consolidation as you pull together your findings and identify ways to actually bring your personal creativity into the business world and the rest of your life. We will address the challenge of *having fulfilling personal and professional relationships*. You will submit your answer to the core questions in your final project, due *in Class* on the last day.

### C.  CLASS MEETINGS

Attend every class session, on time and completely. Since the *sine qua non* of creativity is suspending judgment, grading seems a bit incongruous. However, in this course there is a high correlation between grades and complete attendance and participation. Since many of the activities of this course may appear somewhat strange in a business school setting, it is necessary for you to attend and participate completely with an open mind.

## D. INDIVIDUAL MEETINGS

It has been our experience that when students are given an opportunity to explore issues in their personal and professional lives, they come to appreciate how the tools taught in the course work together and how it is possible to move from confusion or conflict to clarity and new insights in a short time. With this in mind, each of you will have a short individual conference with the professor and with the teaching assistant. These sessions are designed to help you identify a specific issue of concern to you, relating to the core questions, and take that to a new level of understanding by applying the course ideas that you find most useful.

Individual Meeting Schedule
Lorna Catford (L276):   Mon. 4/10, 4/17, 4/24, 5/1; 11:40 a.m.-2 p.m.; Tues. 4/11, 9:20 a.m.-3 p.m.
Tony Anderson (L236):  Mon. 4/10, 4/17, 4/24, 5/1, 5/8, 5/15; 11:40 a.m.-2.20 p.m.

A sign-up sheet for 20-minute meetings will be circulated in class.
Plan to have two or three weeks between your meetings if possible.

## E. CREATIVITY STUDY GROUP

You will be assigned to a Creativity Study Group of approximately eight students, with whom you will participate in small group discussions and class activities. Your creativity group will provide the opportunity for in-depth exploration of your application of the course material not possible in the large classroom format. It is intended that you serve as "allies" for each other on your journeys of self-exploration, and that you communicate weekly with each member of your group outside of class; the format is up to you (phone, e-mail, duos, whole group meeting, etc.).

## F. LIVE-WITHS

Every week you will be asked to "live with" a different heuristic, or rule of thumb, for how to go about your business during the week. The aim of these "Live-Withs" is for you to experience the basic tools for bringing your personal creativity into the world. Each Live-With is designed to give you new insights into your own creativity and the creative process. There is space in the course schedule for you to write in the live with for each week.

Note: You will not be assessed on how well you *understand* each Live-With, but, rather, how much you immerse yourself in *experiencing* it during the week. The Live-Withs are one of the most important pieces of the course and you are expected to fully apply yourself to each one during the week it is assigned.

## G. WEEKLY PAPERS

A brief *typewritten* paper (1-2 pages) is due each week.* Include your experiences of the week's Live-With plus your personal responses to the readings, speakers, and creative tools and activities. The course presents a vast range of material. Try everything, and report on what happens. We hope you will continue to use those activities that are particularly valuable for you, and modify those that seem less appropriate. In fact, your creative challenge is this: for everything we do in class, if it doesn't seem personally meaningful for you, "*cheat*," and make it meaningful!
*Because the emphasis is on substantive involvement and reflection, we acknowledge that you might have some "off" weeks; thus **you are to complete 5 out of 7 possible papers.**

## H. JOURNAL

You are to keep a regular ongoing Creativity Journal in order to record your observations and questions that arise as a result of living with each week's Live-With. This journal is to be your personal experience with using the four basic creativity tools of the course as you explore your everyday challenges. By keeping a regular journal of your "journey" into inner terrain, you will be able to notice repeated interests, concerns, responses, and reflections to living with the course material. This journal will serve as a reservoir of your observations, sensations and experiences for developing your weekly papers and will help you pull together material for your final project.

This journal is for your own personal use and is <u>confidential</u>. Please bring it and your colored markers to every class session, as some activities will require drawing or writing. Bring it to your individual meeting so you can describe how you are using it; however, no-one but you will actually read it.

Blank 8 1/2 x 11 bound journals are available in the Book Store. In the past, students benefited most from developing their own best style of journal-keeping. A partial list of the types of things that you can do with your journal is given below.

Record daily "deep thoughts"
Use it for class notes and class exercises
Do activities described in *The Path of the Everyday Hero*
Make observations / ask questions about yourself (e.g. I noticed...; Why did I react that way?)
Keep track of your "Voice of Judgment" (and the VOJ of others)
Unravel problems and crises
Make notes to yourself about critical decisions you face — actually make your decisions
Write goals and affirmations
Record and interpret dreams
Keep an ongoing creativity log of your ideas for all the projects you are involved in
Record your creative breakthroughs
Take notes on your creativity reading
Draw daily mandalas or mood doodles
Write poetry
Review your day before bed and keeping a log of what you learned about yourself that day

Use a variety of media: regular pens and pencils, crayons, markers, paints, quotes or pictures from magazines, collage.

Organize your journal in whatever way works best for you. You might like to have different sections for different uses — e.g., one for your experience with each of the four tools, one for each of the five major challenges of life, plus sections for goals, inspirational quotes, dream interpretation, inspirational pictures cut from magazines, and a summary section.

Experiment. Have fun!

## I. READINGS

Submerge yourself in the creativity literature, especially during the first half of the Quarter. Later you might find that your reading decreases as you begin to experience creativity more consistently. The creativity literature is vast, and you may have difficulty getting your hands and mind around it. How can you deal with this problem of too much to read and too little time? The book-list is organized in three parts to allow you to make some selections. Let your interests direct you on the reading. Feel free to read something that is not on the list; the list is updated each quarter as students describe new books.

Each week you are to read a few chapters in the **Texts**. In class, we will build on what's there, rather than explain it from scratch. Use your Creativity study group for deeper probing of areas of personal interest.

Second, read the readings in your **Syllabus Packet** for each week that they are assigned. Your packet contains brief pieces to augment the subjects covered in class, plus transcripts of past guest speakers. Include your reaction to the transcripts in your weekly papers. Scan your weekly syllabus packet before class, though you may prefer to read it in depth after the Monday meeting.

Third, peruse the books in the three sections of the attached **Reading List** during the first half of the course (and browse the "creativity" section in a bookstore for new books that catch your eye), and then select one to read in more depth. All of this material just begins to scratch the enormous surface of the literature on creativity.

Along with your weekly paper on **Monday May 1**, submit a one page typed description / personal reaction to the book. We will then compile for you a compendium of interpretations of and reflections on these books. In the past, students have found this resource extremely valuable.

We need your assistance with this. When you find a book you wish to read and contribute to the compendium, write its title, author and your name on the *Creativity Compendium* sign-up sheet posted by Lorna Catford's office door (L276).

Fourth, you will receive occasional **supplementary photocopied material**. Read this as you receive it, especially the biographical information on the guest speakers.

It is true that after a certain point in your development very little reading is needed. As Muktananda's guru, Nityananda, once said to him when he saw him carrying a book, "Did books make the mind or did the mind make books?"

In any case, your reading may lead you to write notes, however brief or extended, that can be part of your weekly paper, included in your journal, or incorporated into your Final Project.

## J. FINAL PROJECT

Your final project is your answer to the questions: Who is my *Self*? What is my *Work*? This project is due in Class on **Monday June 5**, and consists of two related parts, a **paper** and a **creative expression**.

The **paper** (four to six pages, double spaced) is to be a culmination of the self-knowledge you have gained during the 10-week journey of this course, and should provide an answer to the core questions. Use this paper as an opportunity to clarify and articulate who you are, what you deeply care about, what activities would provide you with a driving sense of purpose, and what the elements are of a personal and professional life that would be satisfying and meaningful.

You paper should be a catalyst for you to utilize all the readings, experiences, Live-Withs, and the four tools to answer these questions as they relate to you and your challenges in life. It can also be a document that you can refer back to throughout your life as an aid to keep you clear about what is ultimately most important to you. The presumption of this course is that by answering these questions and then guiding your life according to this self-knowledge, you will *de facto* bring your personal creativity into the business world and, indeed, everything you do.

Whereas your paper presents your analytical response to the core questions, your **creative expression** is to be simply a demonstration or "picture" of your *Self* and your *Work*. Its form is up to you. In the past, students have done the following: photography, sculpture, collage, set of mandalas, dance, art work, poetry, slides, movie, crafts, skit, mime, whole-class activity, even food! You may like to write and illustrate or dramatize your own personal myth, which you can create from the instructions in the epilogue of *The Path of the Everyday Hero*. This piece of your project is to accompany your paper, so the two of them together provide an in-depth communication of your own personal creativity in business. It may be handed in with your paper or presented to the class on **Monday June 5**.

The expressive part of the final project may seem a little ambiguous right now. During the course you will have many opportunities to experiment with a variety of modes of expressing your Self and your Work, which should trigger some inspirations about this part of your project. You will have the opportunity mid-quarter to discuss your ideas for this.

## V  ON LORNA CATFORD

Lorna has helped to teach *Creativity in Business* here for 11 years, and is on the faculty of Sonoma State University, where she teaches various traditional and esoteric psychology courses. She has held creativity seminars in corporate and academic settings for 18 years, and provides research and problem-solving through Catford Creativity Consulting. Her doctorate, completed at Stanford, identifies strategic styles for creative problem solving in business, and alternative approaches for developing personal creativity in business. Practicing what she preaches, Lorna is not particularly good at accepting conventional limitations; she is passionately committed to living out her vision of a full, rich life, inviting others to do likewise. As a licensed psychotherapist, Lorna uses the mythical "Hero's Journey" as a metaphor for living and being creative in one's Self and one's Work. She directs a national project to identify the needs of, and provide support services for, parents of special needs or critically ill infants. The mother of two small children, she is a photographer and artist in her spare (?) time. And is becoming rather expert at juggling!!!

## ON TONY ANDERSON

Tony currently has a small organization development (OD) practice in Sonoma County. His recent clients include the Price Club of Rohnert Part, the Piedmont Recreation Center, the Service Employee International Union, local 535, Old Adobe Developmental Services, and the Early Intervention Program of Napa, Solano, and Sonoma Counties. He draws on a background in Art and Theater in implementing work system redesign projects. His premise is that by trusting the client's creative power and informed intuition, and including as many participants as possible, the system itself, not the consultant, is the most appropriate expert to effectively redesign organizations. In addition, Tony team teaches *Quality of Work Life* and *Total Quality Management* for the graduate OD program in the Business and Psychology Departments at Sonoma State University. He also is involved in various community development projects and works as a case manager for the North Bay Regional Center. Lastly, and most importantly, he is a member of a small family of five in little town called Sebastopol.

# VI COURSE SCHEDULE AND ASSIGNMENTS

> *We shall not cease from exploration*
> *And the end of all our exploring*
> *Will be to arrive where we started*
> *And know the place for the first time.*
>                                     T. S. Eliot

## THE PREPARATION

**Wednesday 4/5**   **INTRODUCTION**
                   **Tool # 1 - FAITH IN YOUR CREATIVITY**

        Read:    *Creativity in Business (CiB):* Introduction, Ch.1-2
                    *Path of the Everyday Hero (Path):* Foreword, Ch. 1-4
                    *Syllabus Packet:* Section 1-2

        Live With: _____

## THE QUEST

**Monday 4/10**   **Tool # 2 - ABSENCE OF JUDGMENT**

        Read:    *CiB: Ch. 3* - Destroy Judgment, Create Curiosity
                    *Syllabus Packet* - Section 3
                    Creativity book of your choice

        Special Assignment: Individual meetings start today.
                  • 1st mtg.: bring self-evaluations from *Path*, Ch. 2, plus statement of your own issue relating to the **Self & Work** theme.
                  • 2nd mtg.: give progress report.

        Live With: _____

**Monday 4/17**   Tool # 3   -   PRECISE OBSERVATION

    Read:   *CiB: Ch. 4* - Pay Attention
             *Syllabus Packet* - Section 4
             Creativity book of your choice (cont.)

    Special Assignment: Individual meetings. See above.

    Live With: _____


**Monday 4/24**   Tool # 4   -   PENETRATING QUESTIONS

    Read:   *CiB: Ch. 5* - Ask Dumb Questions
             *Syllabus Packet* - Section 5
             Creativity book of your choice (cont.)

    Special Assignment: Individual meetings. See above.

    Live With: _____


**Monday 5/1**   Challenge — PURPOSE IN LIFE
                (Tool # 1 - Faith in your Creativity)

    Read:   *CiB: Ch. 6* - Do Only what is Easy, Effortless & Enjoyable
             *Path: Ch. 5* - Discovering and Pursuing your True Purpose
             *Syllabus Packet* - Section 6

    Special Assignment: 1-pg. book synopsis/reaction for *Creativity Compendium*
                              Individual meetings. See above.

    Live With: _____


**Monday 5/8**   Challenge — TIME AND STRESS
                (Tool # 2 - Absence of Judgment)

    Read:   *CiB: Ch. 7* - Don't Think About It
             *Path: Ch. 7* - Living Stress-free in the Here and Now
             *Syllabus Packet* - Section 7

    Live With: _____

**Monday 5/15**   Challenge — **PERSONAL / PROFESSIONAL BALANCE**
(Tool # 3  -  Precise observation)

    Read:    *CiB:* Ch. 8 - Ask Yourself if It's a Yes or a No
                *Path:* Ch. 8 - Achieving Personal and Professional Balance
                *Syllabus Packet* - Section 8

    Live With: _____

**Monday 5/22**   Challenge — **TRUE PROSPERITY**
(Tool # 4  -  Penetrating Questions)

    Read:    *CiB:* Ch. 9 - Be Ordinary
                *Path:* Ch. 9 - Finding your Way to Prosperity
                *Syllabus Packet* - Section 9

    Live With: _____

## THE RETURN

**Monday 6/5**   Challenge — **FULFILLING PERSONAL & PROFESSIONAL RELATIONSHIPS**

    Read:    *CiB:* Ch. 10 - Be In The World But Not Of It
                *Path* - Epilogue
                *Syllabus Packet* - Section 10

    Special Assignment: Final Reflective Paper and Creative Expression due

    Lifetime Live With: _____

## VII  READING LIST

I have organized books relating to personal creativity in business into four sections to facilitate your exploration of the literature according to topic. However, this organization is somewhat deceiving, as many books could easily be placed under two or three headings. Use this list as a starting point for your own exploration of the creativity material relevant to your particular interests.

### A. BUSINESS CREATIVITY

John D. Adams, *Transforming Work*, Miles River Press, 1984.

Weston Agor, *Intuitive Management*, Prentice Hall, 1984.

Nancy Anderson, *Work With Passion*, Carrol & Graf, 1984.

Warren Bennis, *On Becoming a Leader*, 1989.

Randy Bright, *Disneyland: Inside Story*, Harry N. Abrams, Inc, 1987.

Lorna Catford, *Creative Problem Solving in Business: Synergy of Thinking, Intuiting, Sensing and Feeling Strategies*, Doctoral Dissertation, Stanford University, 1987.

Owen Edwards, *Upward Nobility: How to Succeed in Business without Losing your Soul*, Crown Publishers, 1991.

Debbie Fields, *One Smart Cookie*, Simon & Schuster, 1987.

Charles Garfield, *Peak Performers: The New Heros of American Business*, William Morro & Co., 1986

Bennett Goodspeed, *The Tao Jones Averages*, Dutton, 1983.

Stephen Grossman *et al.*, *Innovation, Inc.: Unlocking Creativity in the Workplace*, Plano, TX, Wordware Publishing, 1988.

Robert Grudin, *The Grace of Great Things: Creativity and Innovation*, Ticknor & Fields, 1990.

John Heider, *The Tao of Leadership,: Leadership Strategies for a New Age*,

Willis Harman & John Hormann, *Creative work: The Constructive Role of Business in Transforming Soociety*, Indianapolis, Knowledge Systems, Inc., 1990.

John Kao, *Managing Creativity*, Prentice-Hall, 1991.

John Keil, *The Creative Mystique: how to Manage it, Nurture it, and Make it Pay*, Wiley & Sons, 1985.

William C. Miller, *The Creative Edge*, Addison-Wesley, 1987.

John Naisbitt, *Megatrends*, Warner Books, 1982.

John Naisbitt & Patricia Aburdenne, *Megatrends 2000: Ten New Directions for the 1990's*

Tom Peters & Robert Waterman, *In Search of Excellence*, Harper & Row, 1982.

Michael Phillips, *The Seven Laws of Money*, Wordwheel and Random House, 1979.

John Renesch (Ed.), *New Traditions in Business: Spirit and Leadership in the 21st Century*, San Francisco, CA, Sterling & Stone, Inc., 1991.

Mary Riley, *Corporate Healing*, Deerfield Beach, Florida, Health Communications, Inc., 1990.

Everett M. Rogers, *Diffusion of Innovations*, The Free Press, 1983.

Rowena Rowan, *The Intuitive Manager*, Little, Brown & Co., 1986

Robert Roskind, *In the Spirit of Business*, Berkeley, CA., Celestial Arts, 1992.

Peter Senge, *The Fifth Discipline*, New York, Doubleday, 1990

Peter Senge et al., *The Fifth Discipline: The field book*, New York, Doubleday, 1994

Marcia Sinetar, *Do What You Love: The Money will Follow*, Paulist Press, 1987.

S. Srivastra, *The Executive Mind*, Jossey-Bass, 1983.

Gary Steiner, *The Creative Organization*, University of Chicago Press, 1965.

Tarthang Tulku, *Skillful Means: Patterns for Success*, Berkeley, CA, Dharma Publishing, 1991.

Marvin Weisbord, *Discovering Common Ground*, Berrett-Koehler

David Whyte, *The Heart Aroused: Poetry and the Preservation of the Soul in Corporate America*, Bantam, Doubleday, Dell Group, 1994.

"World Business Academy Perpectives" Quarterly Journal published by WBA and Berrett-Koehler (see below) covering "New Paradigm" business issues.

See Berrett-Koehler Publishers Catalog for recent "Creativity in Business" books. This is all they publish. Steven Piersanti (CEO), 155 Montgomery St., San Francisco, CA 94104-4109. 1-800-929-2929.

## B. STANDARD CREATIVITY BOOKS

Russell Ackoff, *The Art of Problem Solving*, Wiley, 1978.

James L. Adams, *Conceptual Blockbusting*, Freeman, 1974.

_____,*The Care and Feeding of Ideas*, Addisson-Wesley, 1986.

Weston Agor, *The Logic of Intuitive Decision-Making*, Quorum Books, 1986.

Theresa Amabile, *The Social Psychology of Creativity*, Springer-Verlag, 1983.

Robert Bly, *Iron John*, 1990.

Tony Buzan, *Use Both Sides of Your Brain*, Dutton, 1983.

Richard E. Byrd, *A Guide to Personal Risk Taking*, American Management Association, 1974.

Leslie Cameron-Bandler et al., *Know How: Guided Programs for inventing your own Best Future*

Edward DeBono, *Lateral Thinking*, Harper & Row, 1970.

David Feinstein and Stanley Kripner, *Personal Mythology*, Tarcher, 1988.

Robert Fulghum, *All I really Need to Know I Learned in Kindergarten*,

Howard Gardner, *Frames of Mind: The Theory of Multiple Intelligences*, Basic Books, 1983.

John Gardner, *Self Renewal: The Individual and the Innovative Society*, Norton, 1981

Jean-Louis Gassee, *The Third Apple*, Harcourt, Brace & Jovanovich, 1987.

O. Gingerich, *Scientific Genius and Creativity: Readings from Scientific American*, W. H. Freeman & Co., 1987.

Phillip Goldberg, *The Intuitive Edge*, Tarcher, 1983.

Ellen Goodman, *American Artists on Art*,

Jacques Hadamard, *The Psychology of Invention in the Mathematical Field*, Dover, 1954.

David Keirsey and Marilyn Bates, *Please Understand Me: Character Temperament and Types*

Arthur Koestler, *The Act of Creation*, Hutchinson, 1984.

Marilyn & Robert Kriegel, *The C Zone: Peak Performance Under Pressure*

Thomas Kuhn, *The Structure of Scientific Revolutions*, University of Chicago Press, 1963.

Harold Kushner, *When All You've ever Wanted Isn't Enough: The Search for a Life that Matters*, Simon & Schuster, 1986.

Michael LeBoeuf, *Imagineering*, McGraw-Hill, 1980.

Rollo May, *The Courage to Create*, W. W. Norton: New York, 1975.

Michael Meyer, *The Alexander Complex*, Times Books, 1989.

Anne Morrow Lindbergh, *Gift From the Sea*,

Isabel & Paul Myers, *Gifts Differing*, Consulting Psychologists Press, 1985.

P. Ranganath Nayak & John M. Ketteringham, *Breakthroughs*, Rawson Associates, 1986.

Alex Osborne, *Applied Imagination: Principles and Procedures of Creative Problem Solving*, Charles Scribner's Sons, 1963.

Helen Palmer, *The Enneagram*, Harper & Row, 1988.

Harold Rothbart, *Cybernetic Creativity*,

Albert Rothenberg and Carl R. Housman, *The Creativity Question*, Duke University Press, 1975.

Gabrielle Rico, *Writing the Natural Way*, Tarcher, 1983.

Don Richard Riso, *Personality Types*, Houghton Mifflin, 1987.

Roger Schank, *The Creative Attitude*, Macmillan, 1988.

Robert Sternberg, *The Nature of Creativity*, Cambridge University Press, 1988.

Sally Swift, *Centered Riding*, Trafalgar Square Books.

Richard Von Oech, *A Whack on the Side of the Head*, Creative Think, 1983.

_____, *A Kick in the Seat of the Pants*, Harper & Row, 1986.

Robert Weisberg, *Ceativity: Genius and Other Myths*, W. H. Freeman, 1986.

## C. PERSPECTIVE-CHANGING BOOKS

Miriam and José Arguellos, *Mandala*, Shambala Books, 1972.

Richard Bach, *Illusions: The Adventures of a Reluctant Messiah*, Delacorte, 1977.

Melody Beattie, *CoDependent No More: How to Stop Controling Others and Start Caring for Yourself*,

Jean Shinoda Bolen, *Goddesses in Every Woman*, Harper & Row, 1984.

_____, *Gods in Every Man*, Harper & Row, 1989.

Joan Borysenko, *Minding the Body, Mending the Mind*, Addison-Wesley, 1987.

Joseph Campbell, *The Hero with a Thousand Faces*, Princeton University Press, 1973.

Joseph Campbell & Bill Moyers, *The Power of Myth*, Doubleday, 1988.

Leslie Cameron-Bandler, David Gordon & Michael Lebeau, *Know How: Guiided Programs for Inventing Your Own Best Future*,

Lucia Capacchione, *The Creative Journal: the Art of Finding Yourself*, Newcastle Publishing, 1989

Kim Chernin, *Reinventing Eve: Modern Woman in Search of Herself*, Random House, 1987.

Arthur Deikman, *The Observing Self*, Beacon Press, 1982.

Gayle Delaney, *Living Your Dreams*, Harper & Row, 1979.

Antoine de Saint-Exupéry, *Airman's Odyssey*,

_____, *The Little Prince*,

Karlfried Durkheim, *Hara*, Samuel Weiser, 1977.

David Feinstein & Stanley Krippner, *Personal Mythology: the Psychology of your Evolving Self*, Tarcher, 1988.

Howard Ferguson, *The Edge*, Getting the Edge Co., Cleveland, OH, 1988

Marilyn Ferguson, *The Aquarian Conspiracy*, Tarcher, 1980.

Timothy Gallwey, *The Inner Game of Tennis*, Random House, 1974.

_____, *The Inner Game of Golf*, Random House, 1981.

Patricia Garfielld, *Creative Dreaming*, Ballantine Books,

Shakti Gawain, *Creative Visualization*, New York: Whatever Publishing, Inc., 1978.

Natalie Goldberg, *Writing Down the Bones*, Shambal Press, 1989

Joseph Goldstein, *The Experience of Insight*, Unity Press, Santa Cruz, 1976.

Charles Hampden-Turner, *Maps of the Mind*, Macmillan, 1981.

Willis Harman and Howard Rheingold, *Higher Creativity*, Tarcher, 1985

David Harp, *The Three-Minute Meditator*, 1988.

Eugene Herrigel, *Zen and the Art of Archery*

Lex Hixon, *Coming Home: The Experience of Enlightenment in Sacred Traditions*, New York: Anchor, 1978.

Benjamin Hoff, *The Tao of Pooh*, New York, Dutton, 1982.

_____, *The Te of Piglet*, New York, Dutton, 1992.

Douglas Hofstadter, *Goedel, Escher, Bach: An Eternal Golden Braid*, Vintage, 1980.

Jean Houston, *The Possible Human: A Course in Enhancing your Physical, Mental and Creative Abilities*, Tarcher, 1982.

_____, *The Search for the Beloved*, Tarcher, 1987.

Sam Keen & Anne Valley-Fox, *Your Mythic Journey: Finding Meaning in your Life through Wriiting and Storytelling*, Tarcher, 1989

Don Koberg & Jim Bagnall, *The Universal Traveler*, William Kaufman, 1972.

Harold Kushner, *When All You've Ever Wanted isn't Enough: The Search for a Life that Matters*,

Stephen La Berge, *Lucid Dreaming: Awake in Your Dreams*, Tarcher, 1985.

Maxwell Maltz, *Psychosybernetics*

Abraham Maslow, *Religions, Values and Peak Experiences*, Ohio University Press, 1968.

Robert Masters & Jean Houston, *The Varieties of Psychedelic Experience*, Holt, Rinehart & Winston, 1966.

Rollo May, *The Cry for Myth*, Norton & Co., 1991

Jane Middleton-Moz, *Children of Trauma*,

Dan Millman, *The Warrior Athlete: Body, Mind and Spirit*, Stillpoint Publishing, 1979.

_____, *Way of the Peaceful Warrior, a Book that Changes Lives*, H. J. Kramer, 1984.

Maureen Murdock, *The Heroine's Journey: Woman's Quest for Wholeness*, Shambhala, 1990.

Michael Murphy, *Golf in the Kingdom*, Delta,

Donald Norman, *The Psychology of Everyday Things*,

Carol Ochs, *Women and Spirituality*,

Robert Ornstein, *The Psychology of Consciousness*, Harcourt, Brace, Jovanovich, 1977.

_____, *Multimind*, Houghton Mifflin, 1986.

Carol Pearson, *The Hero Within*, (2nd. Edition), Harcourt Brace, 1989

M. Scott Peck, *The Road Less Travelled*, Simon & Schuster, 1980.

Roger Penrose, *The Emperor's New Mind*, Oxford University Press, 1989

Robert M. Pirsig, *Zen and the Art of Motorcycle Maintenance*, Bantam, 1976.

Ilya Prigogine & Isabelle Stengers, *Order out of Chaos: Man's New Dialog with Nature*, Bantam, 1984.

Ayn Rand, *The Fountainhead*,

Don Richard Riso, *Personality Types: Using the Enneagram for Self-Discovery*, Houghton Mifflin, 1987.

Gabrielle Roth, *Maps to Extasy: Teachings of an Urban Shaman*, New World Library, 1989.

Deane Shapiro, Jr. *Precision Nirvana*, Prentice-Hall, 1978.

E. F. Schumacher, *A Guide for the Perplexed*, Harper, 1977.

Robert Shiarella, *Journey to Joy*, Matrika Publications, 1982.

Starhawk, *Truth or Dare: Encounters with Power, Authority and Mystery*,

Sally Swift, *Centered Riding*, Trafalgar Square Farm Book,

SyberVision, *The Neuropsychology of Weight Control*, Tapes and book, SyberVision Systems, Inc., Pleasanton, CA, 1988.

Alvin Toffler, *The Third Wave*, William Morrow, 1980.

Frances E. Vaughan, *Awakening Intuition*, Anchor Books/Doubleday, 1979.

John H. Walsh, *Tales of the Greek Heross*,

Alan W. Watts, *The Wisdom of Insecurity*, Vintage Books/Random House, 1972.

Ken Wilber, *No Boundary*, Center Publishing, 1979.

R.L. Wing, *The I Ching Workbook*, Doubleday, 1979.

## D. SOME CLASSICS FROM OTHER TRADITIONS

*The Bhagavad Gita*, Vintage Books division of Random House, 1977.

Ralph Blum, *The Book of Runes*, St. Martin's Press, 1987

Taisen Deshimaru, *The Zen Way to the Martial Arts*, Dutton,

Aldous Huxley, *Perennial Philosophy*, Harper Colophon, 1945.

J. Krishnamurti, *The Flight of the Eagle*, Harper & Row, 1971.

_____, *On Thinking These Things*, Harper & Row

Muktananda, *The Play of Consciousness*, Harper & Row, 1971.

_____, *I Am That*, SYDA Foundation, 1982.

_____, *Where Are You Going?* SYDA Foundation, 1981.

P. D. Ouspensky, *The Psychology of Man's Possible Evolution*, Vintage, 1974.

Patanjali, *Yoga Sutras*, Mentor Books: New American Library, 1969.

Shunryn Suzuki, *Zen Mind, Beginner's Mind*, Weatherhill, 1970; paperback edition, 1976.

Chogyam Trungpa, *Shambhala: The Sacred Path of the Warrior*, Shambhala Publications, 1984.

Tarthang Tulku, *Skillful Means*, Dharma Publications, 1978.

Terrence Webster-Doyle, *Karate: The Art of the Empty Self*,

Paramahansa Yogananda, *The Autobiography of a Yogi*, Self-Realization Fellowship, 1974.

Graduate School of Business Administration
University of Virginia
Box 6550
Charlottesville, Virginia 22906-6550
(804) 924-4841

John L. Colley, Jr.
The Almand R. Coleman
Professor of Business Administration

TO: Second Year Students

FROM: Professors Colley and Fair

DATE: November 22, 1994

SUBJ: Course Details for Reading Seminar in Management I, II, & III, 1994/95

The lists of readings (Book List I and Book List II) and the detailed schedules for the three Seminars (I, II & III) are attached to this memorandum.

Please note:

1. Each section (A & B) will be randomly divided into two discussion groups, with one group meeting on Monday and the other on Tuesday.

2. Each group will meet once a week for 1-1½ hours. **After reading the book, you should jot down your brief reaction to the discussion questions to be turned in to the instructor each week.** The total time for two class preparations and two class meetings should provide the time necessary each week to read the book, reflect on and respond to the discussion questions, and meet once for discussion.

3. **Each group will thus meet on either Monday or Tuesday, but not both.**

4. All groups will meet in Room 334.

5. Attendance is very important because of the limited number of meetings. You are, of course, free to attend another section if you have an unavoidable conflict.

6. A paper will be required on some aspect of the readings. The paper should draw on at least two (2) of the readings in regard to some management topic. The length of the paper should not exceed 2,000 words, excluding footnotes and bibliography. *Copies of outstanding papers have been placed on reserve in the library.*

7. *Papers are due on the dates specified on the attached schedules.*

8. If you are not a Darden student, please see the DEMS office to arrange for a mailbox.

## READING SEMINARS IN MANAGEMENT ('94-'95)

| Title | Author | Publisher |
|---|---|---|

### Book List I - 2nd half, Fall Semester - Colley

| | | |
|---|---|---|
| *The Portable Machiavelli* (The Intro. & The Prince) | Machiavelli | Penguin Books |
| *Succeeding Against the Odds* | Johnson with Bennett, Jr. | Warner Books |
| *Den of Thieves* | James B. Stewart | Simon & Schuster |
| *Prophets in the Dark* | Kerns and Nadler | Harper Business |
| *To The End of Time* | Richard M. Clurman | Simon & Schuster |
| *It Doesn't Take a Hero* | H. Norman Schwarzkopf | Bantam Books |

### Book List II - 1st half, Spring Semester - Colley

| | | |
|---|---|---|
| *American Steel* | Richard Preston | Prentice Hall |
| *Body and Soul* | Anita Roddick | Crown |
| *Control Your Destiny or Someone Else Will* | Tichy and Sherman (Jack Welsh/GE) | Doubleday |
| *Confessions of an S.O.B.* | Al Neuharth | Doubleday |
| *Barbarians at the Gate* | Burrough and Helyar | Harper & Row |
| *The Art of War* | Edited by Clavell | Dell Publishing |

### Book List I & II - 2nd half, Spring Semester - Fair

Both Book Lists will be offered; Book List I on Mondays at 2:30 p.m. and 4:00 p.m. and Book List II on Tuesdays at 2:30 p.m. and 4:00 p.m.

## READING SEMINARS IN MANAGEMENT ('94-'95)

### Detailed Schedules

#### Reading Seminar I - 2nd half, Fall Semester - Colley

| Week of | Book |
|---|---|
| October 24, 25 | *The Portable Machiavelli* |
| October 31, November 1 | *Succeeding Against the Odds* |
| November 7, 8 | *Den of Thieves* |
| November 14, 15 | *Prophets in the Dark* |
| November 21, 22 | *To The End of Time* |
| November 28, 29 | *It Doesn't Take a Hero* |
| December 6, 4:30 p.m. | *Course papers due* |

#### Reading Seminar II - 1st half, Spring Semester - Colley

| Week of | Book |
|---|---|
| January 9, 10 | *American Steel* |
| January 16, 17 | *Body and Soul* |
| January 23, 24 | *Control Your Destiny...* |
| January 30, 31 | *Confessions of an S.O.B.* |
| February 13, 14 | *Barbarians at the Gate* |
| February 20, 21 | *The Art of War* |
| February 28 4:30 p.m. | *Course papers due* |

#### Reading Seminar III - 2nd Half, Spring Semester - Fair

| Week of | A Section Book | B Section Book |
|---|---|---|
| March 20, 21 | *The Portable Machiavelli* | *American Steel* |
| March 27, 28 | *Succeeding Against the Odds* | *Body and Soul* |
| April 3, 4 | *Den of Thieves* | *Control Your Destiny...* |
| April 10, 11 | *Prophets in the Dark* | *Confessions of an S.O.B.* |
| April 17, 18 | *To The End of Time* | *Barbarians at the Gate* |
| April 24, 25 | *It Doesn't Take a Hero* | *The Art of War* |
| May 2, 4:30 p.m. | *Course papers due* | *Course papers due* |

# READING SEMINAR IN MANAGEMENT

*Suggested Discussion Questions*

## The Portable Machiavelli

1. How would you define "Machiavellian"? When you see or hear it used, what do you think it means?

2. From your personal business experiences, can you cite examples of "Machiavellian" practices?

3. Discuss Machiavelli's view that "civilization itself is a corrupting influence."

4. In Chapter 3, Machiavelli suggests that when the Prince conquers a people dissimilar in language, customs, laws, etc., it is wise for the Prince to go live there or to colonize the new territory. How could this apply to business?

5. What actions does Machiavelli write about that can be applied to the new manager? To his/her selection of staff? To his/her management of staff?

6. How can we explain the enduring fascination with Machiavelli?

7. What parallels can be drawn between Machiavelli's Prince and current CEO's of large corporations?

## READING SEMINAR IN MANAGEMENT

### *Suggested Discussion Questions*

### Succeeding Against the Odds

1. What is the current status of John Johnson's various interests?

2. What is Johnson doing today? Who is running the company? How successful are his businesses?

3. Throughout, Johnson develops the "the advantage of the disadvantage." What did he mean by this and what examples of this does he give?

4. What "principles" did Johnson practice and exploit favorably in the establishment of Ebony?

5. Is Johnson's approach for selling advertising to Zenith one you would recommend? What do you think of this approach in general? Can you think of other areas where it would be useful? harmful?

6. "Going first class is the best leverage." Is this true for you? Differentiate between class and style.

7. Would Machiavelli be proud of Johnson?

8. Do you feel that Johnson has a responsibility to the African-American community? If so, have his actions fulfilled this obligation?

## READING SEMINAR IN MANAGEMENT

### *Suggested Discussion Questions*

### Den of Thieves

1. If you did a personality check on Milken, Boesky, Siegel and Levine, what would you report?

2. Was it unfair, as many Wall Streeters suggest, to single out one firm and/or one individual for prosecution?

3. How was the pre-1970 "clubbly world" of investment banking different from investment banking in the 1980's?

4. Did Drexel work for Milken or Milken work for Drexel? What was Drexel management's responsibility for the Milken problem?

5. Milken said, "My business was creating and saving jobs, not destroying them." Do you agree?

6. What effect did public relations (the press, the media in general) have on Drexel's reputation? the financial community's? Joseph's, Milken's, and others'?

7. How does this book alter your impressions of Wall Street? Milken says the book is a "fairy tale". What do you think?

8. Milken, Drexel and Wall Street have their defenders. Some have even called Milken a National Treasure. How can that be? What do you think?

For additional information, see:
**The Predators' Ball**, Connie Bruck, Penguin Books
**Liar's Poker**, Michael Lewis, W.W. Norton and Company
**Burning Down the House**, James Sterngold, Summit Books

# READING SEMINAR IN MANAGEMENT

*Suggested Discussion Questions*

## Prophets in the Dark

1. Why did David Kearns have mixed emotions about being named CEO of a large, well-known American corporation.

2. What factors led Kearns to leave IBM for XEROX? Does a company have more of an obligation for ensuring lifetime employment to employees than the loyalty employees have to the company?

3. How did XEROX let its prominent market position slip away?

4. How many ways did "chance" intervene to assist Kearns' elevation to the CEO job.

5. How much do you think the internal struggle between the XEROX faction and the Ford faction contributed to XEROX's near-fatal plunge?

6. How did XEROX survive its string of technical disasters?

7. How much of running a company is intellectual (figuring out what to do) versus the force, drive, and long hours required to effect the changes?

8. Was Kearns too dependent on consultants?

9. Did Total Quality Management resurrect XEROX or did its presence focus managers back on the "basics"?

## READING SEMINAR IN MANAGEMENT

*Suggested Discussion Questions*

### To The End of Time

1. How would you characterize/contrast the management skills, abilities, and results of the Time and Warner executive teams?

2. How did the corporate values of Time and Warner reflect those of the respective CEOs? Could these values or corporate cultures ever merge without one set or the other changing? Could the Co-CEO structure work?

3. Is shareholder value the ultimate, controlling corporate objective?

4. Is "exorbitant" executive compensation "obscene" and "un-American"?

5. What if the "magnanimous" compensation is largely tied to stock price (shareholder value) through options?

6. Is a level of debt four times the annual cash flow inherently bad?

7. What is Steve Ross' current situation? Nick Nicholas'? How is Time Warner doing now?

8. How did the "church and state" type of organization practiced at Time, Inc. work? Is it an idealistic approach to running a business?

9. Do you agree with Judge Allen's decision?

## READING SEMINAR IN MANAGEMENT

*Suggested Discussion Questions*

**It Doesn't take a Hero**, by H. Norman Schwartzkopf with Peter Petre, Bantam Books

1. How important do you think childhood events were in his ideas about leadership and responsibility?

2. Would you characterize him as tough?

3. Do you think he enjoyed war and combat, a la Patton, for instance?

4. Was he a general "ahead of his time?"

5. How did he approach team-building with military and political leaders of other countries?

6. Was he a model in terms of managing diversity?

7. What could a business executive or student learn about leadership from Schwartzkopf?

## READING SEMINAR IN MANAGEMENT

*Suggested Discussion Questions*

### American Steel

1. How can a $1 Billion company he managed by a corporate office of 17?

2. Is the macho image with a "hot metal" mystique a key success factor for Nucor?

3. How would you describe Iverson's leadership and management style?

4. Did Nucor drift into the steel business? Were they helped or hindered by Big Steel?

5. Would an MBA be likely to gamble on the untrained, unskilled workers in S.C.? What role did the work teams and bonuses play in Nucor's avoidance of unions and its rapid success?

6. How much risk did Nucor take in purchasing the German machine?

7. How prevalent do you suppose low-level "cooporation" is among competitors about which the management knows nothing.

8. Few experiences compare to the start-up of a unique machine or process. What examples of leadership made an impression on you during the risky and dangerous start-up?

9. How much pressure does Nucor's success at Crawfordsville put on "Big Steel"?... on foreign competitors?

## READING SEMINAR IN MANAGEMENT

*Suggested Discussion Questions*

### Body and Soul

1.  What were the key decisions Anita Roddick made during the first two years of The Body Shop's existence?

2.  How does Anita Roddick explain The Body Shop as a force for social change? Why do you think she feels this way? Do you agree and should this attitude apply to all businesses? Why? Why not?

3.  Describe The Body Shop's marketing strategy. Why do you think it is successful?

4.  The morale and motivation of the company's staff seems to be high. How does this come about?

5.  She describes several trips she's taken to unusual or exotic places. How do these help, hurt, or have any effect on her business?

6.  How is The Body Shop doing now? For those of you who have visited the one in Charlottesville's Fashion Square, what do you think?

7.  What does Ms. Roddick have to say about women in business? Do you agree?

8.  What rights or avenues of complaint would a minority shareholder have who might object to the spending of company funds on environmental concerns?


For other discussions of women and business, see:

**The Female Advantage,** Sally Helgesen, Doubleday Currency
**Wall Street Women,** Anne Fisher, Knopf
**In a Different Voice,** Carol Gilligan, Harvard University Press

## READING SEMINAR IN MANAGEMENT

*Suggested Discussion Questions*

### Control Your Destiny, (to page 251)

1. How do you feel about Welch's drive to create the world's strongest enterprise? Is that a reasonable goal for any CEO to set?

2. Are his approaches of improvement, open debate, and all bets are off compatible with your notion of leadership?

3. How do you feel about the "business engine," the rapid restructuring through acquisitions and divestitures, and the continuous improvement in performance?

4. Is the change from an expectation of "lifetime employment" to "providing opportunity" a realistic reflection of global competition?

5. Has Welch changed the basic modus operandi of a modern U.S. corporation?

6. Can a company have his "pluses" without his negatives?

7. How has GE performed recently recent time periods?

8. Are his values of "candor, forcing reality, and lean-and-agile" appropriate for any business today?

## READING SEMINAR IN MANAGEMENT

*Suggested Discussion Questions*

### Confessions of an S.O.B.

1. Why did Neuharth write this book?

2. Was he "Machiavellian"?

3. How did you feel about his approaches to women and minorities in management?

4. What factors gave Gannett inherent advantages in launching <u>USA Today</u>?

5. Was Neuharth adequately compensated?

6. How would you value his "perks" relative to his salary?

7. Was Neuharth an S.O.B., or did he just fancy the image?

8. Tom Peters (at Darden in 1989-90) and Neuharth say that everyone should fail (or get fired) once before they're forty. Do you foresee that happening to you?

9. Neuharth says that "life is a test." What did he mean by that? How does it affect you?

10. Is Neuharth a feminist? What is his secret to managing women?

# READING SEMINAR IN MANAGEMENT

*Suggested Discussion Questions*

## Barbarians at the Gate

1.  How would you characterize Ross Johnson's rise to power?
    What makes Ross Johnson tick?

2.  Was RJR a well-run company?

3.  Should the special desires of the Winston-Salem clique have been of over-riding concern to management or the board?

4.  How was Johnson able to neutralize or control the board?

5.  Did his attitudes toward the LBO change after he had the "parachutes" in place?

6.  How much was this carnival worth to RJR shareholders? to KKR?

7.  Many investment bankers and their firms were involved here. What impressions did you get of this industry and the individuals involved from reading <u>Barbarians at the Gate</u>?

## READING SEMINAR IN MANAGEMENT

*Suggested Discussion Questions*

### The Art of War

1. Why has this book endured for centuries?

2. Have we really made little progress since antiquity?

3. Do you agree with him on delegation of authority?

4. Discuss Sun Tzu's offensive strategies (Chapter III) and compare them to the recent Gulf War. To Vietnam.

5. Are there other comparisons that you can think of between what Sun Tzu recommended 2000 years ago and what happened in the Gulf War?

6. Compare his generalship comments with modern generals you may know about.

7. How would you compare the philosophy of Sun Tzu and that of a modern corporate CEO? Are there areas for comparison? What are they?

8. What does Sun Tzu say about factors that affect an organization's morale? Have you experienced examples of this?

# UCLA ANDERSON GRADUATE SCHOOL OF MANAGEMENT
## MBA PROGRAM

MANAGEMENT 251: MANAGEMENT OF HUMAN RESOURCES
WINTER, 1995

| | |
|---|---|
| Instructor: | Eric Flamholtz |
| Office: | 5317 GSM |
| Telephone: | (310) 825-4956 |
| | |
| Assistant: | Norma Sutcliffe |
| Telephone: | (310) 227-8799 |
| | |
| Materials: | Flamholtz, Eric: Human Resource Accounting, by Jossey-Bass Publishers, Inc., San Francisco, CA, 1985 (Flamholtz, "HRA") |

- Flamholtz, Eric: Growing Pains: How to Make the Transition from an Entrepreneurship to a Professionally Managed Firm, Jossey-Bass Publishers, Inc., San Francisco, CA 1990 (Flamholtz, "Professional Management")

- Phyllis F. Schlesinger, Vijay Sathe, Leonard A. Schlesinger, and John P. Kotter, John : Organization (3rd Edition), Irwin, Homewood, Illinois, 1992 (Schlesinger, et al."Organization")

- Robbins, Stephen P.: Essentials of Organizational Behavior (3rd Edition), Prentice Hall, Englewood Cliffs, New Jersey, 1991. (Robbins, "Organizational Behavior").

- Readings Binder

## Course Description, Objectives and Framework

This course focuses upon the management of people in organizations. It is intended for managers rather than for human resource professionals, and the perspective that is adopted is that of a senior general manager or the senior VP of Human Resources. The term "human resource management" ("HRM") implies a view that people are an organizational resource and ought to be managed as such.

This course deals with the human resource management process at three related levels: 1) the day-to-day issues, problems, and considerations facing managers in dealing with and managing people in organizations, 2) the role and functions of the human resource management system, and 3) the broader, strategic issues involved in managing people as resources from an organization wide viewpoint.

Some of the specific goals for the course are:

1. To provide a framework for thinking about the role and functions of human resource management;

2. To provide you with an opportunity to familiarize yourself with some concepts, ideas and research findings which are relevant to the management of people in organizations;

3. To provide you with the opportunity to develop skills in analyzing human resource issues and problems facing virtually all organizations at some stage of their development; and

4. To give you an opportunity to think systematically about your own human resource management style and (hopefully) to improve your present or potential effectiveness as a manager.

Given this perspective, the course outline is organized at three related but distinct levels of analysis:

1. The day-to-day utilization of people as organizational resources to achieve optimal productivity, satisfaction, retention and development;

2. The "personnel" or "human resource management" function that performs specialized human resource management support tasks; and

3. Broader issues facing senior management involving the use of people as organizational resources.

## Teaching Methods, Grading, Assignments

During this course, we shall be developing two types of approaches to thinking about HRM issues. One approach will be largely behavioral and process oriented. The other will be more analytical and decisions-oriented. Both are relevant to different aspects of human resource management.

M251/Flamholtz
Winter, 1995

**The Behavioral Approach**

Many of the HRM issues involve the use of conceptualization and action-taking skills. Bottom line effectiveness in human resource management involves the development of skills for: 1) problem recognition, 2) analysis of practical ways of dealing with people, 3) appreciation of the potential relevance of behavioral concepts and research findings, and 4) the personal skills in using insights to influence the behavior of people. Unfortunately, none of this can be reduced to formulae in a meaningful way.

My approach to assisting you to help develop or enhance these skills is to serve more as a "learning manager," rather than as a traditional instructor. More specifically, my strategy is to attempt to apply the Bowers & Seashore Four-factor Theory of Leadership to the management of the learning process in Management 251. This involves: 1) Goal Emphasis, 2) Interaction Facilitation, 3) Work Facilitation, and 4) Support. For those who wish to read ahead, see Chapter 11 ("Professional Management"). Alternatively, we shall deal with these concepts in session 2.

This approach to teaching makes certain assumptions about our respective roles. In brief, my job is to help create the environment in which you have the opportunity to do your own learning. Thus, readings are presented because I believe that they are potentially relevant to you as managers. I will assume that you have read them, and do not intend to discuss many of the readings in class except in so far as they are relevant to a particular case or problem under discussion. I am not interested in rote recall per se; however, you will have an opportunity to demonstrate your familiarity with the concepts and ideas in the readings. The goal is to motivate you to become familiar with the language of HRM.

**The Analytical Approach**

At present, the field of human resource management has been conceptualized quite differently than many other fields you will study at AGSM. Specifically, the field tends to be based upon the behavioral tradition rather than formal analytical models. However, during the past few years a new approach to human resource management has been evolving from an emerging school of thought that has come to be known as "Human Resource Accounting" (HRA). This has been an area of great personal and professional interest to me since my doctoral studies.

Although the area of HRA and its application to Human Resource Management is still in its relative infancy, I plan to use an HRA perspective in this course as well as the more traditional behavioral perspective. The HRA perspective is becoming more widespread.

M251/Flamholtz
Winter, 1995

## The Combined Approach

Taken together, these two perspectives provide a potentially powerful lens to view human resource management issues. The former provides a background for day-to-day operational actions, while the latter provides a frame of reference for broader, more systematic issues.

## Methods

I will use a combination of methods throughout the course, including lectures, cases, films, and a term research project. The aim is to strike a balance between theory and practice. Since one of the purposes of the course is to provide you with a forum to discuss human resource management issues and philosophies, not all of the classroom activities or exercises are aimed at your "mind-set" or appreciation of the human resource management process as much as at your retention of details. What I am saying is that, at least in part, the medium of the course is part of its message.

It ought to be noted that the course has been designed in such a way that to derive optimal benefit it will be necessary for you to go through all of the relevant readings, exercises and experiences from beginning to end. Stated differently, the course is not modularized so that the pieces are independent of each other. The learning is cumulative. However, you will need to provide some of the connections through your own efforts. Although this statement may not seem fully clear to you now, I believe it will be clear by the end of the course if you invest the required effort. I also recommend that you reread this statement on methods once or twice during the quarter.

## Grading

The grading will be based as follows:

1. Final Term Research Project         80%
2. Class Preparation & Participation   20%

The term project, described in assignment 13, must be turned in by the last session to receive full credit.

M251/Flamholtz
Winter, 1995

**Final Comment**

I am personally enthusiastic about this course and look forward to getting to know each of you and working with you this quarter. I hope you find the course interesting and of personal and professional value.

M251/Flamholtz
Winter, 1995

## WEEKLY TOPICS AND ASSIGNMENTS

**SESSION DATE**     **TOPIC**

1 Tuesday    I.   Introduction and Overview of the Management of Human Resources
1/10/95

           A.   Need for Human Resource Management Skills
           B.   Nature of Human Resource Management

      II.   Making the Transition to the Managerial Role

Required Reading [in advance]
a)   Robbins, Organizational Behavior, Chapters 1-3
b)   Flamholtz and Randle, "The Inner Game of Management," Reading #1
c)   Flamholtz, HRA, Chapter 1
d)   Flamholtz, Professional Management, Introduction, Chapters 1 and 9.

Problems, Cases, Exercises
a)   Case: Peter Prinzi, Reading #2
b)   Case: Bay Markets Corporation (A-D), Reading #3
c)   Assignment #1 (class discussion)
d)   Assignment #2 (class discussion)

2 Tuesday    II.   Making the Transition to a Managerial Role (Cont'd)
1/17/95
      III.   Organizational Effectiveness, Stages of Organizational Growth

           A.   Critical Elements of Organizational Effectiveness

           B.   HRM at Different Stages of Organizational Growth

Film: "The Bob Knowlton Story"

Required Reading [in advance]
a)   Flamholtz, Professional Management, Chapters 2-5
b)   Schlesinger et al., Organization, pp. 103-124 (ch.4), 459-469 (ch.8)

M251/Flamholtz
Winter, 1995

Problems, Cases, Exercises
a) Case: People Express, Schlesinger et al., pp. 125-153
b) Assignment #3 (Class Discussion)
c) Exercise: Bob Knowlton (class discussion)
d) Flamholtz, "Toward a Holistic Model of Organizational Effectiveness and Organizational Development at Different Stages of Growth," Reading #4

---

**3 Tuesday**    **IV. Motivation and Leadership**
**1/24/95**

    A. Individual Motivation, Productivity, Satisfaction, and Turnover (cont'd)

    B. Leadership, Group Dynamics, Communication Skills

        Film:    "Motivation, and the Self-fulfilling Prophecy - The Pygmalion Effect"

Required Reading [in advance]
a) Flamholtz, Professional Management, Chapter 11
b) Robbins, Organizational Behavior, Chapters 4-5, and 9
c) Scott, "Activation Theory and Task Design," Reading #5
d) Kotter, Schlesinger, & Sathe, Organization, pp. 5-27

Problems, Cases, Exercises
a) Case: Sturdivant Electric Corporation, Reading #6
b) Assignment #4 (Written, 3-4 pages)
c) Exercise: Pygmalion Effect (class discussion)

---

**4 Tuesday**    C. Leadership and Authority: Managing Upward Without Formal
**1/31/95**        Power

        Film: "Twelve Angry Men"

    Required Reading [in advance]
    a) Robbins, Organizational Behavior, Chapters 10 and 11
    b) Likert, "The Nature of Highly Effective Groups," Reading #7
    c) Gabarro and Kotter, "Managing Your Boss," Reading #8
    d) Rogers and Roethlisberger, "Barriers and Gateways," Reading #9

M251/Flamholtz
Winter, 1995

e) Nichols and Stevens, "Listening to People," Reading #10

**5 Tuesday**
**2/7/95**

Problems, Cases, Exercises
a) Exercise: "Twelve Angry Men" (In class exercise and discussion).
b) Assignment #5 (class discussion)

**6 Tuesday**
**2/14/95**

D. Leadership, Group Dynamics, Communication Skills

Required Reading [in advance]
a) Robbins, "Organizational Behavior," Chapters 7 and 8
b) Kerr and Jermier, "Substitutes for Leadership," Reading #11
c) Schlesinger et al., Organization, pp. 260-273 (ch.5)

Problems, Cases, Exercises
a) Case: Strike in Space, Reading #12
b) Assignment #6 (class discussion)

**7 Tuesday**
**2/21/95**

V. Strategic Planning, Strategic Human Resource Management, and Control

A. The Corporate Strategic Planning Process

B. Strategic Human Resource Management

C. Control Systems

Required Reading [in advance]
a) Flamholtz, Professional Management, Chapter 7,8 and 10
b) Flamholtz, Randle, & Sackmann, "Personnel Management," Reading #13
c) "Conversation with Jones and Doyle," Reading #14
d) Tichy, et al., "Strategic Human Resource Management," Reading #15
e) Robbins, Organizational Behavior, Chapter 14
f) Daft and Macintosh, "The Nature and Use of Formal Control Systems, "Reading #16

M251/Flamholtz
Winter, 1995

Problems, Cases, Exercises
a) Case: Continental Can, Reading #22
b) Assignment #7 (class discussion)

---

**8 Tuesday
2/28/95**

C. Control Systems (Cont'd)

VI. Human Resource Accounting

A. The Nature and Purpose of Human Resource Accounting

B. Human Resource Accounting Measurement Models I

Required Reading [in advance]
a) Flamholtz, HRA, Chapters 5-7, 10

Problems, Cases, Exercises
a) Case: Excellent Electronics Company (A), HRA, pp. 69-71
b) Assignment #8 (class discussion)

---

**9 Tuesday
3/7/94**

C. Human Resource Accounting Measurement Models II

D. Applications of Human Resource Accounting

Required Reading [in advance]
a) Flamholtz, HRA, Chapters 12-13

Problems, Cases, Exercises
a) Case: Lester Witte (A), Reading #17
b) Assignment #9 (class discussion)

VII. Corporate Culture and Human Resource Management

Required Reading [in advance]
a) Flamholtz, Professional Management, Chapters 6 and 12
b) Marsland et al., "Note on Japanese Management," Reading #18
c) Robbins, Organizational Behavior, Chapter 15
d) "Corporate Culture," Reading #19
e) Schlesinger et al., Organization, pp. 552-568 (Sathe, "How to Decipher and Change Corporate Culture"), pp. 341-355 (Ch.5)
f) Silverszweig and Allen, "Changing the Corporate Culture" Reading #21
g) Robbins, Organizational Behavior, Chapter 16.

M251/Flamholtz
Winter, 1995

      <u>Problems, Cases, Exercises</u>
         a) Case: Nippon Steel Corporation, Reading #20
         b) Assignment #10 (class discussion)
         c) Assignment #11 (class discussion)

---

**10 Tuesday**    VIII.   Challenge and Special Topics
**3/14/95**

      <u>Problems, Cases, Exercises</u>
         a) Assignment #12 (class discussion)
         b) Assignment #13, Term Project

M251/Flamholtz
Winter, 1995

## READINGS

| # | Description |
|---|---|
| 1 | Flamholtz and Randle, "The Inner Game of Management" |
| 2 | Case: Peter Prinzi, Westec (A) |
| 3 | Case: Bay Markets Corporation (A-D) |
| 4 | Flamholtz, "Toward a Holistic Model of Organizational Effectiveness and Organizational Development at Different Stages of Growth" |
| 5 | Scott, "Activation Theory and Task Design" |
| 6 | Case: Sturdivant Electric Corporation |
| 7 | Likert, "The Nature of Highly Effective Work Groups" |
| 8 | Gabarro and Kotter, "Managing Your Boss" |
| 9 | Rogers and Roethlisberger, "Barriers and Gateways to Communication" |
| 10 | Nichols and Stevens, "Listening to People" |
| 11 | Kerr and Jermier, "Substitutes for Leadership" |
| 12 | Case: Strike in Space |
| 13 | Flamholtz, Randle, and Sackmann, "Personnel Management: the Tenor of Today (and Tone of Tomorrow)" |
| 14 | "Conversation with Jones and Doyle" |
| 15 | Tichy et al., "Strategic Human Resource Management" |
| 16 | Daft and MacIntosh, "The Nature and Use of Formal Control Systems" |
| 17 | Case: Lester Witte (A) |
| 18 | Marsland et al., "Note on Japanese Management" |
| 19 | "Corporate Culture" |
| 20 | Case: Nippon Steel |
| 21 | Silversweig and Allen, "Changing Corporate Culture" |
| 22 | Case: Continental Can Company of Canada, Ltd. |

M251/Flamholtz
Winter, 1995

## MANAGEMENT 251 -- HUMAN RESOURCE MANAGEMENT
## ANNOTATED BIBLIOGRAPHY

The following is an annotated bibliography of selected additional readings for topics covered in the course.

### Organizational Life Cycles

Baty, G. B. *Entrepreneurship for the 80's*. Reston, Va.: Reston, 1981. This book provides a catalogue of concerns for new entrepreneurial ventures It is not a reference tool for problem solving; rather, it provides a quick overview of potential problems and suggests appropriate information sources.

Cameron, K.S., Sutton, R.I., and Whetton, D.A. *Readings in Organizational Decline*. Cambridge, Mass.: Ballinger Publishing, 1988. This collection of readings presents both the theory of organizational decline as well as empirical studies that examine the decline process from a sociological as well as a psychological or behavioral perspective. It also includes articles that describe the steps organizations can take to prevent or overcome the problems encountered at this stage of growth.

Carland, J.W., and others. "Differentiating Entrepreneurs from Small Business Owners: A Conceptualization." *Academy of Management Review*, April 1984, pp. 354-359. This review of the literature describes the characteristics of both the entrepreneur and the entrepreneurial ventures and proposes two conceptualizations: one for differentiating entrepreneurial ventures from small businesses and another for differentiating entrepreneurs from small business owners/managers. The critical distinctions found between the two involve the entrepreneurs' greater innovative abilities and such entrepreneurial traits as goal orientation, internal locus of control, and the need for independence, responsibility, and power. Risk-taking behavior is rejected as a distinguishing characteristic of entrepreneurship. Definitions of small business venture, entrepreneurial venture, small business owner, and entrepreneur are presented.

Dalton, D.R. and Kesner, I.F. "Organizational Growth: Big Is Beautiful," *Journal of Business Strategy*, Volume 6(1), Summer 1985, pp. 38-48. The observation that bigger is better for the business enterprise is a controversial one. An attempt is made to: 1. review growth as an organizational phenomenon and a near universal goal, 2. discuss the supposed association between size and organizational performance, and 3. develop an argument that growth and absolute size should be legitimate goals of an organization whether or not size can be meaningfully related to performance. While it is clear that the size of the organization is not related to performance, financial and otherwise, there are many nonfinancial advantages that accrue to the larger organization, such as: 1. pure clout, 2. larger executive salaries, 3. recognition, and 4. ability to afford specialists in all fields. There is also a downside to bigness, though. For example, larger firms are subject to closer scrutiny, greater social responsibility is expected of them, and problems of coordination and allocation of resources become more complex.

Kennedy, A. "Every employee an Entrepreneur." *Inc.*, April 1984, pp. 108-117. In this interview, Allen Kennedy, coauthor of *Corporate Cultures* (see previous entry), explains this theory in an anthropological perspective, claiming that each company has its own policy and internal behavior that strongly affects its business practice. He predicts a trend away from major corporations and toward entrepreneurship and decentralization. Kennedy discusses his own entrepreneurial venture.

Kimberly, J.R., Miles, R.H. and Associates (eds.) *The Organizational Life Cycle*, San Francisco: Jossey Bass Publishers, Inc, 1980. This is a collection of works on the nature of organizational birth, transformations, decline and the challenges organizations face at each stage in their life cycle. Many of the articles presented are empirical studies of how organizations or populations of organizations and how they have or have not solved growth-related problems.

Motz, R. "Entrepreneurial Managers in Large Organizations." *Business Horizons*, September/October 1984, pp. 54-58. This article highlights the importance of entrepreneurial managers in complex, well-established organizations. An entrepreneurial manager can constantly monitor and potentially redefine the organization's objectives as well as meet a changing environment full of new opportunities. How company can adapt to the entrepreneurial personality is discussed, and strategies for producing innovation within a large company are presented.

Peters, T.J., and Waterman, R.H. *In Search of Excellence: Lessons from America's Best Run Companies*. New York: Harper & Row, 1982. Based on a study of large U.S. corporations, this book outlines eight basic practices that the authors argue are found consistently in excellent organizations. The authors selectively illustrate the occurrence of these practices in a variety of companies.

Powell, J.D., and Bimmerle, C.F. "A Model of Entrepreneurship Moving Toward Precision and Complexity." *Journal of Small Business Management*, January 1980, pp. 33-36. This article reviews the entrepreneurial process through the use of a model emphasizing the complexity of the venture initiation decision. The model outlines entrepreneurial descriptors, precipitating factors, and venture specific factors, as steps leading to the final entrepreneurial venture. Previous, simplistic models are criticized as having limited predictive utility.

Tushman, M.L. and Romanelli, E. "Organizational Evolution: A Metamorphosis Model of Convergence and Reorientation. In *Research in Organizational Behavior, Volume 7*. B. Staw and L.L. Cummings (eds.). Greenwich, CT: JAI Press, pp. 171-222. The author is presenting a model of organizational change that suggest firms grow and change in a revolutionary rather than evolutionary fashion. They also examine the impact succession of top management teams organizational success.

Tushman, M.L. and Nadler, D. "Organizing for Innovation," *California Management Review*, Spring 1986, pp. 74-92. This article provides a practical discussion of the steps management can take to develop an organization which facilitates innovation and creativity.

Barbara Blumenthal & Philippe Haspeslagh. *Toward a Definition of Corporate Transformation*. Sloan Management Review, Spring 1994. What is corporate transformation and how can we define a successful one? The authors propose a definition based on behavioral changes throughout the organization and suggest a framework, built on their analysis of cases and interviews, for comparing transformations among firms.

## Organizational Effectiveness at Different Stages of Growth

Ditlea, S., and Tanjorra, J. "The Birth of an Industry." *Inc.*, January 1982, pp. 64-70. The development of the completely new personal computer software industry is described through examples of the growth of the seven original companies in the field. Case studies of the companies are presented, starting from their inception and working through to their current problems, which involve decisions on how to structure their organizations, what products to make, and how to sell those products.

Drucker, P.F. *Innovation and Entrepreneurship: Practice and Principles*. New York: Harper & Row, 1985. Peter Drucker describes a new, dynamic, entrepreneurial economy in America. Through systematic management of organized activity, innovation is no longer left to chance. Drucker examines seven sources of innovative opportunities and explains the practice of entrepreneurship.

Gumpert, D.E., and Stevenson, H.E. "The Heart of Entrepreneurship." *Harvard Business Review*, March/April 1985, pp. 85-94. The steps of the entrepreneurial process are outlined, along with the necessary structure and characteristics a firm should have to maintain an entrepreneurial environment. The administrative state of mind, whose focus involves guarding resources and reducing risk, is contrasted with that of the entrepreneur.

Harrigan, K.R. "Managing Declining Businesses," *Journal of Business Strategy*, Volume 4(3), Winter 1984, pp. 74-78. Firms often face the problem of preventing strategic business unit (SBU) performance from flagging in a declining business. Success frequently depends on differences in attitude and infrastructure. This study addresses the aspects of managing declining demand which require special attention. There are a number of ways to reap profits within declining SBUs. If analysis indicates that the declining business' profitability potential is low because of inferior strategic posture or if the firm lacks the planning infrastructure and managerial skills, then the firm should exit. Repositioning the SBU can be an untidy solution, while divestiture constitutes a clean break. Both industry and organizational factors can hinder the firm's progress in dealing with the declining SBU. Appointing a manager who has the skill to deal with the affected SBU is important, and the company must clearly communicate its policy.

Howy, F., and Vaught, B.C. "The Rural Entrepreneur: A Study in Frustration." *Journal of Small Business Management*, January 1980, pp. 18-24. This study of 150 rural Texas entrepreneurs lists the major problems faced by these businesses and shows that there are certain types of problems—such as personnel problems, government regulations, and economic conditions—that because of their external nature frustrate managerial attempts to overcome them. Entrepreneurs cite these issues as major problems inhibiting the successful operation of their businesses, yet they do not seek outside help. They do seek outside help for what they perceive as the most significant types of problems over which they feel they have control, such as marketing-related problems. They study concludes that more education is needed in the area of goal expectancy. Goal accomplishment, as opposed to the skills training, should be emphasized so that frustration will be minimized as awareness of control is gained by management.

Kidder, T. *The Soul of a New Machine*. New York: Avon, 1981. This narrative explores the development of a new computer at Data General Corporation. It illustrates the dynamics of new product development within an entrepreneurial organization.

"Prophets of the New Age." *Inc.*, April 1984, pp. 81-91. Case studies are presented that depict the beginnings and subsequent successes of six entrepreneurs who have formed highly profitable corporations. Included among the six are Steven Jobs of Apple Computer and Fred Smith of Federal Express.

Richman, T. "Going Their Way." *Inc.*, December 1982, pp. 70-76. This article reviews the achievements of America's fastest growing private companies, named in the "Inc. 500." Brief case studies of the top twenty-five entrepreneurial companies are presented, and characteristics shared by all the companies are described.

Scully, J. *Odyssey*. New York: Harper & row, 1987. The author, CEO of Apple Computer, Inc., describes the problems his firm faced and how they were overcome as Apple Computer made the transition from an entrepeneurship to a professionally managed firm.

James P. Womack and Daniel T. Jones. *From Lean Production to the Lean Enterprise*. Harvard Business Review. March/April 1994. The next step after implementing lean-production techniques is linking these breakthroughs up and down the value chain, creating a lean enterprise. The lean enterprise is a group of individuals, functions, and legally separate but operationally synchronized companies that create, sells, and services a family of products. Few companies have created a lean enterprise, and understandably. Individuals, functions, and companies have needs that conflict with each other and with those of the lean enterprise. The strengths and weaknesses of German, U.S., and Japanese industrial traditions suggest that trade-offs between these three entities are inevitable.

## Strategic Planning

Brandt, S.C. *Strategic Planning in Emerging Companies*. Reading, Mass.: Addison-Wesley, 1981. This book provides the basic perspective necessary for strategic planning and outlines its various dimensions. The author integrates comments on organizational units and corporate culture within the framework of strategic planning.

Eisenhardt, K.M. "Making Fast Strategic Decisions in High Velocity Environments," *Academy of Management Journal*, Volume 32 (3), 1989, pp. 543-576. Eisenhardt examines how executive teams make strategic decisions in the high velocity environment of the microcomputer industry. She finds that fast decision-makers use more, not less information than do slower decision-makers. They tend to develop more, not fewer, alternatives, and use a two-tiered advice process. Conflict resolution and integration among strategic decisions and tactical plans are also critical to the pace of decision-making. Most importantly, these faster decision processes lead to superior performance in the market.

Glueck, W.F., and Jauch, L.R. *Strategic Management and Business Policy.* New York: McGraw-Hill, 1984. This text walks the reader through the strategic management process, emphasizing the need for continuous planning. Focus is on the environment and internal competitive advantages. Choices and evaluation of strategy provide a firm understanding of the model.

Lorange, P. *Implementation of Strategic Planning.* Englewood Cliffs, N.J.: Prentice-Hall, 1982. Lorange provides and overview of the issues involved in implementing strategic plans. In addition, a considerable amount of discussion relating to planning systems provides a framework to evaluate a strategic planning system.

Porter, M.E. *Competitive Advantage: Creating and Sustaining Superior Performance.* New York, NY: The Free Press, 1985. Porter develops an integrated framework for analyzing strategic problems. He helps the reader frame strategic problems and develop the appropriate analyses.

Tylee, W.J. "Strategic Planning at R.J. Reynolds Industries," *Journal of Business Strategy*, Volume 6(2), Fall 1985, pp. 22-28. Despite recent criticisms of strategic planning and its effectiveness, R.J. Reynolds Industries Inc. (RJR) views strategic planning as a necessity for business success. Practical and visionary strategic planning is responsible for the firm's high level of profitability. At RJR (Winston-Salem, North Carolina), the emphasis of strategic planning is development of practical, relevant plans that are feasible to implement and contribute to the evolution of the firm. Planning is integrated into the operations of the firm at all levels of management. Through strategic planning, RJR has established its basic mission as a consumer products firm and identified product/market segments for strategic development. Both internal and external growth strategies are pursued, with internal strategies focused on spurring excellence in existing businesses and external strategies focused on solidifying market position through acquisitions.

Steiner, G.A. *Top Management Planning.* New York: MacMillan, 1969. Steiner offers readers an important foundation in an overview of corporate planning terminology and concepts. A top management perspective places the emphasis on overall results for the business while also discussing planning in many of the functional areas.

Gary Hamel and C.K. Phahalad. *Strategy as Stretch and Leverage.* Harvard Business Review. May/June 1993. The authors take strategic planning beyond just pursuing opportunities that fit the company's resources. They are interested in the dynamics of competition and how some companies are more successful than others by creating new forms of competitive advantage by utilizing a strategic mindset where "stretch" supplements fit and they leverage the strategic allocation of resources. There are five basic ways to leverage: by concentrating resources around strategic goals; by complementing one kind of resource with another; by conserving resources whenever they can; and by recovering resources from the marketplace as quickly as possible. To contend with hungry rivals, managers must master the art of resource leverage and recognize that creating stretch -- a gap between where a company is and where it wants to be -- is the most important task.

James F. Moore. *Predators and Prey: A New Ecology of Competition.* Harvard Business Review. January/February 1994. James Moore sets up a new metaphor for competition drawn from the study of biology and social systems to replace the metaphor that companies go head-to-head in an industry battling for market share. A company should be viewed not as a member of a single industry but as part of a business ecosystem that crosses a variety of industries. In this business ecosystem companies "coevolve" around a new innovation, working cooperatively and competitively to support new products and satisfy customer needs. In any larger business environment, several ecosystems may vie for survival and dominance, such as the IBM and Apple ecosystems in personal computers. In fact, it's largely competition among business ecosystems, not individual companies, that is fueling today's industrial transformation. Executives must understand the evolutionary stages all ecosystems go through, and more important, how to direct these changes.

Henry Mintzberg. *The Fall and Rise of Strategic Planning.* Harvard Business Review. January/February 1994. Mintzberg argues that what is needed is not strategic planning but strategic thinking. Strategic planning is analysis or breaking down a goal into steps, formalizing those steps, and articulating the expected consequences. Strategic thinking, in contrast, is about synthesis which involves intuition and creativity. The outcome of strategic thinking is an integrated perspective, a not too precisely articulated vision of direction that must be free to appear at any time and at any place in the organization. Traditional strategic planning or strategic programming can augment strategic thinking by supplying the formal analyses that strategic thinking requires, helping managers think strategically and helping to specify the steps needed to carry out the vision.

## Organizational Structure

Galbraith, J.R. *Designing Complex Organizations*, Reading MA.: Adison-Wesley, 1973. This book presents an analytical framework for the design of complex organizations. It focuses primarily on organizations with complex lateral relationships and matrix components. The ambiguous levels authority and responsibility created in this type of organization warrants the special attention Galbraith provides.

Merrell, D.W. "The Impact of Restructuring on Employees," *Journal of Buyouts and Acquisitions*, Volume 4 (1), 1986, pp. 60-62. The impact of restructuring on employees is often overlooked. The organization will suffer during a restructuring as long as workers are uncertain about their future. The lack of information and failure to communicate with employees during this process intensifies feelings of uncertainty. This results in insecurity and a loss of motivation as well as a desire to sabotage the restructuring effort. This article describes some steps which management can take to minimize these negative consequences.

Miner, J.B. *Theories of Organizational Structure and Process*, Chicago, Il.: The Dryden Press, 1982. This book provides a survey of the major bodies of theoretical literature concerning organizational structure and processes. It includes a discussion of Likert's System 4, Sociotechnical Systems theory, Technology, Administrative behavior, organizational structure and a variety of other major theories.

Robey, D. *Designing Organizations, 2nd Edition*, Homewood, Il.: Irwin, 1986. Robey provides a useful conceptual bridge between the macro and micro views of organizational design. Thus, he balances the literature on organization theory and strategy, with that of organizational behavior (which relies on the work group as the level of analysis. In the second edition, he includes extended materials on strategy, life cycles, power, culture, and information processing.

Ian I. Mitoff, Richard O. Mason and Christine M. Pearson. Framebreak: The Radical Redesign of American Business, San Francisco: Jossey-Bass. 1994. The authors of this book reveal how nothing less than a total, broad-ranging reconceptualization of American business can save corporations from rampant upheaval and turmoil. They explain how nineteenth organizational structures— with their self-contained units such as marketing, finance, and operations— are no longer the building blocks of organizations. The authors propose a strikingly new, dramatically different design for organizations based on four key dimensions of business life and success: knowledge and learning, recovery and development, service and spirituality, and world-class operations. The outcome is an approach to business that has never been articulated before: total ethical management.

Jon R. Katzenbach and Douglas K. Smith. *The Discipline of Teams*. Harvard Business Review, March/April 1993. This article which is drawn from the book, *The Wisdom of Teams*, looks at a organizational structure design that is becoming more popular at high performance organizations -- the team. What makes a team different from other kinds of working groups? When should the team option be utilized? A team differs from other working groups because the teams performance is greater than simply the sum of the individual contributions. To achieve high performance, the best teams invest a tremendous amount of time in shaping its purpose and translating its purpose into specific performance goals. Members of successful teams pitch in and become accountable with and to their teammates. Three types of teams are identified: teams that recommend things such as task forces; teams that make or do things such as operations teams; and teams that run things such as overseeing a functional activity. Team potential exists anywhere hierarchy or organizational boundaries inhibit good performance.

Richard Rapaport. *To Build a Winning Team: An Interview with Head Coach Bill Walsh*. Harvard Business Review, January/February 1993. In this interview, Bill Walsh discusses how he produced winners through his structured and businesslike approach which maximized the potential of his players and his coaches. He discusses how he developed meticulous long-range strategic and personnel plans where he defined responsibilities, objectives and priorities for everyone in the organization. He discusses the "arc of utilization" where he projects what each player can do throughout their expected life cycle in the organization.

## Management Development

Cox, C., and Beck, J. *Management Development*. New York: Wiley, 1984. Through a selection of articles, the book deals with many current issues of management development. Issues treated include women in management, managerial obsolescence, and responsibility for training.

Katz, R.L. "Skills of an Effective Administrator," In People: Managing Your Most Important Asset a collection of Harvard Business Review classics, Boston, MA: Harvard Business Review, 1988. Mr. Katz identifies and examines three basic skills; technical, human, and conceptual, that every successful manager must have. He suggests, however, that these skills are required in varying degrees, according to the level of management at which he or she is operating.

London, M. Developing Managers. San Francisco: Jossey-Bass, 1985. Throughout this study of career motivation, guidelines and issues are brought to the attention of management. In addition, it review types of training programs and their potentials and includes a description of strategies for coping with mid-career crises.

Lopez, F.E., Rockmore, B.W., and Kesselman, G.A. "The Development of an Integrated Career Planning Program at Gulf Power Company," In H.G. Heneman and D.T. Schwab (eds.), Perspectives on Personnel/Human Resource Management (Homewood, Ill.: Irwin, 1982). This article provides a model and case study for developing a career matrix for management development.

Whetten, D.A., and Cameron, K.S. Developing Management Skills, Glenview, Il.: Scott, Foresman and Company, 1984. Competence in interpersonal skills is a critical prerequisite for a successful career in management. Strong analytical and quantitative skills are important, but not sufficient. This book can be best described as a management practicum which includes a combination of conceptual learning and behavioral practice, since both are necessary for effective skill development.

T. George Harris. The Post-Capitalist Executive: An Interview with Peter F. Drucker. Harvard Business Review, May/June 1993. Drucker argues that managers must learn to negotiate a new environment with a different set of work rules and career expectations. Companies currently face downsizing and turmoil with increasing regularity. Once built to last like pyramids, corporations are now more like tests. Managers must relearn how to manage. In the new world of business, information is replacing authority as the primary tool of the executive. One embarks on the road toward information literacy not by buying the latest technological gadget but by identifying gaps in knowledge. Also the manager must begin to take individual responsibility for himself or herself. To that end, the managers must explore their personal competencies such as competencies, abilities, likes, dislikes, and goals.

Davis Krackhardt and Jeffrey R. Hansen. Informed Networks: The Company Behind the Chart. Harvard Business Review. July/August 1993. While the formal organizational chart shows who's the boss, it does not reveal which people confer on technical matters or discuss office politics over lunch. Much of the real work in any company gets done through this informal organization with its complex networks of relationships that cross functions and divisions. By diagramming three types of networks managers can harness the true power in their organization. These networks are: the advise network, which reveals the people to whom others turn to get work done; the trust network, which uncovers who shares delicate information; and the communication network, which shows who talks about work-related matters. These networks which are generated through employee questionnaires are useful in getting to the root of many organizational problems such as resistance to change because team members of a task force are not central to the trust network.

## Leadership

Bennis, W. On Becoming a Leader. Reading, Mass.: Addison-Wesley, 1989. Using a series of interviews with people such as director Sydney Pollack, Ms. editor Gloria Steinem, and Apple CEO John Scully, the author examines the nature of leadership. Bennis also describes the differences between managers and leaders and provides suggestions for how organizations can help develop effective leaders.

Likert, R. The Human Organization. New York: McGraw-Hill, 1967. A classic, this book deals with leadership styles and their effects on the management and value of human resources. Likert postulates four different styles or systems of management, which parallel the first four styles of management described in Chapter Ten of the present book.

Maccoby, M. *The Leader.* New York: Simon & Schuster, 1981. Maccoby challenges the traditional concepts of management and proposes a picture of the leaders who will come to dominate in the United States. Through descriptions of six types of leaders, both in business and government, the author documents leadership principles and then goes further to discuss the development of leadership.

Nitin Nohria and James D. Berkley. *Whatever Happened to the Take-Charge Manager.* Harvard Business Review, January/February 1994. Nohria and Berkley argue that in the 1980's managers in their quest to be take-charge actually abdicated their managerial responsibility by relying too much on consultants, gurus, and the latest fad of the week to answer all their problems. They feel that the first place to start in taking back their responsibility and becoming truly take-charge is to become more pragmatic. They need to become more sensitive to their company's context and be more open to uncertainty. Pragmatic managers need to avoid three common pitfalls; the "let's do it better this time" syndrome, the "flavor of the month" syndrome, and the "let's go for it all" syndrome.

H. Kent Bowen, Kim B. Clark, Charles A. Holloway and Steven C. Wheelwright. *Make Projects the School for Leaders.* Harvard Business Review, September/October 1994. The authors argue that using development projects for product development where the members are from the various functional groups can not only result in superior products but in developing superior future leaders. They argue that the senior management provided the project teams with powerful guiding visions for business strategy, project, and product. These visions were reinforced and internalized by the project team members. The project leaders expanded significantly in their capacity for leadership.

Manfred F. R. Kets de Vries. Leaders, Fools and Imposters: Essays on the Psychology of Leadership, San Francisco: Jossey-Bass, 1992. In this book of insightful essays, Kets de Vries explodes the myth that rationality is what governs the behavior of leaders and followers. Probing the careers of Robert Maxwell, John DeLorean, and others, he examines the addictiveness of power, why so many leaders have difficulty sharing it, and what causes some leaders to abuse it. This book gives consultants and managers the tools to detect and act on problems in leadership, offers organizational behaviorists a better understanding of the leader-follower dynamic, and gives leaders the means to transform themselves.

## Control Systems

Koenig, J., Flamholtz, D.T., and Flamholtz, E.G. *Organizational Control Systems.* New York: Touche Ross & co., 1985. A monograph that outlines control and control systems, this book also addresses the role of accounting and organizational control. It considers the organization's need for control and how to evaluate this need.

Newman, W.H. *Constructive Control.* Englewood Cliffs, N.J.: Prentice-Hall, 1975. This book describes how managerial control can obtain positive responses through ties to desired results. The structural and behavioral elements of control are explored along with their applications in a variety of operations. Finally, systems to coordinate controls are reviewed.

David A. Garvin. *Building a Learning Organization.* Harvard Business Review, July/August 1993. Garvin argues that before people and companies can improve they must first learn the new behaviors. To do this, they must look beyond rhetoric and high philosophy and focus on the fundamentals of learning. Key to becoming a learning organization is the establishment of learning audits which measure the cognitive and behavioral changes from learning new skills.

## Corporate Culture

Dalziel, M.M., and Schoonover, S.C. *Changing Ways: A Practical Tool for Implementing Change Within Organizations,* New York, NY: AMACOM, 1988. The authors present detailed strategies for managing change in organizations. They focus on three critical questions associated with the change effort: 1) How can I get my organization ready to change? 2) How do I ensure a smooth and successful implementation plan? and 3) What types of people do I need to make the implementation successful?

Kilmann, R.H., Saxton, M.J., Serpa, R., and Associates. *Gaining Control of the Corporate Culture*. San Francisco: Jossey-Bass, 1985. This book presents the state of the art on corporate culture today. It includes the work of leading scholars, managers, and consultants. Through this combined effort it brings forth an integrated approach toward culture management. The book focuses on a number of actual case studies such as AT&T, NCR, Atari, and Levi Strauss to demonstrate their points.

Deal, T.D., and Kennedy, A.A. *Corporate Cultures: The Rites and Rituals of Corporate Life*. Reading, Mass.: Addison-Wesley, 1982. In this book the authors suggest that long-term corporate success is dependent on company culture. Specifically, the company's culture must match its strategy. Moreover, a person's success within a company can be a direct result of how well he or she interprets that culture. Through numerous examples the book portrays aspects and types of culture.

Sathe, V. *Culture and Related Corporate Realities*, Homewood, Il.: Irwin, 1985. Sathe provides a comprehensive text on the definition, implications, assessment, and management of organizational culture. The book includes text and cases to help understand the relevant problems and issues associated with the management of organizational culture.

Schein, E.H. *Organizational Culture and Leadership*. San Francisco: Jossey-Bass, 1985. Schein defines corporate culture and describes how it evolves over time in response to organizational changes. He also provides a framework for identifying and analyzing corporate culture.

## Role of the Entrepreneur

Burgelman, R.A. "A Process Model of Internal Corporate Venturing in the Diversified Major Firm." *Administrative Science Quarterly*, June 1983, pp. 223-244. The focus of this field study is the process through which a diversified major firm transforms R&D activities into a new business through internal corporate venture (ICV). The relationship between project development and business development is specifically examined, as well as how new organizational units developed around new businesses become integrated into the operating system of the corporation. The components necessary for a successful ICV effort are presented.

Grove, A.S. *High Output Management*. New York: Random House, 1983. The president of Intel who is one of its founders describes his concept of Intel's management philosophy. The book stresses an output-orientation and introduces the concept of management leverage team management. Finally, an analogy to sports is drawn to illustrate obtaining peak individual performances among the business team.

Levinson, H., and Rosenthal, S. *CEO*. New York: basic Books, 1984. This book outlines the practice of leadership by CEOs. Through documented interviews at six will-known companies, the authors provide a glimpse of what leadership involves in a highly organized setting.

Steiner, G.A. *The New CEO*. New York: MacMillan, 1983. This book reviews the changing social and political environment of U.S. business and the extent to which the forces that shape it compel the CEOs of large firms to involve themselves in external affairs. These new responsibilities, particularly in the public policy area, require CEOs to have a variety of talents and the ability to balance constituent interests.

Amar Bhide. *How Entrepreneurs Craft Strategies that Work*. Harvard Business Review. March/April 1994. Bhide reports on the research on more that 200 thriving ventures. The research found four relevant guidelines for budding entrepreneurs. Successful entrepreneurs screen out unpromising ideas as soon as possible using judgment and reflection, not using extensive data analysis. Second, they are realistic about their financial situation, personal preferences and goals. Third, to conserve their limited time and money, they minimize the resources devoted to researching ideas. Last, they realize they do not need all the answers in order to act.

## Family Business

Buchalter, G. "A Desert Fox" *Forbes* Volume 144 (8), October 16, 1989, pp. 244-250. Twenty-five years ago, Laughlin, Nevada, located across the Colorado River from Bullhead City, Arizona, did not exist. There was just an unnamed strip of bleached-out desert with a few inhabitants and a rundown tavern with a few slot machines. Today, town founder Donald Laughlin presides over a booming gambling town of 4,000 residents that attracted 2 million tourists in 1988. When Laughlin came to the area in 1964, he saw potential revenues in every direction. He opened Riverside Resort Hotel & Casino in 1966. In 1988, the Riverside Resort had revenues of $79 million and netted some $7 million. Laughlin has become the 4th-largest gambling city in the US. The town's growth attracted established gaming syndicates, such as Circus Circus Enterprises, Sahara, and Harrah's. Don Laughlin has had problems with Nevada's gaming laws. These include the placement of family members in key positions and the drug problems of family members. Laughlin owns the town's movie theaters and convention hall, the town's 2 banks, a local bus company, ferry boats, and other real estate in Nevada and Arizona.

Deveny, K. "How Leonard Lauder Is Making His Mom Proud," *Business Week* (Industrial/Technology Edition), September 4, 1989, pp. 68-73. Leonard A. Lauder, son of Estee Lauder, has been the chief executive of Estee Lauder Inc. (New York) for the past 7 years. Long before then, he began transforming the mom-and-pop business into a cosmetics empire. Thanks to Leonard, the firm now boasts top-notch training programs for employees and strict financial controls. He insists that he has an edge on his publicly held rivals, pointing out that the firm's net margin consistently tops the industry average. The push is on to polish the image of the company's flagship Estee Lauder brand. The company's basic formula is to sell in upscale department stores and avoid new brands that only steal sales from existing ones. The ability to develop consistent brand images gives the firm big advantages over its less-focused rivals. Leonard Lauder supports the strategy by assiduously cultivating retailers. In part, that means giving them exclusive promotions. He has built an idiosyncratic corporate culture that marries the paternalism of a small family operation with the marketing power of a big company. Tables.

Goldwasser, T. *Family Pride: Profiles of Five of America's Best-Run Family Businesses*, New York, NY: Dodd, Mead & Co., 1986. The best-run family businesses have always upheld the principles of quality, serving the customer, and treating employees with respect. Business critics of American industry are now looking at these companies with renewed interest. This book examines five family businesses which are still run by the founder or members of his family: Hallmark, Noxell Corporation, Marriott Corporation, H&R Block, and S.C. Johnson & Son. Goldwasser examines each company's beginnings, growth, diversification, cultures, and strategies.

Donna Fenn. *Are Your Kids Good Enough to Run Your Business.* Inc. August 1994. This short article details the trend towards children coming into the family business. Considering this possibility can start while the children are still young. The author gives some references where family entrepreneurs can get advice on the problems peculiar to family businesses.

Donna Fenn. *Pass It On.* Inc. August 1994. Fenn presents the case history of Capsco Sales, a family business with three of the founder's children on the payroll. The founder's difficulties in planning the succession after her retirement are detailed.

## Shifting Control of the Firm

Albo, W.P., and Henderson, A.R. *Mergers & Acquisitions of Privately Held Businesses* (2nd Edition), Canadian Institute of Chartered Accountants: Toronto, Ont, 1989. This book provides a comprehensive guide through all steps of corporate acquisitions of small to mid sized firms. It examines a variety of critical factors is significant depth including: acquisition planning, planning of the sale, pricing, tax considerations, negotiation, financing, and post acquisition integration.

Buono, A.F., and Bowditch, J.L. *The Human Side of Mergers and Acquisitions: Managing Collisions Between People, Cultures and Organizations*, San Francisco: Jossey-Bass Publishers, Inc., 1989. This book analyzes the human factor in mergers and acquisitions. It describes the uncertainty involved in the change as well as the implications of individual managers' actions throughout the process. The authors examine the hidden costs in combining organizations in addition to the turmoil brought about by shifting values, beliefs, and norms.

Golden, W.J. and Little, A.D. "Leveraged Buyouts as a Corporate Development Tool," *Journal of Business Strategy*, Volume 6(1), Summer 1985, pp. 7-14. Large-scale divestitures, especially those involving businesses in mature industries, are difficult to implement. The leveraged buyout (LBO) has proven very useful for such divestitures because it gets around the major implementation obstacles. However, it has not been used much by corporations, partly because LBO planning is perceived as too costly and time-consuming. The purchase of a firm in an LBO is largely financed by debt. The technique makes the most sense when a corporation expects to be unable to sell a business unit on a timely basis at a fair price. The most common buyer group in an LBO is the management of the unit to be divested. In the next 5 years, there will be a dearth of divestiture candidates qualified for LBOs relative to the number of interested buyers and the available supply of financing. Thus, corporations will be in a good position to negotiate favorable terms of sale for qualified candidates using the LBO technique. Areas that must be reviewed prior to beginning LBO negotiation include: 1. pension effect, 2. documentation of operating risks, 3. objectives, and 4. valuation technique.

Holmes, R.E. "How to Retain Work Forces When Firms are Acquired" *Mergers & Acquisitions* March/April, 1988, pp. 61-63. In the sale of a small or mid-sized business, one of the key elements is the workforce. Good communication is critical during the acquisition process, and attempts at secrecy may be detrimental to the internal selling process.

Rosen, C. "The Growing Appeal of the Leveraged ESOP," *Journal of Business Strategy*, January/February 1989, pp. 16-20. Rosen discusses how more and more companies are linking their leveraged buyouts to an employee stock ownership plan. Three of the primary reasons are: 1) to create shareholder loyalty, 2) to encourage superior performance, and 3) There are some very significant tax incentives which reward this type of transaction.

Schweiger, D.M., Ivancevich, J.M, and Power, F.R. "Executive Actions for Managing Human Resources Before and After Acquisition" *Academy of Management Executive*, Volume 1, May 1987, pp. 127-138. The authors conducted extensive interviews in target firms finding: 1) a loss of identity, 2) anxiety and a lack of information, 3) an obsession with self-survival, 4) the loss of talent through the loss of co-workers, and 5) family repercussions. Effective managerial actions to soften these consequences included: 1) maintain commitment to employees, 2) be honest, 3) show a sincere understanding for employee concerns, 4) refusing to permit political behavior, 5) handling terminations and outplacements in a dignified manner, and 6) actively managing the aftermath of the acquisition.

M251/Flamholtz
Winter, 1995

## EXERCISES

### (in-class worksheets)

1. "The Bob Knowlton Story" (worksheet)
2. "Motivation and the Self-fulfilling Prophecy-The Pygmalion Effect" (worksheet)
3. "Twelve Angry Men" (worksheet and case)

M251/Flamholtz
Winter, 1995

## The Bob Knowlton Story - Worksheet

1. Using concepts from class and readings, specifically those presented in the <u>Inner Game of Management</u>, identify the specific problems Bob Knowlton is having in making the transition to a managerial role.

2. What Inner Game Syndrome(s) is Bob Knowlton suffering from? Explain.

3. Assume you are Bob Knowlton. What goals should you set to improve your effectiveness as a manager?

4. What specific action steps should you take to achieve these goals?

5. How did Bob's manager (Gerald) contribute to Bob's problems in this situation?

6. What could Gerald have done to help avoid this situation?

M251/Flamholtz
Winter, 1995

## The Pygmalion Effect - Worksheet

1. Describe an example of the Self-Fulfilling Prophecy in your organization.

2. List at least five ways a manager can relay positive expectations and five ways negative expectations can be conveyed to an employee.

3. Which workers are most susceptible to the Pygmalion Effect? What are the implications for management?

4. In what ways can workers convey their expectations to their bosses?

5. What cautions should be kept in mind as you apply the Pygmalion Effect?

M251/Flamholtz
Winter, 1995

## Twelve Angry Men

During this session you will be watching the film titled "Twelve Angry Men." The following questions will be discussed during the session:

1. How well did the appointed (formal) leader of the group function as a leader? Explain.

2. Who were the informal leaders who emerged during the jury's deliberation?

3. In what specific ways did each of the informal leaders attempt to influence the behavior and decisions of the group? Give examples.

4. How effectively did each of the people listed in Columns B-E of Exercise 1 perform each of the leadership functions listed in Column A?

5. To what extent did each of the people listed in Columns B-E of Exercise 2 demonstrate each of the leadership skills listed in Column A?

6. What group management strategy and tactics did Henry Fonda use? Why was he successful?

7. What factors affected the way people voted during the first vote at the beginning of the film? List.

8. In what ways did the group exercise control over the behavior of its members during the jury's deliberations? Give examples.

9. Can you cite any examples of how the ideas in the film might be useful to you as a manager?

M251/Flamholtz
Winter, 1995

Exhibit 1
Twelve Angry Men
Cast of Characters

COACH
(FOREMAN)
Martin Balsam

ADVERTISING MAN

MILD MANNERED
BANK CLERK

WATCH-MAKER

MESSENGER
SERVICE OWNER-
Lee J. Cobb

GARAGE OWNER
(with cold)-
Ed Begley

BROKER (with
frameless glasses)-
E.G. Marshall

OLD MAN

MAN FROM THE SLUMS-
Jack Klugman

ARCHITECT-
Henry Fonda

HOUSE PAINTER

BASEBALL FAN-
Jack Warden

M251/Flamholtz
Winter, 1995

## Exercise 1

### How Well Did Each Person Perform Leadership Functions?

| Col. A | Col. B | Col. C | Col. D | Col. E |
|---|---|---|---|---|
| | Henry Fonda | Lee J. Cobb | E.G. Marshall | Martin Balsam |
| Leadership Functions | Architect | Messenger Service Owner | Stockbroker | Coach (Foreman) |
| 1. Get the group to set and reach its goal (goal emphasis). | _____ _____ _____ _____ _____ _____ | _____ _____ _____ _____ _____ _____ | _____ _____ _____ _____ _____ _____ | _____ _____ _____ _____ _____ _____ |
| 2. Get the group to work together effectively (interaction facilitation). | _____ _____ _____ _____ _____ _____ | _____ _____ _____ _____ _____ _____ | _____ _____ _____ _____ _____ _____ | _____ _____ _____ _____ _____ _____ |
| 3. Help the group to get its job done (work facilitation). | _____ _____ _____ | _____ _____ _____ | _____ _____ _____ | _____ _____ _____ |

M251/Flamholtz
Winter, 1995

4. Support members of the group (support).

M251/Flamholtz
Winter, 1995

Exercise 2

To What Extent Did Each Person Have
Leadership Skills? (High, Medium, or Low)

| Col. A<br>Leadership Skills | Col. B<br>Henry Fonda<br>Architect | Col. C<br>Lee J. Cobb<br>Messenger Service Owner | Col. D<br>E.G. Marshall<br>Stockbroker | Col. E<br>Martin Balsam<br>Coach (Foreman) |
|---|---|---|---|---|
| **A. Communication Skills:** | | | | |
| Ability to listen carefully? | _____ — | _____ — | _____ — | _____ — |
| Ability to avoid making people angry at him? | _____ — | _____ — | _____ — | _____ — |
| Ability to persuade? | _____ — | _____ — | _____ — | _____ — |
| Ability to keep people quiet? | _____ — | _____ — | _____ — | _____ — |
| **B. Team Building skills:** | | | | |
| Ability to give support? | _____ — | _____ — | _____ — | _____ — |

M251/Flamholtz
Winter, 1995

**Ability to get allies?**

M251/Flamholtz
Winter, 1995

## Exercise 3

### Applying the Ideas in "12 Angry Men"

Cite three examples of how the ideas in this film concerning leadership, group dynamics, and communication might be useful to you as a manager?

1. _____

   _____

   _____

   _____

2. _____

   _____

   _____

   _____

3. _____

   _____

   _____

   _____

M251/Flamholtz
Winter, 1995

# MANAGEMENT 251: MANAGEMENT OF HUMAN RESOURCES

## Assignment Set

1. Case: Peter Prinzi, Westec (A)
   Required: Answer the following questions.  (Class discussion)

   a. What kinds of activities give Peter Prinzi the most job satisfaction?

   b. To what extent has Pete made a successful transition from Installation Supervisor to Operations Manager?

   c. In what areas is Pete the most skilled?

   d. What kinds of skills does he need to develop?

   e. What could the Branch Manager do to help Pete make a successful transition to Operations Manager?

2. Case: Bay Markets Corporation (A-D)
   Skim the case, focusing on the managerial problems of Stan Grant.
   Required: Answer the following questions.  (Class discussion)

   a. Why was Stan Grant unsuccessful in his job as Director of Information Services?

   b. What types of personal and professional changes would grant have had to make to become effective as Director of Information Services?

   c. Is Lew Fox likely to be effective in managing the DP Organization? Why or why not?

   d. Describe Lew Fox's management style and compare it with Stan Grant's style.

3. Case: People Express
   Required: Answer the following questions.  (Class discussion)

   a. What were the major principles guiding People Express' human resource function?

   b. How did growth pressures affect the human resource strategies and personnel at People Express?

M251/Flamholtz
Winter, 1995

   c. What approach, if any, could Dubose have taken to mitigate the organizational and personal problems experienced by People Express and its employees?

4. **Case: Sturdivant Electric Corporation**
   Required: Answer the following questions.     (Written Analysis, 3-4 Pages)

   a. What leadership style does Eden use to manage Abrams?

   b. What problems does Eden create by using this style?

   c. What leadership style should Eden use?

   d. To what extent does Eden perform the five key leadership tasks in managing Al? (goal emphasis, work facilitation, interaction facilitation, supportive behavior, personnel development)

   e. What could Eden have done to improve his leadership effectiveness with Abrams?

5. **Twelve Angry Men**
   Required: Answer the following questions.     (Class discussion)

   How did Henry Fonda's leadership style reflect the fact that he didn't have authority over the others. If he did have authority, what type of style would have been appropriate (given the nature of the task and the people involved)?

6. Case: Strike in Space
   Required: Answer the following questions.     (Class discussion)

   a. What were the causes the strike?

   b. When the astronauts turn the radio back on, what will you say to them? What should your objective be in the ensuing discussions?

   c. After it was all over, Neil Hutchinson, the Flight Director, said, "We learned a marvelous lesson on how to manage people." What lesson do you think he learned?

   d. What lessons did you learn about managing people?

M251/Flamholtz
Winter, 1995

7. Case: Continental Can Company of Canada
   Required: Answer the following questions. (Class discussion)

   a. Describe the management control system at Continental Can.

   b. Is the control system effective in motivating the behavior of people at the plant to achieve their profit goals? Explain.

   c. Does the control system lead to an efficient and effective plant? Explain.

   d. What recommendations do you have for improving the control system?

8. Case: Excellent Electronics Company (A)
   Required: Answer the questions at the end of the chapter. (Class discussion)

9. Case: Lester Witte (A)
   Required: Answer the following questions. (Class discussion)

   a. Who should be chosen for the audit assignment:

      1) Jackson or 2) Williams?

   b. Explain your choice.

10. Case: Nippon Steel Corporation (A & B)
    Required: Answer the following questions. (Class discussion)

    a. Do you feel that NSC should change its personnel policies?

    b. What do you recommend that NSC should do in this situation?

    c. What do you think they will do?

11. Corporate Culture

    Required: Describe the corporate culture within your company, focusing on its impact on human resources. (Class Discussion)

M251/Flamholtz
Winter, 1995

12. "Challenge 251: (see attached)

13. **Term Project: (see attached)**

M251/Flamholtz
Winter, 1995

## CHALLENGE 251

Challenge 251 is intended as a form of self-guided course review without the stress associated with final exams or the monotony of a lecture. Clearly, one objective here is to have some fun!

 You will work in teams based on your study groups for the International Field Study. The top three teams will receive some extra credit and the top two teams will get a prize to be announced.

### How it Works
Each team begins with 100 points. Teams will take turns challenging the other groups with questions based on the course materials. For example, your group might challenge another group for 5 points. The other group will have 2 minutes to write the answer to your question on a flipchart. If they answer correctly, they get 5 of your points, if not, you get 5 of their points. There will be a final bonus round with a 20 point limit. In the end, of course, the groups with the greatest number of points win.

### Preparation
Each group should develop a set of at about 20 questions (please be prepared to turn in one copy though you will not be graded on it). In addition, as described above, there will be a final bonus round -- save your toughest one for this. It is important that you word your questions to minimize ambiguity.

### Domain for Challenge Questions
The Challenge questions may come from reading materials, class discussions/lectures, films, or videos. However, case materials and specific examples are not acceptable. As such, you need to stick to the models and theory presented throughout the course materials. Thus example 1 is unacceptable while example 2 is appropriate:

1. Inappropriate question:
   Q: Who was Al Abrams' boss?

   A: Bill Eden

2. Appropriate question:
   Q: In which stage of growth must a company place the most emphasis on managing its corporate culture?

   A: Stage IV -- Consolidation.

M251/Flamholtz
Winter, 1995

## TERM PROJECT ASSIGNMENT

**Description**

The purpose of this project is to provide you with the opportunity to study one or more of the concepts discussed in a class in more depth. Your assignment is to select a human resource management topic and then do research in that area.

**Required**

1. Select a human resource management area and prepare a term project report that:

    a) summarizes the state-of-the-art in the area, and

    b) explains the implications for human resource management and corporate management.

2. Prepare a written one page summary of your proposed topic and turn it in on 1/24/94.

3. You may work in a team if you wish.

**Procedure**

1. The final written (typed) paper is due on 3/14/95. To maintain fairness to all class members, the paper must be turned in on the date due by the end of the class in order to receive full credit.

2. The term project may range from 20-30 pages in length (<u>typed and double spaced</u>).

3. Topics that may be addressed in these projects include (but are not limited to):

    a) Motivation and Productivity
    b) Leadership Styles and Effectiveness
    c) Group Dynamics
    d) Strategic Planning for Human Resource Management
    e) Control Systems
    f) Human Resource Accounting
    g) Corporate Culture
    h) Environmental Trends and Their Implications

# SUGGESTED ADDITIONAL READINGS

## Organizational Life Cycles

**Barbara Blumenthal & Philippe Haspeslagh.**
**Toward a Definition of Corporate Transformation.**
<u>Sloan Management Review.</u> **Spring 1004.**
What is corporate transformation and how can we define a successful one? The authors propose a definition based on behavioral changes throughout the organization and suggest a framework, built on their analysis of cases and interviews, for comparing transformations among firms.

## Organizational Effectiveness at Different Stages of Growth

**James P. Womack and Daniel T. Jones.**
**From Lean Production to the Lean Enterprise.** <u>Harvard Business Review.</u> **March/April 1994.**
The next step after implementing lean-production techniques is linking these breakthroughs up and down the value chain, creating a lean enterprise. The lean enterprise is a group of individuals, functions, and legally separate but operationally synchronized companies that create, sells, and services a family of products. Few companies have created a lean enterprise, and understandably. Individuals, functions, and companies have needs that conflict with each other and with those of the lean enterprise. The strengths and weaknesses of German, U.S., and Japanese industrial traditions suggest that trade-offs between these three entities are inevitable.

## Strategic Planning

**Gary Hamel and C.K. Phahalad.**
**Strategy as Stretch and Leverage.** <u>Harvard Business Review.</u> **May/June 1993.**
The authors take strategic planning beyond just pursuing opportunities that fit the company's resources. They are interested in the dynamics of competition and how some companies are more successful than others by creating new forms of competitive advantage by utilizing a strategic mindset where "stretch" supplements fit and they leverage the strategic allocation of resources. There are five basic ways to leverage: by concentrating resources around strategic goals; by complementing one kind of resource with another; by conserving resources whenever they can; and by recovering resources from the marketplace as quickly as possible. To contend with hungry rivals, managers must master the art of resource leverage and recognize that creating stretch -- a gap between where a company is and where it wants to be -- is the most important task.

**James F. Moore.**
**Predators and Prey: A New Ecology of Competition.** <u>Harvard Business Review.</u> **January/February 1994.**
James Moore sets up a new metaphor for competition drawn from the study of biology and social systems to replace the metaphor that companies go head-to-head in an industry battling for market share. A company should be viewed not as a member of a single industry but as part of a business ecosystem that crosses a variety of industries. In this business ecosystem companies "coevolve" around a new innovation, working cooperatively and

## SUGGESTED ADDITIONAL READINGS

competitively to support new products and satisfy customer needs. In any larger business environment, several ecosystems may vie for survival and dominance, such as the IBM and Apple ecosystems in personal computers. In fact, it's largely competition among business ecosystems, not individual companies, that is fueling today's industrial transformation. Executives must understand the evolutionary stages all ecosystems go through, and more important, how to direct these changes.

**Henry Mintzberg.**
**The Fall and Rise of Strategic Planning. Harvard Business Review. January/February 1994.**
Mintzberg argues that what is needed is not strategic planning but strategic thinking. Strategic planning is analysis or breaking down a goal into steps, formalizing those steps, and articulating the expected consequences. Strategic thinking, in contrast, is about synthesis which involves intuition and creativity. The outcome of strategic thinking is an integrated perspective, a not too precisely articulated vision of direction that must be free to appear at any time and at any place in the organization. Traditional strategic planning or strategic programming can augment strategic thinking by supplying the formal analyses that strategic thinking requires, helping managers think strategically and helping to specify the steps needed to carry out the vision.

## Organizational Structure

**Ian I. Mitoff, Richard O. Mason and Christine M. Pearson.**
**Framebreak: The Radical Redesign of American Business.**
**San Francisco: Jossey-Bass. 1994.**
The authors of this book reveal how nothing less than a total, broad-ranging reconceptualization of American business can save corporations from rampant upheaval and turmoil. They explain how nineteenth organizational structures--- with their self-contained units such as marketing, finance, and operations--- are no longer the building blocks of organizations. The authors propose a strikingly new, dramatically different design for organizations based on four key dimensions of business life and success: knowledge and learning, recovery and development, service and spirituality, and world-class operations. The outcome is an approach to business that has never been articulated before: total ethical management.

**Jon R. Katzenbach and Douglas K. Smith.**
**The Discipline of Teams. Harvard Business Review. March/April 1993.**
This article which is drawn from the book, The Wisdom of Teams, looks at a organizational structure design that is becoming more popular at high performance organizations -- the team. What makes a team different from other kinds of working groups? When should the team option be utilized? A team differs from other working groups because the teams performance is greater than simply the sum of the individual contributions. To achieve high performance, the best teams invest a tremendous amount of time in shaping its purpose and translating its purpose into specific performance goals. Members of successful teams pitch in and become accountable with and to their teammates. Three types of teams are identified: teams that recommend things such as task forces; teams that make or do things

## SUGGESTED ADDITIONAL READINGS

such as operations teams; and teams that run things such as overseeing a functional activity. Team potential exists anywhere hierarchy or organizational boundaries inhibit good performance.

**Richard Rapaport.**
  **To Build a Winning Team: An Interview with Head Coach Bill Walsh.**
  **Harvard Business Review, January/February 1993.**
In this interview, Bill Walsh discusses how he produced winners through his structured and businesslike approach which maximized the potential of his players and his coaches. He discusses how he developed meticulous long-range strategic and personnel plans where he defined responsibilities, objectives and priorities for everyone in the organization. He discusses the "arc of utilization" where he projects what each player can do throughout their expected life cycle in the organization.

## Management Development

**T. George Harris**
  **The Post-Capitalist Executive: An Interview with Peter F. Drucker.**
  **Harvard Business Review, May/June 1993.**
Drucker argues that managers must learn to negotiate a new environment with a different set of work rules and career expectations. Companies currently face downsizing and turmoil with increasing regularity. Once built to last like pyramids, corporations are now more like tents. Managers must relearn how to manage. In the new world of business, information is replacing authority as the primary tool of the executive. One embarks on the road toward information literacy not by buying the latest technological gadget but by identifying gaps in knowledge. Also the manager must begin to take individual responsibility for himself or herself. To that end, the managers must explore their personal competencies such as competencies, abilities, likes, dislikes, and goals.

**Davis Krackhardt and Jeffrey R. Hansen.**
  **Informed Networks: The Company Behind the Chart.**
  **Harvard Business Review, July/August 1993.**
While the formal organizational chart shows who's the boss, it does not reveal which people confer on technical matters or discuss office politics over lunch. Much of the real work in any company gets done through this informal organization with its complex networks of relationships that cross functions and divisions. By diagramming three types of networks managers can harness the true power in their organization. These networks are: the advise network, which reveals the people to whom others turn to get work done; the trust network, which uncovers who shares delicate information; and the communication network, which shows who talks about work-related matters. These networks which are generated through employee questionnaires are useful in getting to the root of many organizational problems such as resistance to change because team members of a task force are not central to the trust network.

SUGGESTED ADDITIONAL READINGS

## Leadership

**Nitin Nohria and James D. Berkley.**
   **Whatever Happened to the Take-Charge Manager.**
   **Harvard Business Review.** **January/February 1994.**
Nohria and Berkley argue that in the 1980's managers in their quest to be take-charge actually abdicated their managerial responsibility by relying too much on consultants, gurus, and the latest fad of the week to answer all their problems. They feel that the first place to start in taking back their responsibility and becoming truly take-charge is to become more pragmatic. They need to become more sensitive to their company's context and be more open to uncertainty. Pragmatic managers need to avoid three common pitfalls; the "let's do it better this time" syndrome, the "flavor of the month" syndrome, and the "let's go for it all" syndrome.

**H. Kent Bowen, Kim B. Clark, Charles A. Holloway and Steven C. Wheelwright.**
   **Make Projects the School for Leaders.**
   **Harvard Business Review.** **September/October 1994.**
The authors argue that using development projects for product development where the members are from the various functional groups can not only result in superior products but in developing superior future leaders. They argue that the senior management provided the project teams with powerful guiding visions for business strategy, project, and product. These visions were reinforced and internalized by the project team members. The project leaders expanded significantly in their capacity for leadership.

**Manfred F. R. Kets de Vries.**
   **Leaders, Fools and Imposters: Essays on the Psychology of Leadership.**
   San Francisco: Jossey-Bass, 1992.
In this book of insightful essays, Kets de Vries explodes the myth that rationality is what governs the behavior of leaders and followers. Probing the careers of Robert Maxwell, John DeLorean, and others, he examines the addictiveness of power, why so many leaders have difficulty sharing it, and what causes some leaders to abuse it. This book gives consultants and managers the tools to detect and act on problems in leadership, offers organizational behaviorists a better understanding of the leader-follower dynamic, and gives leaders the means to transform themselves.

## Corporate Culture

## Control Systems

**David A. Garvin.**
   **Building a Learning Organization.**
   **Harvard Business Review.** **July/August 1993.**
Garvin argues that before people and companies can improve they must first learn the new behaviors. To do this, they must look beyond rhetoric and high philosophy and focus on the fundamentals of learning. Key to becoming a learning organization is the establishment of

# SUGGESTED ADDITIONAL READINGS

learning audits which measure the cognitive and behavioral changes from learning new skills.

## The Role of the Entrepreneur

**Amar Bhide.**
**How Entrepreneurs Craft Strategies that Work.**
**Harvard Business Review.** March/April 1994.
Bhide reports on the research on more that 200 thriving ventures. The research found four relevant guidelines for budding entrepreneurs. Successful entrepreneurs screen out unpromising ideas as soon as possible using judgment and reflection, not using extensive data analysis. Second, they are realistic about their financial situation, personal preferences and goals. Third, to conserve their limited time and money, they minimize the resources devoted to researching ideas. Last, they realize they do not need all the answers in order to act.

## Family Business

**Donna Fenn.**
**Are Your Kids Good Enough to Run Your Business.**
**Inc.** August 1994.
This short article details the trend towards children coming into the family business. Considering this possibility can start while the children are still young. The author gives some references where family entrepreneurs can get advice on the problems peculiar to family businesses.

**Donna Fenn.**
**Pass It On.**
**Inc.** August 1994.
Fenn presents the case history of Capsco Sales, a family business with three of the founder's children on the payroll. The founder's difficulties in planning the succession after her retirement are detailed.

## Shifting Control of the Firm

# DIFFERENCES THAT WORK:
## MANAGERIAL EFFECTIVENESS THROUGH DIVERSITY

Dr. Mary C. Gentile, Lecturer
HARVARD UNIVERSITY
Graduate School of Business Administration
George F. Baker Foundation

Spring 1995

# DIFFERENCES THAT WORK:
## MANAGERIAL EFFECTIVENESS THROUGH DIVERSITY
Spring 1995
Mary C. Gentile, Lecturer

## Course Rationale

If we take a look at even a short list of key trends facing business leaders today -- the growth of global business competition; the changing demographics of the workforce; the questioning of business, government and community roles and relationships; trends in organizational structures toward more interdependent, cross-functional, flexible and less layered forms; rapidly evolving technologies; shifts in the nature of work toward more service and information-based jobs -- it becomes apparent that the diversity of the workforce, of the customer base, and of business context is both a common element or influence in these trends, and also a critical lever for responding to them.

Given this reality, and given the increasing diversity of our own student body at Harvard Business School, it comes as no surprise that student interest in learning how to manage and optimize the impacts of all forms of diversity on their businesses and their personal careers is growing. The Leadership and Learning study on the Learning Environment reported that students requested greater curricular attention to diversity in the workplace and that faculty were interested in learning more about how to teach such material.

This course, **Differences That Work: Managerial Effectiveness Through Diversity**, is offered as a response to both of these interests, as it provides a laboratory for interested students to probe the subject in some depth even as faculty can test new materials and pedagogical approaches.

## Course Point of View

The course, **Differences That Work: Managerial Effectiveness Through Diversity**, is based upon an underlying premise that diversity in the workplace, if attended to with intelligence, can serve as a bellwether of and a lever toward inevitable change and potential

**Differences That Work**, Spring 1995

opportunity. Many courses on "managing diversity" are rooted in a moral imperative and thereby attend to an agenda of "consciousness-raising" around the particular realities of different identity groups and a debate around the concept of fairness as perceived and as intended. Other curricular efforts shift the emphasis toward an outright appeal to self-interest, but from a defensive and reactive posture in response to legal constraints, demographic projections and competitive pressures.

**Differences That Work** reframes this issue, proactively, as a resource and a process for new learning, for innovation, and for individual and organizational growth. Such a reframing requires a capacious definition of diversity, recognizing its inevitability, its ubiquity, and its inclusiveness. Thus defined, we recognize that workplace diversity is nothing new, but what is new is the impossibility of denying or suppressing its existence. What is gained through such a definition is the ability to include all constituencies ("majority" and "minority") among the beneficiaries of management attention to diversity. This is not to deny the moral, legal or competitive imperatives confronting business leaders nor the reality of differential access to power, but rather to provide a vision of diversity's usefulness as a creative resource, rather than a reproach for past practice or a constraint upon present action.

## Course Objectives

- To enhance our ability to recognize and understand the manifestations and impacts of all forms of diversity in the business context.
- To enhance readiness and ability to reflect upon our own reasoning tendencies around questions of diversity.
- To identify and practice strategies and skills for maximizing the potential benefits of operating in an increasingly diverse context.
- To enhance our readiness and ability to take leadership roles in addressing diversity within business organizations.

**Differences That Work,** Spring 1995

**MODULE ONE: THINKING ABOUT DIVERSITY AND BUSINESS**

Identifies the major diversity-related challenges facing managers and offers a framework for thinking and problem-solving about diversity which will be used throughout the course.

**CLASS ONE:**

PREPARE:
--"Elementary Diversity" from Richard Bernstein's <u>Dictatorship of Virtue: Multiculturalism and the Battle for America's Future.</u> (NY: Alfred A Knopf, 1994) Chapter 1, pp.15-36.
--"How To Make Diversity Pay" by Faye Rice, FORTUNE, August 8, 1994, pp.78-86.

STUDY QUESTIONS:
(1) What are the major arguments and beliefs/assumptions that Bernstein presents in "Elementary Diversity"?
(2) Which ones do you buy? not buy? Why?
(3) What are the major arguments and beliefs/assumptions that Rice presents in "How To Make Diversity Pay"?
(4) Which ones do you buy? not buy? Why?
(5) What are the major motivators/reasons for businesses and managers to attend to diversity? What are the major barriers or reasons not to?

**CLASS TWO:**

PREPARE:
--Ways of Thinking About and Across Difference, HBS Case No. N9-395-117

This note provides a framework for thinking and problem-solving about diversity, as well as a descriptive critique of the reasoning pitfalls we too often encounter when considering this topic.

STUDY QUESTIONS:
(1) Can you think of examples of the reasoning pitfalls (described in the note) that you have heard, read or thought in response to managerial issues of diversity?

(2) Using the model for reframing diversity, can you generate alternative analyses of these same managerial issues?

## MODULE TWO: INDIVIDUAL CHOICES -- SKILLS & PERSPECTIVES

Focuses on three critical managerial interactions -- entry into the organization, professional development, and interpersonal conflict -- where differences (race, gender, cultural background, etc.) can influence relative success and effectiveness.

### CLASS THREE: ENTRY

**PREPARE:**
--Anne Livingston and Power Max Systems, HBS Case Nos.
(A)   N9-395-067
(B1)  N9-395-068
(B2)  N9-395-069
(C1)  N9-395-070
(C2)  N9-395-071
(D1)  N9-395-072
(D2)  N9-395-073
(E1)  N9-395-074
(E2)  N9-395-075

This five part series of short caselets follows the entry and early experiences of engineer Anne Livingston, an African American woman, as she joins Power Max Systems in 1991 as Software Engineering Manager for the new product development group. Power Max is facing stiff competition and wants to be first to market with what is being billed as a revolutionary mass media product. Livingston faces the challenge of bringing a product focus and customer orientation to the largely young, white, male staff of engineers that is reponsible for designing and developing this new broad-based consumer product.

**STUDY QUESTIONS:**
(1) A Case: Should Livingston accept the job with Power Max Systems, if offered? Under what conditions?
(2) B1 Case: How well has Livingston managed her initial entry into the firm?
(3) C1 Case: How should Livingston respond to Dixon and to the software team's doubts?

(4) <u>D1 Case:</u> Should Livingston hire Leung?
(5) <u>E1 Case:</u> What should Livingston do now?
(6) In what ways is Livingston different from the majority of her co-workers? Have these differences affected her entry experience into the firm? If so, how?

## CLASS FOUR: WORKSHOP ON COMMUNICATING ABOUT AND ACROSS DIFFERENCE

### <u>Prepare Pre-Workshop Written Assignment for Class Four</u>

In this class, we will engage in small group and full class discussions designed to address <u>four objectives:</u>
- to become aware of our own group memberships and the ways they affect our experiences, assumptions and perceptions;
- to become aware of how others' group memberships affect their experiences, asssumptions and perceptions;
- to explore the similarities and differences between different types of group identities (cultural, racial, ethnic, gender, sexual orientation, social, functional, etc.)
- to build skills in talking directly about differences.

**TASK:**

- Reflect on your experience entering one of your past jobs, or your FY section at HBS, and think of a <u>significant</u> way in which you were in the MINORITY among your peers. In <u>one or two pages</u> (feel free to use bullet points), answer the following questions:

1) What impact did this identity have on **my early behaviors**? Did I make action choices differently than I might have if I had been in the majority?

2) What impact did this identity have on **others' perceptions of me?** What evidence did I have of this? What were the implications/consequences of these perceptions?

3) What impact did this identity have on **my perceptions of others**? On what evidence did I base these perceptions? What were the implications/consequences of these perceptions?

- **THEN,** reflect on your experience entering one of your past jobs, or your FY section at HBS, and think of a <u>significant </u>way in which your were in the MAJORITY among your peers. In <u>one or two pages</u> (feel free to use bullet points), answer the following questions:

1) What impact did this identity have on **my early behaviors**? Did I make action choices differently than I might have if I had been in the majority?

2) What impact did this identity have on **others' perceptions of me**? What evidence did I have of this? What were the implications/consequences of these perceptions?

3) What impact did this identity have on **my perceptions of others**? On what evidence did I base these perceptions? What were the implications/consequences of these perceptions?

Bring your papers to class. They wil serve as the basis of small and large group discussions, and they will be collected.

**CLASS FIVE: DEVELOPMENT**

PREPARE:
--Jensen Shoes: Lyndon Twitchell's Story, HBS Case No. N9-395-121, and Jensen Shoes: Jane Kravitz' Story, HBS Case No. N9-395-120

These cases detail the experiences of Jane Kravitz (Caucasian female), Strategic Product Manager, and Lyndon Twitchell (African American male), a member of her staff at Jensen Shoes, a successful producer and marketer of casual and athletic footwear. They are assigned to new positions and to each other at the start of the story, and the cases present their very different points of view on their first couple months working together. Performance feedback, stereotypes, and self-fulfilling prophesies are a few of the topics the cases raise.

The cases can be taught in a variety of ways, with all students receiving both cases; half receiving one and half receiving the other; or a third of the class receiving both, a third receiving one and a third receiving the other.

STUDY QUESTIONS:
(1) What were Twitchell's assumptions about Kravitz' abilities, attitudes and motivations? On what were these assumptions based?
(2) What were Kravitz' assumptions about Twitchell's abilities, attitudes and motivations? On what were these assumptions based?
(3) What would Twitchell and Kravitz have had to do differently to result in a more effective working relationship?

## CLASS SIX: CONFLICT

PREPARE:
--Managing Conflict in a Diverse Workplace (**Parts I-- IV**), HBS Case Note No.N9-395-090

    This is a collection of caselets illustrating aspects of diversity-related interpersonal conflict in the workplace. The caselets are organized into seven categories: Intent vs. Perception; Power and Access; Is Equal Fair?; Constructive Conflict; Bystanders and Third Parties; Freedom of Expression; The Implications of Involvement. The caselets in each category are followed by suggestive commentary (or "discussion points") in the form of excerpts from managers, scholars, lawyers, etc.

STUDY QUESTIONS:

Please reflect on the following questions and then consider the discussion points that follow each vignette and their impact on your analysis.
(1) <u>Antoinette Mayer:</u> Should Strong have "known better"? Should Mayer have "understood"? Is anyone at fault? Does that matter?
(2) <u>Nikki Bliss:</u> How should Bliss interpret and respond to Law's behavior?
(3) <u>Moses Wu:</u> Is Wu a viable candidate for management in this environment?
(4) <u>Julia "Mack" MacKenzie:</u> What is MacKenzie worried about? What might be the "unforeseen costs" she is beginning to see?
(5) <u>Cassandra Barton:</u> Does a "diverse" team result in better product? Why or why not? Under what conditions?

- **DUE IN CLASS: One paragraph final paper proposal.**

## CLASS SEVEN: CONFLICT

PREPARE:
--Managing Conflict in a Diverse Workplace (contd., **Parts V--VII**), HBS Case Note No. N9-395-090

STUDY QUESTIONS:
Please reflect on the following questions and then consider the discussion points that follow each vignette and their impact on your analysis.
(1) <u>Everett Evans:</u> Should Evans care or take action if the African-American managers are unconcerned? Why or why not?
(2) <u>Dwight Stewart:</u> What is at stake for Stewart, for Cumberland and for the firm?
(3) <u>Jillian Reese:</u> How important is this decision for Reese? Why?
(4) <u>Jacqueline La Rue:</u> Is LaRue's demand reasonable? Would anything change if the joke had been made by LaRue's superior within the firm?
(5) <u>Nahum Prager:</u> How should Stern respond?
(6) <u>Terry O'Leary:</u> Why was O'Leary "benched"? Was this censorship?
(7) <u>Andie Ottway:</u> How should Ottway weigh what is at stake in his decision?
(8) <u>Maggie Reynolds, Letitia Spiller, and Abby Addams:</u> Do Reynolds, Spiller and Addams have a responsibility to help other women and African-Americans succeed in business?

## MODULE THREE: ORGANIZATIONAL CHOICES -- CULTURE BUILDING

Focuses on organizational case studies using a four-part framework (Motives, Methods, Measures, Mindset) for understanding and responding to the impacts of different forms of diversity on businesses.

PREPARE: (over the course of the next two weeks)
--Managerial Effectiveness and Diversity: Organizational Choices, HBS Case Note No. N1-395-020

This note provides a descriptive framework for identifying and analyzing organizational responses to diversity in the workforce and consumer base.

## CLASS EIGHT: CUSTOMER BASE

PREPARE:
--The Miami Herald Publishing Company, HBS Case No. N9-395-022

David Lawrence, publisher of the Miami Herald, considers whether to separate El Nuevo Herald (the Spanish language insert) from the Miami Herald in response to changing demographics in Dade County. Is this a way to counteract the challenges facing the newspaper industry? Will it sacrifice the mission of the paper--to build community--as Dave Lawrence sees it? Case provides a chance to discuss the challenges and opportunities presented by a diverse consumer base.

STUDY QUESTIONS:
(1) How should Lawrence define his paper's market and his paper's role in the Miami community?
(2) How do these definitions serve Knight-Ridder?
(3) How do these definitions serve the different communities there?

## CLASS NINE: WORK FORCE

PREPARE:
--Accountants and Business Advisors, Inc., City Office, HBS Case No. 9-490-033

Over the past several years both the share of women receiving accounting degrees and the share of women entering public accounting have risen substantially. However, the number of women holding senior positions, such as partner, remains low. This case provides data on retention of females in a large metropolitan office of a public accounting firm, asks whether the lower retention rate (relative to male associates) is a business problem for the firm, and if so, asks what the managing partner should do about it.

STUDY QUESTIONS:
(1) Is retention of women a problem for the City Office? What dimensions of the business are relevant?
(2) What factors contribute to the lower retention rates for women?
(3) What does Shaughnessy learn from the the four partners?
(4) What should Shaughnessy do? Do your remedies represent fundamental or marginal changes for the firm?

## CLASS TEN: WORK FORCE

PREPARE:
--Kurt Landgraf and Du Pont Merck Pharmaceutical Company (A), HBS Case No. N9-394-202

Kurt Landgraf, newly named CEO of Du Pont Merck Pharmaceutical Company, addresses complaints of discrimination from African-American scientists in R&D during a time of significant downsizing and dramatic changes within the pharmaceutical industry.

STUDY QUESTIONS:
(1) How should Landgraf respond to the African-American Core Team's concerns and the threat of a lawsuit?
(2) Should the issues raised by the African-American scientists impact downsizing decisions? If so, how?
(3) What should Landgraf's priorities be and how should he communicate them?

## CLASS ELEVEN: WORK FORCE

PREPARE:
--Lotus Development Corporation: Spousal Equivalents (A), HBS Case No.9-394-197

A group of Lotus employees propose extending all health care and other benefits to the spousal equivalents of lesbian and gay employees. The vice president of human resources considers the proposal during a reorganization and period of financial uncertainty. The case provides an opportunity to discuss the limits and competitive implications of a business's appropriate role in responding to diverse employee needs.

STUDY QUESTIONS:
(1) Why is Campanello considering the proposal?
(2) What would be the likely costs and benefits of Lotus offering benefits to employee spousal equivalents -- for gay/lesbian employees? for straight employees? for Campanello? for the firm?
(3) What kind of response can Campanello and Lotus expect from the market, from investors? from competitiors? from employees?

## CLASS TWELVE: AFFIRMATIVE ACTION

PREPARE:
--The FCC and License Auctions for Emerging Technologies (A), HBS Case No. N9-395-139

This case describes the FCC's efforts to respond to a Congressional mandate to "create meaningful opportunities for women and minority-owned business" in structuring competitive auctions of Spectrum allocation for emerging PCS businesses. The FCC must consider potential Constitutional challenges, responses from both the established industry players (i.e., regional Bell operating companies) and potential new entrants, as well as the optimal course for U.S. competitiveness and the end-users. The case provides an opportunity to consider questions of "affirmative action" in the contemporary context of an emerging and potentially very significant industry.

STUDY QUESTIONS:
(1) What ought the objectives of Congress and the FCC be, if any, with regard to designated entities and the Spectrum auctions?
(2) Are the FCC auction policies for designated entities likely to work as intended?
(3) If they do work, who benefits? who loses?
(4) Is there a better alternative?

## MODULE FOUR: REDEFINING LEADERSHIP

Focuses on the personal characteristics and managerial capabilities required of leaders who step up to the challenge of diversity and suggests ways in which individuals have developed the inner strength to do so.

## CLASS THIRTEEN:

PREPARE:
--Monitor Company: Personal Leadership on Diversity, HBS Case No. N9-395-049

The case presents the voices of several individuals at Monitor Company, ranging from relatively junior consultants to directors and a founding partner, discussing the firm and their efforts to build and nurture a more diverse work environment there. The speakers represent a variety of identities -- men and women, racial and and ethnic diversity, sexual orientation, age -- and they each comment on the personal experiences that helped them to become leaders around issues of diversity. The case provides an opportunity to consider both the many and sometimes conflicting definitions of diversity held even by those who are committed to the issue, and to explore the varied sources of personal motivation for taking leadership positions on it.

STUDY QUESTIONS:
(1) What motivates the different individuals profiled in the case to take a leadership role around diversity? How do they each define diversity? Are there conflicts between these definitions and the goals they engender?
(2) Can the Monitor culture and value system accommodate diverse styles of learning and leadership without sacrificing its distinctive identity?

- **FINAL PAPERS DUE IN CLASS.**

**Differences That Work,** Spring 1995

SUGGESTED READING: (included in your course packets)

For a general overview of some of the relevant research, I recommend:
-- "Race and Ethnicity" by Taylor Cox, Jr. and Stella Nkomo, in Handbook of Organizational Behavior, edited by Robert T. Golembiewski, Marcel Dekker, Inc., 1993, pp. 205-229.
-- "Women and Minorities in Management" by Ann M. Morrison and May Ann Von Glinow, American Psychologist, February 1990, vol. 45, No.2, pp. 200-208.
-- Chapter 7, "Cultural Differences" and Chapter 8, "Ethnocentrism" from Cultural Diversity in Organizations: Theory, Research & Practice, by Taylor Cox, Jr., Berrett-Koehler Publishers 1993, pp. 105-136.

FOR FURTHER STUDY:

-- Taylor Cox, Jr., Cultural Diversity in Organizations: Theory, Research & Practice. (San Francisco, CA: Berrett-Koehler Publishers, Inc., 1993).
-- Mary C. Gentile, ed. Differences that Work: Organizational Excellence through Diversity. (Boston, MA: Harvard Business School Press, 1994).
-- Rosabeth Moss Kanter, Men and Women of the Corporation. (New York: Basic Books, Inc., 1977).

ADDITIONAL READING, BY TOPIC

If you have a particular interest in research on a specific identity group or commentary on a specific topic or issue (i.e., affirmative action, sexual harassment, legal and regulatory guidelines related to diversity, diversity training, and so forth), I would be happy to direct you toward appropriate reading sources. Simply call me to schedule an appointment.

GRADING

Grades for the course will be based 40% on class participation and 60% on the final paper. Class participation involves regular attendance and preparation, as well as active and thoughtful contribution to class discussions.

15

**Differences That Work**, Spring 1995

FINAL PAPER ASSIGNMENT

Final papers may take one of the following forms:

- Identify a management challenge (interpersonal or organizational in scope) related to diversity that you have experienced or witnessed in your own career, or that you have learned about from peers or the business press. Using research and interviews with involved and/or knowledgeable parties as well as reflective individuals from among your own colleagues: describe the challenge fully; present the various responses available; analyze those responses using frameworks and insights drawn from the course/readings/interviews; and present and explain your action plan.

- Identify two reflective, articulate and knowledgeable individuals who hold conflicting views around an issue related to diversity and management. They might be former colleagues, teachers, classmates, etc. Prepare a carefully framed statement of the issue you wish them to debate and tape record their discussion (minimum one hour, maximum two hours). Using research as well as the frameworks and insights drawn from the course, present their key arguments, the points of contention, and the reasoning methods used by each party. Present and explain your reframing of the discussion, offering an analysis that you believe may break the logjam between your discussants. Finally, share briefly the response of each of your discussants to your proposed reframing of the issue.

- You may pursue an alternate topic with instructor approval.

Papers may be completed by individual students or in teams of two.

Length: 10-12 typed double-spaced pages

## UNIVERSITY of VIRGINIA

Managerial Psychology
Spring 1995
Prof. Alexander Horniman

| Date | Class | Topic | Material |
|------|-------|-------|----------|
| Jan. 11 | 1 | Managerial Model of Personality | *TA Today* - Parts I and II pp. 3-58 |
| Jan. 12 | 2 | Managerial Model of Personality | *TA Today* - Part III pp. 59-98 and pp. 99-145 |
| Jan. 18 | 3 | Managerial Model of Personality | *TA Today* - Part V pp. 148-167 |
| Jan. 19 | 4 | Managerial Model of Personality | *TA Today* - Part VI pp. 207-259 |
| Jan. 25 | 5 | TA in Action - No Assignment | Film Case Study |
| Jan. 26 | 6 | TA in Action - No Assignment | Film Case Study |
| Feb. 2 | 7 | The Psychological Basis of Meaning | *Man's Search for Meaning* - Victor Frankl |
| Feb. 3 | 8 | The Psychological Basis of Meaning | *Man's Search for Meaning* - Victor Frankl |
| Feb. 8 | 9 | Taking Control | *7 Habits of Highly Effective People* pp. 1-182 |
| Feb. 9 | 10 | Taking Control | *7 Habits of Highly Effective People* pp. 183-284 |
| Feb. 10 | 11 | Taking Control (Dyad - Discussion Session) | *7 Habits of Highly Effective People* pp. 287-313 |
| Feb. 15 | 12 | Dynamics of Superior - Subordinate Relationships | Joe Peterson (9-480-048) Human Dilemmas of Leadership (*HBR* 63414) |
| Feb. 16 | 13 | Dynamics of Superior - Subordinate Relationships (Dyad - Partner Day No Class) | Al Westerfield (9-479-007) Dynamics of Subordinacy (*HBR* 65313) |

| Date | Class | Topic | Material |
|------|-------|-------|----------|
| Feb. 22 | 14 | Managing In Context | *Modern Madness* - D. LaBier (on reserve) Forward V-X and Chapters 1-3 |
| Feb. 23 | 15 | Managing in Context | *Modern Madness* - D. LaBier (on reserve) Chapters 4-6 - pp. 216-224<br>Tony Santino (A) (9-482-045) |
| Mar. 22 | 16 | Gender Issues | *Talking From 9 to 5* - D. Tannen, pp. 11-131 |
| Mar. 23 | 17 | Gender Issues | *Talking From 9 to 5* - D. Tannen, pp. 132-310 (long assignment - skim read) |
| Mar. 29 | 18 | Gender Issues | *Engendered Lives* - E. Kaschak, pp. 1-129 |
| Mar. 30 | 19 | Gender Issues | *Engendered Lives* - E. Kaschak, pp. 131-226 |
| Apr. 5 | 20 | Racial Issues | *The Content of Our Character* - S. Steele, pp. 1-75 |
| Apr. 6 | 21 | Racial Issues | *The Content of Our Character* - S. Steele pp. 76-173 |
| Apr. 12 | 22 | Racial Issues | *Race Matters* - C. West (entire book) |
| Apr. 13 | 23 | Racial Issues | *Race Matters* - C. West |
| Apr. 19 | 24 | Men and Women Together | *Men Are From Mars Women Are From Venus* J. Gray |
| Apr. 20 | 25 | Men and Women Together (Dyad Day) | *Men Are From Mars Women Are Fran Venus* J. Gray |
| Apr. 27 | 26 | Managing Genius | *Uncommon Genius* - D. Shekerjian |
| Apr. 28 | 27 | Managing Genius | *Uncommon Genius* - D. Shekerjian |
| May 3 | 28 | Creativity | *What A Great Idea* (whole book distributed in class) - Guest Speaker |

| Date | Class | Topic | Material |
|------|-------|-------|----------|
| May 4 | 29 | Adult Development | *The Adult Years* - F. M. Hudson<br>Chapters 1-3 |
| May 5 | 30 | Adult Development | *The Adult Years* - F. M. Hudson<br>pp. 199-227 |

HARVARD UNIVERSITY
Prof. Ibarra

**LEAD**
Spring 1995

I. INTRODUCTION

| | | |
|---|---|---|
| *Tuesday,*<br>*January 31* | 1. | ●Erik Peterson (A) (B)<br>●LEAD Overview Note #1:  "An Introduction to Leadership and Organizational Behavior" |
| *Thursday,*<br>*February 2* | 2. | ●*Erik Peterson (C) (D) (E)<br>●*Richard Jenkins |

II. LEADING PEOPLE

| | | |
|---|---|---|
| *Friday,*<br>*February 3* | 3. | ●Jan Carlzon<br>●Overview Note #2:  "Leading People"<br>    Video:  Jan Carlzon |
| *Monday,*<br>*February 6* | 4. | ●*A Force For Change*, Chapters 1-3<br>●Fill out Motivation Questionnaire<br>    Video:  Martin Luther King - "I Have a Dream" |
| *Tuesday,*<br>*February 7* | 5. | ●Sir John Harvey-Jones<br>    Video:  Sir John Harvey-Jones |
| *Thursday,*<br>*February 9* | 6. | ●Charlotte Beers at Ogilvy & Mather Worldwide (A) *(B)<br>    Video:  Charlotte Beers |
| *Monday,*<br>*February 13* | 7. | ●William Davis<br>●Fill out Myers Briggs Type Indicator<br>    Video:  Twelve Angry Men |
| *Tuesday,*<br>*February 14* | 8. | ●*A Force For Change*, Chapters 4-6<br>    Video:  Twelve Angry Men |
| *Monday,*<br>*February 20* | 9. | ●International Telephone & Telegraph (A) |
| *Wednesday,*<br>*February 22* | 10. | ●Kyocera Corporation |
| *Tuesday,*<br>*February 28* | 11. | ●People Express (A)<br>    Video:  Donn Burr<br>    Video:  What a Way to Run an Airline |

## III. MANAGING PERFORMANCE

| | | |
|---|---|---|
| *Thursday,*<br>*March 2* | 12. | ●Crompton Greaves Ltd.<br>●Overview Note #3: "Managing Performance" |
| *Friday,*<br>*March 3* | 13. | ●Foster Manufacturing Company<br>●*A Business Review Meeting Viewer's Guide<br>    Video: Foster Manufacturing Company |
| *Monday,*<br>*March 6* | 14. | ●"From Control to Commitment in the Workplace" article<br>    Video: Foster Manufacturing Company (continued) |
| *Wednesday,*<br>*March 8* | 15. | ●Brainard, Bennis and Farrell |
| *Thursday,*<br>*March 9* | 16. | ●Old Colony Associates<br>●James Cranfield<br>●Eugene Kearney |
| *Wednesday,*<br>*March 15* | 17. | ●Orientation for Viewing the Cranfield-Kearney Performance Appraisal Interview<br>    Video: Jim Cranfield/Gene Kearney Performance Appraisal Interview (Old Colony Associates) |
| *Thursday,*<br>*March 16* | 18. | ●Königsbräu-Hellas A.E. (Abridged) |
| *Friday,*<br>*March 17* | 19. | ●Cordoba (A)<br>    Video: George Pla<br>    Video: Maria Mehranian |

## IV. MIDTERM REVIEW

| | | |
|---|---|---|
| *Monday,*<br>*March 27* | 20. | ●Soul of a New Machine |
| *Thursday,*<br>*March 30* | 21. | ●Feedback Exercise |

## V. RENEWING AND TRANSFORMING ORGANIZATIONS

*Tuesday,*  22. ●History of Xerox Corporation
*April 4*         ●Overview Note #4: "Renewing and
                    Transforming Organizations"
                  ●"Transforming Organizations: Why
                    Firms Fail" article
                        Video:    Fred Henderson
                        Video:    Renn Zaphiropoulos
                        Video:    Xerox Customer Service
                        Video:    David Kearns

*Thursday,*  23. ●John Reed at First National City Bank
*April 6*          Operating Group (A), (B), (C)
                        Video:  John Reed

*Friday,*  24. ●Orit Gadiesh: Pride at Bain & Co. (A)
*April 7*        *(B)
                        Video:  Orit Gadiesh

*Monday,*  25. ●Black Caucus Groups at Xerox Corporation (A)
*April 10*       *(B)
                        Video:  Black Caucus

*Tuesday,*  26. ●Orientation for Viewing "Twelve O'Clock
*April 11*        High"
                  ●"Turn-Arounds and Change Strategies" note
                        Video: Twelve
                        O'Clock High shown at 3:00 and 6:00 on
                        April 10

*Thursday,*  27. ●Thurgood Marshall High School
*April 13*

*Wednesday,*  28. ●Taco Bell Corp. (A)
*April 19*


## VI. LEADERSHIP AND CAREER DEVELOPMENT

*Monday,*  29. ●Recruiting at Bowles Hollowell Connor & Co.
*April 24*      ●Overview Note #5: "Leadership and
                  Career Development,"
                        Videos:  Bowles Hollowell Interviews
                        with HBS Students

*Wednesday,*  30. ●Myers Briggs Type Indicator
*April 26*       ●"Early Career," Chapter 7 from *Power &
                    Influence*

*Thursday,*  31. ●Success Exercise
*April 27*

| | | |
|---|---|---|
| *Wednesday,*<br>*May 3* | 32. | ●Jack Thomas<br>●"Managing Your Boss" article |
| *Friday,*<br>*May 5* | 33. | ●Donna Dubinsky at Apple Computer, Inc. (A)<br>●"How High Potential Executives Derail" note |
| *Monday,*<br>*May 8* | 34. | ●Suzanne de Passe at Motown Productions (A)<br>*(B) |
| *Thursday,*<br>*May 11* | 35. | ●Arnie Elifson |
| *Friday,*<br>*May 12* | 36. | ●Wrap Up |
| *Monday,*<br>*May 15* | | Final Exam |

*Will be distributed separately

1-5-95

## POWER AND INFLUENCE IN ORGANIZATIONS
## BA 421
## SPRING, 1995 - TERM 1

Toby Y. Kahr, Ph.D.  
705 Broad Street, Room 103  
684-2826 (Office)  
929-9128 (Home)

Class Hours  
Mondays & Thursdays  
8:00 a.m. - 10:15 a.m.  
Classroom D

Office Hours: Before and after class for short discussions. Other times by appointment.

**Power and Influence in Organizations** is designed to equip the student with a mature understanding of the realities of the strategic use of organizational power. Readings in management and academic literature are integrated with case analysis and discussion to afford the student the opportunity to enhance personal skills in the strategic side of management.

The course examines the complex interplay of power and influence in organizational settings with particular emphasis on the use of influence strategies in managerial decision making. Specific topics to be included are understanding the role of power in organizations, its sources and conditions for use, political strategies and tactics and specific organizational issues such as resource allocation, career politics, building power bases, organizational change and crisis management.

### READINGS

Text: Pfeffer, Jeffrey. Managing with Power, Politics and Influence in Organizations. Harvard Business School Press, 1992.

In addition, there is a packete of readings and cases which will be distributed in class.

### EVALUATION

Calculation of your final grade will be on the basis of the following components:

1. Class performance or paper     20%
2. Team Presentation     20%
3. Mid-term exam     20%
4. Case write-ups (2)     40%

### Class Performance Option

An option to the grade for class performance is available for individuals who are uncomfortable with participating in class discussions. I have found from previous experience that some very excellent students end up having their overall grade lowered because they feel inhibited by the size of the class, competition for air time, or the belief that what they have to say is not worth the time of the class. I rely heavily on class discussion of cases, films and readings to teach the analytical skills the course is set up to impart. A certain percentage of students opting out of class discussion will not be a problem, provided I know who they are at the beginning of the semester.

A student may select a book, with my prior approval, which provides material which can be used for a paper that applies the basic analytical principles which will be covered in the first part of the semester. The paper would be 10 pages in length and due by the next to last class session. The paper would be an in depth analysis, using a political framework, of the characters and events described in the book. Biographies of corporate leaders or company histories provide some of the best background material for power strategies, but I'm open to other sources as well.

### Team Presentations

A portion of the grade (20%) will be based on a team analysis and presentation of the topic matter for one of the class sessions. Preassigned teams will select from one of nine sessions and prepare a 20 minute presentation on the case or film indicated for that day. A five page double spaced paper summarizing the main points will be required as part of the assignment.

### Case Writeups

Two case writeups will be assigned for the second half of the term. The first will be due on February 16, 1994, the second on the last day of class. The writeups will be between 7 and 10 double spaced pages in length.

Revised 1/24/95

## BA 421 COURSE OUTLINE
## POWER AND INFLUENCE IN ORGANIZATIONS

| DATE | TOPIC | READINGS | CASES |
|---|---|---|---|
| 1/16/95 | Political Management | *"Power, Success & Organizational Effectiveness" Kotter; Pfeffer, Chapter 1 | |
| 1/19/95 | Ethical and Moral Considerations | *Can a Corporation have a Conscience Goodpaster & Matthews | **Moral Men–Immoral Decisions; *Mike Miller (A)(B) |
| 1/23/95 | Assessing Power in Organizations | Pfeffer, Chapter 2,3; *"Inertial Forces within Organizations" | *Shootout at Johns-Manville Corral; **Missouri Campus |
| 1/26/95 | Sources of Power | Pfeffer, Chapter 4, 6-9 | World of David Rockefeller (videotape); **The Best Bill Drafter |
| 1/30/95 | Language & Symbols | *Making Sense with Symbolism" Pfeffer Chapter 5 | **Oliver North (videotape); *The Split |
| 2/2/95 | Race/Gender Issues MIDTERM | +Men & Women of the Corporation, Kanter Chapter 3 & 8 | Speaker - Judith S. White, Ph.D. |

**BA 421 Course Outline Continued...**

| **DATE** | **TOPIC** | **READINGS** | **CASES** |
|---|---|---|---|
| 2/6/95 | Strategies & Tactics<br>**Case 1 Handout** | Pfeffer, Chapter 10-13 | *Managing US Supersonic Transport A&B<br>*Air Traffic Controllers |
| 2/9/95 | Power & Resource Allocations | *"New Directions in Organizational Behavior" Staw & Salancik<br>Pfeffer, Chapter 5 | **British Steel–The Korf Contract (videotape) |
| 2/13/95 | Power Bases/ Perpetuating Power | **Case 1 Due** | *Job Corps<br>**Loyalty-Team-Play-The System |
| 2/16/95 | Careers: Successions<br><br>**Case 2 Handout** | Pfeffer, pp 317-320<br>+Power in Organizations<br>Pfeffer, pp 264-266<br>+Managing Your Boss<br>Harvard Business Review | **Fall of Lehman Brothers I & II<br>*Management Succession at Ford |
| 2/20/95 | Early Career Issues | +Power & Influence, Kotter Chapter 7, pp 235-265 | **Tom Levick<br>*Textile Corp of America (videotape) |

**BA 421 Course Outline Continued...**

| | | |
|---|---|---|
| 2/23/95 | Crisis Management  Case 2 Due | \*\*Donna Dubinsky & Apple Computer A,B,C,D (videotape)<br>\*Debbie Coleman & Apple Computer |

\* Included in Case Packet
\*\* Team Case
+ On Reserve at Fuqua Library

## BIBLIOGRAPHY

Auletta, Ken. Greed and Glory on Wall Street. New York: Random House, 1986.

Caro, Robert A. The Power Broker: Robert Moses and the Fall of New York. New York: Vintage Books, 1975.

Gabarro, John J. and Kotter, John P. Managing Your Boss, Harvard Business Review, May-June, 1993.

Goodpaster, Kenneth E., and Matthews, John B. Jr. "Can a Corporation have a Conscience?" Harvard Business Review, January-February, 1982. pp 132-141.

Kanter, Rosabeth Moss. Men and Women of the Corporation. New York: Basic Books, 1977.

Kotter, John P. "Power, Success and Organizational Effectiveness", Organizational Dynamics, Winter, 1978, pp 27-40.

Pfeffer, Jeffrey. "Making Sense with Symbolism". Stanford GSB Winter, 1981-82. pp 2-7

Pfeffer, Jeffrey. Power in Organizations. Marshfield, MA., 1981.

Staw, Barry M. and Salancik, Gerald R. New Directions of Organizational Behavior. Chicago, IL: St. Clair Press, 1977.

"The Inertial Forces within Organizations", Harvard Business School. 1984, pp 1-5.

Wright, J. Patrick. On a Clear Day You Can See General Motors. New York: Avon Books, 1980.

# ORGANIZATIONAL LEADERSHIP

Business 379
Political Science 108
Sociology 165

Autumn 1994-1995
Mr. March

---

This course is about leadership in organizations --- business firms, public agencies, military units, voluntary groups, political movements, schools, universities, and churches. Although the course is intended for people who expect to be leaders, or to deal with them, it is not useful in a conventional sense and no claim of immediate relevance is made. The course provides neither techniques for gaining or exercising leadership nor techniques of combating would-be leaders. The emphasis is on the complications involved in becoming, being, confronting, or evaluating a leader in an organization. The main argument is that those complications are echoes of critical issues of life more generally. As a result, the readings are drawn from great literature.

## SOME CENTRAL ISSUES

The course can be seen as an introduction to a handful of central issues:

1. <u>Leadership appreciation</u>. Ultimately, leaders are evaluated in terms of whether they have done good, that is, whether their actions have contributed to improving the human estate. Though conventions of confidence often require evaluations of contemporary leaders to be asserted with conviction, those evaluations are normally not easy to make. Reputations of leaders (as well as attitudes about leadership) are shaped and reshaped by associates, accountants, journalists, competitors, stock analysts, academics, friends, and enemies. Contributing constructively to the social and political process by which leadership reputations are shaped involves understanding the ways evaluations of leaders are formed and how they might be made more meaningful. How do we come to believe that a leader has succeeded or failed? That one leader is better than another? How should we? What should we value in leadership and in individuals who are leaders? What are the ethics and aesthetics of leadership? What makes it beautiful or just? How can we attach sublime evaluative meaning to the mundane features of organizational life?

2. <u>Private lives and public duties</u>. Leaders have private lives from which they draw emotional balance and human sustenance, though they often find their official lives systematically more rewarding. Leadership can destroy both the privacy and the quality of personal life. The importance of position undermines authenticity in personal relations. Self becomes inseparable from standing, making love and hate equally suspect. Leadership also attracts curiosity and gossip, compromising privacy. Followers claim a right to knowledge about a leader's personal life on grounds of its relevance to assessing character and establishing rapport. Finally, private lives complicate the responsibilities of leadership. Personal motives and relations affect the actions of leaders. Personal jealousies and loyalties bend a leader's judgment. Interpersonal trust contributes to, yet corrupts, organizational actions. What are the

possibilities for combining a rich personal life with life as an organizational leader? How are personal feelings to be reconciled with organizational responsibilities?

3. <u>Cleverness, innocence, and virtue</u>. Commentators on leadership are ambivalent about sophistication and cleverness. On the one hand, leaders are often portrayed as astute manipulators of resources and people, praised for their use of superior knowledge and adroitness. They are frequently described as intelligently devious, secretive. We honor their superior abilities to outsmart others. On the other hand, leaders are often pictured not as sophisticated in the usual sense but as possessing an elemental innocence that overcomes the fatuous convolutions of clever people and goes instinctively to the essentials. This capability for simplification is associated not with education, intelligence, and propriety but with an ability to connect, in some uncomplicated way, to the fundamentals of life. In this spirit, leaders are often praised for their naivete and openness, and for their ability to use honesty as a basis for inspiring and extending trust. What is the place of cleverness, innocence, intelligence, and ignorance in descriptions of, or prescriptions for, leadership?

4. <u>Genius, heresy, and madness</u>. Great leaders are often portrayed as geniuses. They are said to see further and more accurately than others. Because of this visionary capability, they dare to take risks that others dare not. They transform organizations through their imagination, creativity, insight, and will. These descriptions of great leaders seem, however, to portray greatness as being associated with heresy, thus to be at variance with the needs of organizations for safer, more reliable behavior. The needs are not perverse. Though heresy sometimes proves, retrospectively, to be the basis for desirable change, most bold new ideas are foolish and properly ignored. They are more likely to destroy an organization than to lead it to new heights of achievement. Thus, great leaders are characteristically heretics who are associated with a transformation of orthodoxy, but most heretics would be disasters as leaders. What is the relation between genius and madness? How do we recognize great leaders among the crazies? How do we nurture genius if we cannot recognize it?

5. <u>Diversity and unity</u>. In everything from problem solving to personnel policies to ideologies, leaders make trade-offs between diversity and unity, between variety and integration, between convergence and divergence. Organizations are collections of individuals and groups often having quite diverse attitudes, backgrounds, aspirations, training, identities, experiences, social ties, and styles. Leadership frequently involves finding ways to minimize the problems of diversity through recruitment from a common background, experience, or education, or through the use of persuasion, bargaining, incentives, socialization, and inspiration to mold multiple talents and backgrounds into a common culture. Such a vision of leadership as forging a unity of harmonious purpose and commitment clashes, however, with an alternative vision of leadership as stimulating and nurturing diversity as a source of organizational and social strength. How do leaders choose between building unity and building diversity? Can they have both? To what extent is unity at one level in an organization a necessary precondition for diversity at another? What are the implications?

6. <u>Ambiguity and coherence</u>. Leadership is generally seen as a force for coherence, as contributing to effective organizational action by eliminating contradictions and preventing confusions. Future leaders are taught to remove inconsistencies, ambiguities, and complexities through precise objectives and well-conceived plans. The modern prototype in a business firm is the idea of business strategy and the development of a "business plan". However, inconsistency and ambiguity have a role in change and

adaptation, and the compulsion toward coherence could be an incomplete basis for understanding or improving leadership and life. In general, effective leadership implies an ability to live in two worlds: the incoherent world of imagination, fantasy, and dreams and the orderly world of pragmatic action. How do we sustain both ambiguity and coherence? Both foolishness and reason? Both contradiction and resolution? To what extent are talents to do so related to literary and poetic imagination? In what ways is poetry a more profound metaphor than economics for interpreting and improving leadership.

7. Power, domination, and subordination. Many modern ideologies treat inequalities in power as illegitimate. Yet, we pursue power and are fascinated by it. We equate personal power with personal self-worth, and powerlessness with loss of esteem and identity. We write history and describe progress in terms of changing patterns of domination and subordination. As a result, we see power as both central to leadership and a complication for it. We recognize a tension between hierarchy and participation, between power and equality, and between control and autonomy. Power is often said to corrupt the holder of it, to transform normally honorable people into monsters. It is also said to condemn, to undermine the ordinary pleasures of honesty in interpersonal relations. At the same time, power is often described as elusive, more a story-telling gimmick than a reality. Insofar as leaders have power, how do they use it? What are its limits? What are its costs? How does a person with little power function in a power-based institution? What are the moral dilemmas of power?

8. Gender and sexuality. Gender and sexuality are well-recognized factors in modern biology, sociology, and ideology. They affect a wide range of behaviors, and intepretations of behaviors, in organizations. In virtually all societies, leadership is linked to questions of sexual identity and gender equality. Most leaders are men; and the rhetoric of leadership is closely related to the rhetoric of manliness. Changes in gender stereotypes with respect to leadership interact with the ways women and men are interpreted to have (or not have) distinctive styles, characters, beliefs, or behaviors, as well as with our understandings of their relations, not only outside hierarchical organizations but also within them. Moreover, leadership appears to intertwined with sexuality. Being a leader and being seen as having power are components of sexual appeal and sexual identity. Sexual relations and accusations of sexual misconduct are endemic around leadership. How do the manifest elements of sexuality and gender in leadership affect the ways we understand, become, and act as leaders?

9. Great actions, great visions, and great expectations. The ideology of leadership emphasizes reason more than foolishness, strategy and vision more than serendipity and improvisation, thinking more than imitation. Action is seen as intentional, driven by an evaluation of its expected consequences. Costs are paid because benefits are anticipated. Within such an ideology, leaders need to have expectations of great consequences to justify the great commitments demanded of them. They need to believe they can make a difference. We ask whether this is an adequate description of leadership behavior or an adequate moral foundation for it. In particular, we examine the implications of justifying great actions by great hopes in a world in which causality is obscure and effectiveness problematic. Within an ethic of consequentiality, how do we sustain commitment in the face of adverse or ambiguous outcomes? How do an organization and a society maintain illusions of efficacy among its leaders? What are the consequences? Are there alternatives?

10. Pleasures of the process. Leadership and leaders are generally justified and understood in instrumental terms. We see leadership as contributing to the ways in which organizations are coordinated and

controlled to improve outcomes. Leaders evaluate themselves, are evaluated, and are (to some extent) compensated in terms of their contributions to those outcomes. At the same time, it is frequently noted that there are pleasures associated with the processes of leadership: the glories of position, the joys of commitment, the excitements of influence, the exhilaration of conflict and danger. These pleasures are, to a substantial extent, independent of their outcomes. As a consequence, understanding leadership often involves recognizing the ways in which the pleasures of the process fit into the calculus of leadership and how they ought to do so. What are the major pleasures of being a leader? How do they affect recruitment into leader roles and behavior within them? How do they affect the way we think about leadership?

It is possible that some of these issues will not be fully resolved by the end of the quarter.

### COURSE FORMAT

The course provides some reading, some opportunities for commentary, and some lectures:

Reading

Four books are required reading (or rereading) during the quarter:

William Shakespeare, Othello
George Bernard Shaw, Saint Joan
Leo Tolstoy, War and Peace .
Miguel de Cervantes, Don Quixote

The course is primarily an excuse to read these four works carefully and completely. Although we will undertake to draw some implications for leadership from the reading, you should avoid focusing on their "leadership" aspects. They should be read as complete works of art, rather than as texts with occasional "relevant" parts. You should immerse yourself in them, engage them, and enjoy them.

Each of the texts is available in the Stanford Bookstore, as well as elsewhere. Where there has been a choice, the Stanford Bookstore has been asked to stock editions with somewhat more fulsome notes than other editions. If you prefer a different (unabridged) edition, use it. Most of the texts are also available on several standard cd-rom collections if you prefer to read them that way and have the necessary equipment.

Bookstores also provide various versions of commercial summaries, study aids, and notes designed to make it easy to avoid doing the reading. Reading such notes bears about the same relation to reading the works to which they refer as reading expert summaries of good wine bears to drinking it -- neither a substitute nor a decent supplement.

## Commentary

At the end of each lecture, the instructor poses a "query". Opportunities for commenting on the queries (and other material in the course) are provided in the discussion period after each lecture, in the discussion sections, and in written essays on one or more of the queries.

The discussion period occupies about 30-45 minutes after each lecture. The focus is on the query posed at the end of the previous day's lecture.

The discussion sections are optional. They provide an opportunity for further discussion of the issues raised in class. They meet on Fridays (except for September 30, November 11, and November 25) at 10, 11, 2:15, and 3:15. You may attend as few or as many sessions as you wish.

The written essays are optional. The details of the assignment are indicated below under the discussion of grading.

## Lectures

The instructor lectures at 8 a.m. each Wednesday and Friday (except for November 11 and November 25)). Each lecture is self-contained. Students are invited to attend. It is understood that 8 a.m. is an unusual experience, and there is no absolute presumption that absence from a lecture or two is incontrovertible evidence of intellectual or moral decadence. However, the same person who invents the lectures also invents the examination and grades the course. The schedule of lectures:

| | |
|---|---|
| September 28 | Lecture # 1: Leadership appreciation |
| September 30 | Lecture # 2: Private lives and public virtues |
| October 5 | Lecture # 3: Othello, I |
| October 7 | Lecture # 4: Cleverness, innocence, and virtue |
| October 12 | Lecture # 5: Othello, II |
| October 14 | Lecture # 6: Genius, heresy, and madness |
| October 19 | Lecture # 7: Saint Joan |
| October 21 | Lecture # 8: Diversity and unity |
| October 26 | Lecture # 9: Ambiguity and coherence |
| October 28 | Lecture #10: War and Peace, I |
| November 2 | Lecture #11: Power, domination, and subordination |
| November 4 | Lecture #12: War and Peace, II |
| November 9 | Lecture #13: Gender and leadership |
| November 11 | NO LECTURE |
| November 16 | Lecture #14: War and Peace, III |
| November 18 | Lecture #15: Sexuality and leadership |
| November 23 | Lecture #16: Don Quixote, I |
| November 25 | THANKSGIVING RECESS |
| November 30 | Lecture #17: Great visions, great actions, great expectations |
| December 2 | Lecture #18: Don Quixote, II |
| December 7 | Lecture #19: Pleasures of the process |
| December 9 | Lecture #20: Leaders as poets and plumbers |

## GRADING

The course may be taken on either a graded or a pass/no credit basis. The rules for recording the pass/no credit option, as well as rules for adding and dropping the course, are the rules of the school in which the course is being taken. Please note that the rules of the Graduate School of Business differ from the rules of the School of Humanities and Sciences, the School of Engineering and the School of Education.

The grade depends on three things:

1. Performance on a <u>final examination</u>. The final examination is given <u>only</u> at the regularly scheduled time. It is required. If you will be unable to take the examination at the regular time, you should not enroll in the course, for you will not be able to complete it successfully. The examination is a three-hour, open-book written examination covering reading, lectures, queries, and discussion. It must be taken in the examination room without access to computers, word processors, electronic data bases, cd-roms, or other similar augmentations.

2. Participation in <u>class discussions</u> (optional). Participation in the discussion of the queries in the Wednesday and Friday lecture periods and in Friday discussion sections will be graded in terms of its relevance, clarity, probity, and imagination. Quality is more critical than quantity, but assessment of the former normally requires a reasonable amount of the latter.

3. <u>Written essays</u> (optional). The assignment is to write five essays, each <u>no more than 400 words in length</u>. The length limitation is firm. The number of words in each essay must be indicated at the end of the essay. If the essay exceeds 400 words, the 400th word must be indicated. For grading purposes, the first 400 words will be treated as the complete essay. Each essay should be a self-contained commentary on one of the queries posed by the instructor. It should reflect knowledge gained through class discussion but should not be simply a summary of that knowledge. The essays may include precisely drawn references to relevant literature, but they are not intended to be research or library reports. Rather they should be comments that would interest someone who knows the literature, has attended this course, has thought about the issues, and is intelligent, educated, and literate. The five essays should be submitted in final, edited form with spelling errors, grammatical atrocities, and expository circumlocutions excised. Grades will be based on the originality and thoughtfulness of the ideas and the parsimony, clarity, and felicity of the writing. Essays must be given to the instructor in class or turned in to 509 CERAS. They are due <u>no later than noon, Wednesday, November 23</u>. Absolutely no extensions of the time deadline will be given. You should anticipate the inevitable disasters that occur near a deadline, including breakdowns in health, computers, or love affairs, and assure you meet the deadline in spite of them.

At the time of the final examination, each student determines the weights to be assigned to the three components in determining his or her grade. Weights must sum to 100% and satisfy the following constraints:

| | | |
|---|---|---|
| Final examination | : | 90%, 80%, 70%, 60%, or 50% |
| Class discussions | : | 30%, 20%, 10%, or 0% |
| Written essays | : | 50%, 40%, 30%, or 0% |

Grades for students taking the course as Business 379 use Graduate School of Business notation (H, P, etc.) and standards. Grades for other students use Stanford standard notation (A, B, etc.) and standards.

STANFORD UNIVERSITY  
Graduate School of Business

Jerry Porras  
David Bradford  
Debra Meyerson  
Jim Thompson

## G370: LEARNING TO LEAD
Spring, 1994

### Overview

There is a growing demand for more and "better" leadership in the US. and the world. Yet, most would agree that leadership is a performing art and that a conceptual understanding of leadership processes is simply not enough to make someone a better leader. Learning to Lead has been developed with these two thoughts in mind.

This course has been designed to bridge across three arenas in which learning about leadership can best take place. The first arena is the traditional classroom in which concepts are presented and discussed through a variety of means such as lectures, case analyses, videos and so on. The second is a workshop setting in which behaviors are precipitated through the use of structured experiential exercises, analyzed and then practiced for improvement. The third is a real life setting in which individuals actually engage in performing tasks and the role of leadership is exercised as people try to accomplish set goals.

We intend to help you learn more about leadership by involving you in a coordinated set of activities occurring in all these three arenas simultaneously. Needless to say, this will not be easy and since this is the first time we (or anybody as far as we know) have tried to do this, things may not always go smoothly. So, we hope you will view these situations as opportunities to learn how to do things more effectively. In doing so, we believe you will learn more about how to lead as we learn more about how to create the conditions that best facilitate your learning. It can be a nice reinforcing cycle if we can pull it off together.

### Course Description

As you already know, this is a two-quarter course (Spring 1994 and Fall 1994) in which you must complete both quarters in order to get credit for either. In addition, we have planned activities for the summer so that you can continue to develop your leadership competency while on your normal summer job. We'll say more about this below.

During the Spring quarter we will introduce you to significant leadership issues by organizing our exploration of them around a series of metaphors about leaders, each of which represents a unique and self contained world view, complete with assumptions about the world, people in the world, and what one should be and do as a leader. These sets of metaphors represent key tensions or controversies underlying different notions of leadership. For instance, the metaphors, Captain, Heroic/Post-Heroic, and Coach, differ in their assumptions about governance and control, about what motivates people, and about the key characteristics of situations.

These metaphors will be dealt with both conceptually (through readings, lectures, guest speakers and case and video discussions) and experientially (through simulations, role plays, and behavioral exercises). In addition to class time, we will require you to participate in one evening meeting each week during which much of the experiential and competence building activities will take place. Finally, during this initial quarter, you will be expected to involve yourself in an out-of-class activity that requires you to exercise influence or leadership. The experience gained from this activity will be folded into the learning processes of the course. This will be accomplished by training you to be more skilled participant observers of leadership situations (both your own and others') and to use these observations as data to be fed into class activities.

Your participant observation skills will provide the basis for continuing your learning during the summer. We expect that in your summer job you will either be in a leadership role or be around others who are leading. Learning to Lead will continue in the summer in two ways. First, we will ask you to systematically collect data on the leading process throughout the summer by observing the behavior of leaders around you (or yourself) and the characteristics of the situations they operate in. These data will provide part of the basis for further developing your model of leadership (which we will help you continue to do in the fall quarter when you return). Second, we will offer a weekend workshop in the middle of the summer giving you an opportunity to gather with your fellow students and integrate your learnings to date as well as plan how to more effectively use the rest of the summer.

Finally, in the fall quarter we will first of all help you integrate all you have learned and then apply your understanding of leadership to situations of change. An action project will be a key ingredient of your learning how to lead change.

## Evening Meetings

Students will be divided into 7-person groups that will meet every Tuesday or Wednesday evening for two hours. (We will attempt to give you your preference in terms of evenings but we need to construct the groups to be maximally heterogeneous).

The objective of these teams are several-fold:

- To provide a smaller-sized setting where you can pursue in more depth issues that have come up from speakers, class discussion or the readings

- To understand the dynamics of small group behavior and learn what you can do to be a more effective group member

- To increase your competencies in handling different leadership situations (including getting coaching on how to better deal with your outside organization).

These objectives will be achieved through a combination of role-plays and exercises with periodic examination of how the team is operating. Starting with the third week, each member will take turns being responsible for developing the agenda and leading the group that evening. In addition, another member (who will be the leader the following week), will serve as process observer to note the team's dynamics and intervene to increase the group's effectiveness. A faculty member will meet with the process observers or the group leaders (in separate meetings) each Friday at noon to coach them on their roles. (A more complete description of the functions of these two roles and of the group will be handed out the first week of class).

For the first two weeks, the faculty will take responsibility for the evening sessions. Since the teams will not be formed the first week, you will have your choice of coming to a Tuesday or Wednesday evening training session (6:30 - 8:30 in room 53) that will deal with <u>interpersonal influence skills</u> (to help you learn how to more constructively influence each other and the faculty!). The second week will be a series of team building activities (that will be fun and challenging) conducted by Outward Bound. By this time your evening groups will have been formed and you will meet with your group on the appropriate evening. This session will be a little longer running from 6:00 - 9:00 p.m.

Course Requirements and Grades

Your course grade will be based on class participation and on the quality of your work in a comprehensive new learning tool we've developed called the **Leadership Map**.

**Class participation (35% of grade)** - We have heavily weighted class participation because the quality of this class is so tightly linked to the quality of students' participation. Participation in this case includes a variety of interrelated activities: 1) relevance and quality of daytime class discussions and exercises, 2) relevance and quality of evening session participation, including (but not limited to) how one performs the functions of group "leader" and "observer" (described in a separate document to be handed out in class) and how one delivers and receives feedback, 3) participation in outside leadership activity, and the quality and rigor with which one applies concepts to their practice and brings their practice back to conceptual discussions.

Evaluation of student participation will be based on three inputs: 1) faculty observations, 2) peer assessments, and 3) self assessments.

**Leadership Map (65%).** The personal "Leadership Map" represents the capstone of the course. It is meant to be an integrating, organic document that will continue to evolve throughout the course, and hopefully beyond. The Map represents a structure through which you can think about and continually examine your own development as a leader; it is a snapshot in time that should be revised in an on-going manner. The Map will capture a series of inputs, including, but not limited to, your 1) personal values and significant contributions you wish to make, 2) conceptual learnings from readings, other classes, observations, etc., 3) personal reflections about your experiences, understandings, competencies, weaknesses, etc., 4) additional learnings derived from any other sources, 5) conceptual model of leadership, and, most significantly, 6) personal development plan for how and why you will go about building knowledge, competency, and experience in those areas in which you determine you wish to focus. We will evaluate your Map not according to whether you have found an "answer," but the thoughtfulness and thoroughness with which you have explored the questions, the quality of your reflections about your leadership experiences, strengths, weaknesses, hopes, and fears and how well you have integrated these reflections with theory and your developing understanding of leadership. More detail about the specific structure of the Leadership Map is provided next.

## Leadership Map

> But the virtues we acquire by first exercising them, as is the case with all the arts, for it is by doing what we ought to do when we have learnt the arts that we learn the arts themselves; we become e.g. builders by building and harpists by playing the harp. Similarly, it is by doing just acts that we become just, by doing temperate acts that we become temperate, by doing courageous acts that we become courageous.
>
> Aristotle, *The Nicomachean Ethics, p. 43.*

And so it is with leadership. The art of leadership is born out of practice. Yet learning and growth take place most effectively when one learns how to observe, capture and reflect upon their own and others' practices and the situations in which these practices occur.

The **Leadership Map** is a tool for you to reflect upon, integrate, and plan from your experiences and the body of conceptual knowledge you will acquire. You will work on the map continually throughout the quarter consolidating in it all of your key learnings. We will collect the Map several times during the quarter to punctuate and provide feedback about a period of learning. It is *not* an "end product." We emphasize this because we want to convey the significance of thinking about leadership development as a lifelong process in which this class intervenes. The Leadership Map is intended to help you along the way. If for some reason the structure of this tool does not work for you, and you think an alternative structure will work better, *please,* by all means explore the option of adapting it to your specific needs with one of the instructors. This is your tool.

The **Leadership Map** should include the following sections, all of which should be reconsidered and revised regularly.

**1) Personal Statement.** This section should help you consolidate your thoughts about why you want to be a leader. For what purpose will you lead? For what purpose or values will you sacrifice? What will give you the internal fortitude and dedication to lead? Why will people want to follow? This section could also explore your own concerns as they relate to your personal statement about leadership. Don't think that once you have made entries into this section you are done. On the contrary, expect to periodically revise your statements as you learn more about yourself and the process of leading. This should be an evolving statement rather than one that is "fixed in stone."

**2) Conceptual Integrations.** In this section we want you to focus on the readings and their significance to you. For each assigned reading pick out the one or two most meaningful ideas to you and elaborate on what they mean and why you think they are significant. Attempt to relate them to your own experiences clarifying whether or not the concepts make sense in light of your leadership practice. Finally, discuss how the ideas relate to other concepts encountered in previously assigned readings, whether they build on or contradict, clarify or confuse, etc.

**3) Weekly Reflections.** This section is crucial. It should be free flowing allowing yourself to explore the wide range of experiences you've had this week. In it you should integrate the learnings you derive from a variety of "data" inputs, including such things as thoughts about class discussions, your own experiences this week, application to your experiences of any of the theories you've captured in Part 2 of your Map, elaborations and critiques of theories based on your experiences, observations of leaders or peers, and feedback you receive from your group, peers in your leadership activity, and instructors.

**4) Other Learnings.** This section compiles insights you want to keep that don't fit in any of the other parts of your Map. These might emerge from a wide variety of sources, including other courses, outside discussions, newspaper or periodical articles, films, etc.

**5) Model of Leadership.** This section is intended to help you make explicit your implicit model of leadership. You have one, everyone does. It is important to surface your model and the assumptions underlying it so that you may more consciously evolve and grow it. This section does not need to include everything. Moreover, you are not expected to develop a parsimonious theory about leadership. A central message of the class, in fact, is that there is no universal parsimonious theory of leadership; there are multiple theories that are more and less relevant depending on the person and situation. What we expect you to do in this section is to develop a tentative conceptual theory of leadership as it relates to you today, in a particular set of circumstances. This may simply be a statement of those theories that seemed most compelling and an explanation of why and when they are most compelling to you. While this section is meant to be conceptual, it also must be personal. It is your working theory today; it necessarily changes as you and your understandings of circumstances do ....

**6) Development plan.** This is perhaps the most action oriented part of the Map. This section should work as a learning guide and should evolve as your needs and interests change. You will use this, in part, as a developmental tool which, in the context of this course, you will re-visit in the mid-summer workshop and at the beginning of the fall quarter. The development plan should build on your conceptual understandings and your experiences. From these reflections you may develop some insight into those areas in which you want to work. Specifically, the plan should consider those areas in which you might like to gain more 1) knowledge, 2) experience, and 3) competency. You should set some developmental goals and then carefully consider how you are going to go about achieving them. Think about courses you may want to take at the GSB, experiences you want to have this summer, readings you would like to do, and so on. We urge you to distinguish areas you can work on in the short term, in this case the summer, and areas you would like to work on over the longer term.

**STANFORD UNIVERSITY**
Graduate School of Business

Jerry Porras
David Bradford
Debra Meyerson
Jim Thompson

### G370: LEARNING TO LEAD
Class Outline - Spring 1994

## GETTING STARTED

**1. Mar. 29th   (T)   Why Lead?**

This session will pose and help you to begin to more deeply think about a series of questions to be addressed individually and as a class throughout the course sequence. Specifically, we will ask: 1) Why is leadership so important? 2) Toward what purpose and with what passion are you motivated to lead? 3) What are you willing to sacrifice to achieve this purpose or fulfill this passion?

Read:   "Foreward" pp. xi -xxii, J. Gardner, Self Renewal

"Self Renewal," pp. 8 - 20, J. Gardner, Self Renewal

"Introduction" pp. xi-xv, J. Gardner. On Leadership

Optional:   "The Servant as Leader," p. 7-17, R. Greanleaf, Servant Leadership.

"Loving the Plateau" pp. 39-49, G. Leonard, Mastery

"The Master and the Fool," pp. 169-176, G. Leonard, Mastery

Do: Take a look at the application you wrote for this class. Examine it carefully. Come prepared to probe deeply into why you want to lead and what concerns you most with the prospect of being a leader.

Speaker:   John Gardner

**2. Apr. 1st   (F)   What is Leadership?**

Leadership and the particular competencies required of leaders have been subject to extensive debate. Learning to Lead is designed to give you several perspectives on leadership through the use of metaphors. This session will introduce the use of metaphors and ask the fundamental question: What is leadership?

Read:   "The Parables of Leadership," W. C. Kim & R. A. Mauborgne, Harvard Business Review.

"What Leaders Really Do," J. Kotter, Harvard Business Review

"We Learn How to See" pp. 21, G. Morgan, <u>Images of Organization</u>

Optional: "The New Managerial Work," R. M. Kanter, <u>Harvard Business Review</u>

"Leadership Theory and Research," pp. 1 - 21, A. Bryman, <u>Charisma and Leadership in Organizations</u> (Skim for background)

Do: Make sure you have made a thoughtful entry into your Leadership Map regarding your own personal leadership statement. Come to class prepared with your hypotheses about what leadership means and what the most essential competencies of leadership are. Enter these into your Leadership Map under "Model of Leadership."

"Eagle Smelting" (Prepare case)

3. Apr. 5th   (T)   **Leader as Captain**

The first metaphor of leadership we will explore is leader as "Captain." Many of the attributes we traditionally associate with highly successful leaders are congruent with this metaphor. This session will look at these qualities and competencies and examine the situations under which this approach to leadership is most effective. We will explore the assumptions a "Captain" holds about people, motivation, and situations. Consider what are the particular advantages and disadvantages of this approach to leadership?

Read: "Classical Management Theory," pp. 25-29, G. Morgan, <u>Images of Organization</u>

"Kick-starting the Revolution," pp. 71-83, N. Tichy & S. Sherman, <u>Control your Destiny or Someone Else Will</u>

"Nothing Sacred," pp. 84-91, N. Tichy & S. Sherman, <u>Control your Destiny or Someone Else Will</u>

"Facing Reality," pp. 92-104, N. Tichy & S. Sherman, <u>Control your Destiny or Someone Else Will</u>

"Driving," pp. 468-495, R. Caro, <u>The Power Broker</u>

"New Paradigm Management," <u>Fortune</u> (handout)

Do: Consider the following: What are the assumptions behind the leader as "Captain" metaphor? What does it mean for a leader to be "in charge"? What are the competencies involved in this approach? In what situations will it work best? Worst?

Come prepared to ask the speaker questions about his own leadership approach particularly about the situations in which this "take charge" approach is most and least appropriate and effective?

Make weekly entry into your Leadership Map

Speaker: George McCown, Managing Partner,
McCown DeLeeuw & Co.

### 4. Apr. 8th (F) Heroic and Post-Heroic Views of Leadership

This session focuses on the "post-heroic" leader, the leader that gets things done by empowering other people to seize control, make decisions, and act. We examine those situations in which this approach is effective and changes in the environment that have led to this leadership approach becoming more appropriate. Since the post-heroic leader often works through teams, we will spend some time discussing teams and processing the work done during the previous evening session.

Read: "The Discipline of Teams," J. Katzenbach & D. Smith, Harvard Business Review

"The Hard Work of Being a Soft Manager," W. Peace, Harvard Business Review

"Post-heroic Leadership," D. Bradford (handout)

Optional: "Speed, Simplicity, Self-Confidence: Interview with Jack Welch," N.Tichy & R. Charan, Harvard Business Review

Do: Assignment will be handed out in previous class

### 5. Apr. 12th (T) Leader as a Coach

This class will continue the work done in the previous class in which we explore how leaders build conditions which enable others to get work done and work as part of effective teams. Since coaches work through teams, this session will build on the theme, "leader as coach," and draw from the insights and experiences of effective coaches.

Read: "To Build a Winning Team: An Interview with Bill Walsh, " R. Rappaport, Harvard Business Review

"Coaching and the Art of Management," R. Evered & J. Selman in Organizational Dynamics.

Optional: "Coaching," Chapter 18 from T. Peters & N. Austin, Passion for Excellence

Do: Make weekly entry into your Leadership Map. Additional assignment will be handed out in previous class.

**148**

3

Speaker: Bill Walsh, Head Football Coach
Stanford University

6. Apr. 15th (F) **Integrating Learnings**

This session will include a discussion that integrates and applies the ideas and approaches discussed thus far in the course. We will also introduce participant observation as a method for collecting information.

Read: Excerpts from "Systematic Observation Methods," K. Weick (handout)

"Conducting Case Studies," Chapter. 4, R. Yin

Do: Bring in your Leadership Map. You will turn it in for feedback and evaluation.

In your evening groups develop an integration of your key learnings up to now. Each team will be responsible for providing significant input into today's discussion.

7. Apr. 19th (T) **Leader as Sense Maker**

This session will challenge traditional notions of leader as either a "doer" or "one that can get others to do" and offer an alternative metaphor based on leader as interpreter. This model of leadership, views the leader's relationship to his/her organization much like the art critic's relationship to a piece of art. This metaphor may be most relevant under conditions of ambiguity, when organizations look more like rapidly changing "anarchies" than stable "machine bureaucracies." Since in many ways the contemporary world is filled with ambiguities, this metaphor of leadership may be more relevant to today's leaders than it first appears.

Read: Leadership in an Organized Anarchy," in M. Cohen & J. G. March, Leadership and Ambiguity,

Short story (hand out)

Do: What assumptions about the environment and the way organizations function does this approach challenge? What competencies does this metaphor suggest are important? Under what conditions might this approach be the most relevant way to think about the process of leading?

Make weekly entry into your Leadership Map

8. Apr. 22nd (F) **Leader as Visionary**

This session will help students understand what organizational vision is and how leaders shape vision. More specifically, we will focus on two types of visionary leaders: charismatic visionaries and organizational visionaries. You will have the opportunity to explore the assumptions behind each type of visionary, the situations in which one type might be most appropriate, and the behaviors and competencies associated with

4

each type. The class will also help students understand themselves better in the context of the two types of visionary leaders. In addition, we will re-visit the personal questions about vision and purpose posed in the first class session.

Read: "Organizational Vision and Visionary Organizations," J. Collins & J. Porras, California Management Review

"Research on the New Leadership and Charisma in Business Organizations," pp. 115 - 139. A. Brysman, Charisma and Leadership in Organizations

"Values Make the Company: An Interview with Robert Haas" in Harvard Business Review

Optional: "The Dark Side of Leadership," J. Conger, Organizational Dynamics

Do: Look at the personal statement you developed following the first class session and revise it in your Leadership Map.

**9. Apr. 26th (T) Leader as Conductor**

Our focus this class will be on the metaphor of leader as conductor, as in orchestra conductor. This metaphor makes central the competencies and functions of planning, organizing, and controlling. We will analyze the underlying assumptions of this metaphor, particularly as they relate to the predictability of the future and an organization's stance toward innovation and change.

Read: "The Work of the Leader," W. Pagonis, Harvard Business Review

"The CEO as Organizational Architect: An Interview with Xerox's Paul Allaire," R. Howard, Harvard Business Review

Do: Be prepared to discuss the following questions: How is a leader like a conductor? What are the assumptions underlying the metaphor of leader as "conductor"? When do we see leaders behaving like conductors? What competencies are required? What are the characteristics of situations in which this approach to leading is most effective? Reflect on your own competencies in these areas.

Make weekly entry into your Leadership Map.

Speaker: To be announced

**10. Apr. 29th (F) Leadership as Improvisation I**

This session views leadership and the social world from the perspective of improvisation. The metaphor of improvisation is powerful, not just in its assumptions about the environment, but in the new set of competencies it demands from group leaders and participants.

Read: "The Aesthetic of Imperfection in Orchestras and Organizations," K. Weick (handout)

"Jazz as a Process of Organizational Innovation," D. Bastien and T. Hostager, Communication Research

"Team Learning," pp. 233-238, P. Senge, The Fifth Discipline

Do: Try to attend or view some sort of improvisational performance or some event that has the qualities of improvisation. What conditions makes improvisation work? Fail? What competencies are required to be good at improvisation? Bring your observations to class.

11. May 3rd    (T)    **Leadership as Improvisation II**

During this session you will work on some of the competencies highlighted in the previous session.

Read: "Whatever Happened to the Take Charge Manager?" N. Nohria & J. Berkeley. Harvard Business Review

"Toward Projects for All," pp. 222 - 225, T. Peters. Liberation Management

"Knowledge Management Structures," pp. 382 - 412, T. Peters. Liberation Management

Do: Make weekly entry in your Leadership Map

Speaker: Pat Ryan, Department of Drama, Stanford University

12. May 6th    (F)    **Language, Symbols and Motivation**

In this section we will look at the various ways in which leaders motivate and influence followers. We will pay special attention to the use of language and symbols in these processes. We will also go back to the source of your own personal motivation and commitment under the premise that leaders must be aware of their own source of motivation before they can motivate others.

Read: "Rhetoric: The Work of Words" in R. Eccles & N. Nohria Beyond the Hype

"Inspiring Others: The Language of Leadership," J. Conger, Academy of Management Executive

"Symbolic Action" in J. Pfeffer, Managing with Power

Do: Observe and analyze the use of language in a press conference or speech (e.g., on CSPAN).

13. May 10th   (T)   Integrating Learnings

This session will include a discussion that integrates and applies the ideas and approaches discussed thus far in the course.

**Do:** Make weekly entries in your Leadership Map and then turn it in for feedback and evaluation.

In your evening groups develop an integration of your key learnings up to now. Each team will be responsible for providing significant input into today's discussion.

14. May 13th   (F)   Influence

Most of what we have been dealing with up to this point is based on a leader influencing subordinates. In this session we will focus specifically on processes of influence laterally and upward, directions very important to leadership but seldom emphasized.

**Read:** To be handed out in class

**Do:** To be handed out in class

15. May 17th   (T)   Leader as "Path breaker"

The leader as "Path breaker" metaphor highlights some essential aspects of leadership: risk-taking, high performance, drive, persistence, focus, tenacity. These qualities are more apparent in some leaders than in others. In this session we will focus on these qualities both at personal and more abstract levels. We will ask, "under what conditions is this approach most appropriate"? What are the costs and benefits of this style? What makes some leaders more "Path breaker" like than others?

**Read:** "Of Means and Ends," pp. 24 - 47, Saul Alinsky, Rules for Radicals.

Excerpts from Atlas Shrugged (handout)

**Optional:** CEO, Sandra Kurtzig

**Do:** Make weekly entries in your Leadership Map. Additional assignment handed out in class.

**Speaker:** Sandra Kurtzig, Chair Emeritus
ASK Group

16. May 20th   (F)   Leader as Protector

One of the functions of leadership is the provision of safety, trust, and stability. Without these qualities, people feel insecure and threatened and are unable to take risks, innovate, and learn. Change demands some stability. Risk requires some safety. This class will examine the ways in which leaders create safety and trust and the impact that this has on followers and leaders capacity to take risks and change.

Read: "Toward a Theory of 'Swift Trust'" D. Meyerson, R. Kramer, & K. Weick (handout)

"The Missing 'X-Factor': Trust," pp. 248-256, T. Peters, Liberation Management

"Trust, Respect, and the Mindful Organization," pp. 459-467, T. Peters, Liberation Management

Do: Assignment to be handed out in class.

17. May 24th (T) Leader as Moral Steward

Business is increasingly becoming the most global institution in the world. That is, no other social institution spans boundaries of nations, religions, politics to the extent that business does. Insofar as some of the most pressing social issues facing the people of the world transcend national boundaries, business and business leaders find themselves increasingly in the position of social and moral stewards of the globe. In this class we will examine what it means for business leaders to assume the role of social and moral steward. How does this figure in with other business responsibilities? What are the responsibilities of business leaders today?

Read: "Conclusion," A. Roddick, Body and Soul

"The Moral Dimension" pp. 67-80, J. Gardner, On Leadership

"Fragmentation and the Common Good," pp. 93-100, J. Gardner, On Leadership

"Choosing Service over Self-Interest, pp. 3-22, P. Block, Stewardship

"Replacing Leadership with Stewardship" pp. 41-51. P. Block, Stewardship

Do: Make weekly entry in your Leadership Map. Additional assignment to be handed out in class.

Speaker: John Gardner

18. May 27th (F) Integrating Learnings

This session will include a discussion that integrates and applies the ideas and approaches discussed thus far in the course.

Read: "Finding Courage in Fear," pp. 39-48, L. Donnithorne, West Point Way of Leadership.

"The Harder Right," pp. 61-72, L. Donnithorne, <u>West Point Way of Leadership.</u>

Excerpts from <u>Saint Joan,</u> G. Shaw. (handout)

**Do:** Make weekly entries in your Leadership Map and then turn it in for feedback and evaluation.

In your evening groups develop an integration of your key learnings up to now. Each team will be responsible for providing significant input into today's discussion.

19. May 31st    (F)    Transition into the Summer

This last session will be used to discuss and develop a perspective for your efforts during the summer. We want you to get the most out of your summer job experience, using it as a laboratory to gain further understanding of the leadership process. We will discuss our plans for a summer leadership workshop as well as structure your data collection approaches to your summer experience.

Work in the 1990's:
The Organization of Women and Men
OB742-2

Professor Debra Meyerson  
Admin. Assist.: Sherry Folsom, fifth floor (4-2304)  
E-mail: Debra Meyerson on mts or  
fmeyerson@gsb-peso.stanford.edu  
Phone: (415) 725-4039 Fax: (415)854-9669  

Times: Mondays & Thursdays  
Oct. 27- Nov. 14, 4:15-5:30  
& Friday and Saturday  
Nov. 18 & 19th, 8:00-4:00

## Course Description

This class will be significantly different from others at the Business School. During the first third of the class will be working together from 2,500 miles apart (I'm at Stanford), using two way video conferencing, email, and telephone. The other two thirds will take place over a two day intense workshop, in a format similar to what we use in executive education. This format has some important implications. First, you should realize that by joining this class you are participating in a process of innovation. Among top tiered business schools, Michigan is at the forefront of experimentation with new ways of delivering education and creating "learning communities." For example, Michigan is in the middle of "exporting" an entire M.B.A. program to executives at Cathay Pacific in Hong Kong. Ours is the first class they will "import." The idea follows from the mandate of globalization: source expertise globally, market customers globally, and so forth. In any case, you are part of an important innovation process and I encourage you to provide as much *constructive* feedback about pedagogy, style, and content as you feel appropriate. This learning is essential to us all, particularly at this stage in the innovation process.

The second implication of this teleconferencing/workshop format is that the sequencing and timing of the assignments is relatively heavy at the beginning and then relatively light. This is partly to compensate for the fact that there is a limit to the amount of preparation you can do for the two day workshop, which constitutes the bulk of the class.

This class also differs from others in its content. We will address some issues central to the organization of work and life -- those related to how women and men work together in organizations. In the process, we will move from a surface-level overview to a deeper analysis of the underlying cultural mechanisms that hold the current system of relations relatively in tact. This deeper analysis is essential; ultimately, it will enable us to chart a course of substantive change aimed at creating more healthy work systems for women and men.

During the first third of the class (that which will be teleconferenced), we start with a basic overview of the organization of women and men at work. We then look at dual career and work/family/leisure concerns and examine those cultural assumptions that shape how organizations manage these issues. We will also look at some of the more innovative solutions to these concerns and we will be visited by a guest who is involved in the implementation of a massive restructuring effort that is aimed, in part, toward using technology to address gender equity issues. As a class, we move into a more general discussion on how women and men "relate" to each other across groups, within groups, and interpersonally. On all topics, and particularly on the topic of work and family, we will emphasize men's stake in this issue, as well as women's.

The two day workshop will be experiential, designed to stimulate feelings about some central issues and work through various "solutions". We will begin this workshop by discussing and experiencing one of the basic phenomena underlying gender relations -- power, privilege and oppression -- and talk about how these relations figure into the various topics we covered throughout the class. On the second day of the workshop we will revisit various perspectives on "differences" and try to understand how gendered relations of power create and sustain these "differences." Throughout, we will be sorting through the implications of various concerns for management in organizations. My hope is that you will come out of the course with a much deeper and more critical understanding of the bases of gender relations in organizations which will enable you to work, affect change, and manage more effectively.

## Course Assignments and Pedagogy

The course offers you the opportunity to learn in a variety of ways: Lectures and readings provide the conceptual framework; cases and video cases will be used to help you analyze situations and propose actions; experiential activities provide the raw material for personal reflection and internalization of some of the deeper and more complex topics. You are encouraged to reflect on your experiences in a variety of ways.

You will be expected to read all assigned readings, participate constructively in class and attend regularly. Evaluation will be based on the following:

a) Participation and Attendance     30%
b) Personal Reflection Paper     30%
c) Research Paper     40%

a) **Participation** and contribution to class discussion is an essential part of your role and responsibility in this class. However, people from some cultures are less comfortable with verbal participation. Although it is essential that all members of this class push themselves and contribute, I realize that we all start from a different place of comfort and can contribute in different ways. It is essential that you read the required reading prior to class and come to class prepared to integrate concepts into class discussion. You are encouraged to participate at the conceptual level as well as the personal level.

b) **Personal reflection papers** are meant to be something in-between article summaries and personal journals. These papers require you to apply a concept or set of concepts from each reading to your own experience or to something you observe in the world around you (that may not directly involve you). In the few cases that readings do not seem relevant to your own life or to the organizational world around you, then simply summarize in a paragraph or two the most important points (to you) that came out of the reading. The point of this paper is to encourage you to apply these concepts to the world that is relevant to you. I encourage you to compile your entries as you go rather than wait until the end. The paper need not be integrated; it should more closely resemble a journal than a term paper. **This is due on the last day of class (Nov. 19) and should include entries on readings assigned through the Friday workshop.**

c) The **research paper** requires you to take a topic covered in class and research it in-depth. I encourage you to use secondary sources (books, articles, etc.) as well as primary sources (e.g., interviews). You can work with one other person in class, if you want. The paper should be no longer than 12 pages. **The paper is due on Nov. 30.**

## Course Outline

**0. Oct. 25, time and place TBA: Pre-class Introduction (I will be on-site)**

**1. Oct. 27: The Organization of Women and Men in Organizations: An Overview**

Read: 1) Women and Men in Management, Ch. 1, G. Powell.
2) "Point-Counterpoint: Discrimination against Women in Management," G. Northcraft and B. Gutek" Women in Management, E. Fagenson (ed.), 1993.
3) "Glass ceiling, Glass Prisons: Reflections on the Gender Barrier," M. Maier, The Diversity Factor, Spring, 1994.

**2. Oct. 31: The Organization of Work, Family, and Leisure: Underlying Issues (IT'S HALLOWEEN)**

Read: 1) Second Shift, pages 1-32, A. Hochschild, 1989.
2) "Changing the Conditions of Work: Responding to Increasing Work Force Diversity and New Family Patterns, " L. Bailyn, in Transforming Organizations, T. Kochan and M. Useem (Eds.).
3) Accountants and Business Advisors, Inc., HBS case.

**Prepare the case:**
1) Is retention of women a problem for the City Office? What dimensions of the business are relevant to this issue?
2) What factors contribute to the lower retention rates for women?
3) What does Shaughnessy learn from the four female partners?
4) What should Shaughnessy do? Do you recommend fundamental or marginal changes for the firm?

**3. Nov. 3: The Flexible Workplace: Is this a Solution?**

Read: 1) "The Flexible Workplace: What have we Learned?" C. Rogers, Human Resource Management, 1992.
2) "The Isolation of the Virtual Worker," San Francisco Examiner, Sept. 25, 1994.
3) "Pathways to Change," L. Bailyn, pages 121-150, in Breaking the Mold.

Prepare: 1) What are the ways in which telecommuting can enhance one's quality of life?
2) How might telecommuting affect the distribution of work and family responsibilities among men and women?
3) What are the benefits and costs of other "flexible" work arrangements?

In Class: Guest Speaker: Barbara Miller, Ford Foundation Project Manager on "New Office Business Environment"

**4. Nov. 7: Structures Power, Access, and Opportunity**

Read: 1) "Note on Power and Difference," Sheila Taylor, Unpublished, Univ. of Chicago.
2) "Organizational Barriers to Gender Equality: Sex Segregation of Jobs and Opportunities," J. Baron and W. Bielby in Gender and the Life Course, Alice Rossi (Ed.).
3) U of M Business School Vital Statistics.
4) "Beyond the Myth of the Perfect Mentor," (pages 11-14)

**Prepare:** 1) What are the ways in which informal processes shape the distribution of women and men in corporations?
 2) Have you had a mentor in your professional life? What was that relationship like and how did it figure into your professional development?

**In Class:** 1) The Karen Green Case (video case)

**5. Nov. 10 Intergroup Relations: Structural and Group Effects
(class today is 4:30- 5:45)**

Read: 1) <u>Men and Women of the Corporation</u>, pages 206-242, R. M. Kanter.

In Class: "Tale of O" (video case)

**6. Nov. 14: Intergroup and Interpersonal Relations between Men and Women**
 1) <u>Women and Men in Management</u>, Chapter 5, G. Powell.
 2) "He Said, She Said," pages 169-196, in <u>Value Judgments,</u> Ellen Goodwin, 1993.
 3) "Managing Cross-Gender Mentoring," J. Clawson and K. Kram, <u>Business Horizons,</u> May-June, <u>1984.</u>
 4) "The Case of the Hidden Harassment," D. Niven, <u>Harvard Business Review,</u> March/April, 1992.
 5) "Sexual Harassment in the Workplace, " E. Wagner, American Management Assn.*(as reference - skim for class)* (HANDOUT)

**Preparation:**
 1) Come prepared with a position on the Hidden Harassment case.

=================

**7. Friday, Nov. 18: Relations of Power between Groups (Workshop)**
 (8 a.m. to 4 p.m. with 1 hour lunch break)

**Read (at least one from each category):**
**On Power Relations (generally) and Sexuality**
 1) "Changing perspectives on power," b. hooks, Ch. 6 from <u>Feminist Theory: From Margin to Center, 1984.</u>
 2) "Sexuality in the workplace: Key issues in social research and organizational practice," B. Gutek, in <u>The Sexuality of Organization,</u> J. Hearn, D. Sheppard, P. Tacred-Shiriff, and G. Burrell (eds.), 1990. ( HANDOUT )
**On Dominance**
 3) "Men who do and Men who Don't" in <u>Second Shift,</u> A. Hochschild.
 4) "White privilege: Unpacking the Invisible Knapsack," <u>Independent School,</u> P. McIntosh.
**On Oppression**
 5) "Myths, Stereotypes, and Realities of Black Women: A Personal Reflection," E. Bell, <u>Journal of Applied Behavioral Science,</u> 1992.


**8. Saturday, Nov. 19: Workshop on Differences, Gender Relations, and Change**
 (8 a.m. to 4 p.m. with 1 hour lunch break)

**Read (<u>one</u> from each category):**
**On Differences**

1) "Women in Management: An Exploration of Competing Paradigms," S. Riger, P. Galligan, American Psychologists, 1980.
2) "Talking Trouble," A. Roiphe, Working Woman, Oct. 1984.

**On Gender**
1) "Gendering Organization Theory," J. Acker in Gendering Organizational Analysis, A. Mills and P. Tancred (eds.), 1992.
2) "The Gender we Think, The Gender we Do in Our Everyday Organizational Lives," S. Gherardi, Human Relations, June, 1994.

**On Building Alliances and Affecting Change**
1) "Comrades in Struggle," b. hooks, in Feminist Theory: From Margin to Center, 1984.
2) "Tempered Radicalism and the Politics of Ambivalence and Change," D. Meyerson and M. Scully, Organization Science, forthcoming.
3) "Stepping into Old Biographies or Making History Happen," A. Hochschild, Second Shift.*(optional.)*

**Prepare:**
1) How do you "do" gender in your everyday lives?
2) How do you see gender relations operate within the Michigan Business School?

The University of British Columbia
Faculty of Commerce and Business Administration
Autumn, 1994

## Commerce 426
Organizational Change and Development

**Instructor**: Larry Moore
**Office**: HA 561; phone: (O) 822-8381; (H) 228-8617
**Office Hours**: Wed. and Fri. 3:00-4:00 or by appointment

Course Description:

   The focus of this course is on exploring the realities of organizational change from the vantage point of the OD practitioner. Much of the class time will be dedicated to discussion of readings, cases and other materials. A sampling of views, relevant skills, issues and approaches is provided in the readings. These have an advantage over a textbook in that we can see the differences between approaches rather than have them reported to us. There will be some lecturettes to provide an overarching perspective into which the wide variety of cases, readings, and other materials can be fitted and applied. The scheme is to apply course material to particular situations (cases, field work) and to examine in depth the OD issues that arise during the course.

Course Objectives:

(1) To develop a diagnostic framework (the Environmental CELL Model) and utilize it.

(2) To understand the role of "change agents" and the skills and activities related to that role.

(3) To understand various "interventions" and how then can contribute to facilitating change in a variety of situations.

(4) To introduce the student to the diagnosis, analysis, and reporting of organizational change through participation in a field project team effort.

Grading Plan:

| | | |
|---|---|---|
| Team Case (written) | (due Sept. 23) | 10% |
| Written case #1 | (due Oct. 21) | 15 |
| Written case #2 | (due Nov. 18) | 15 |
| Participation | | 20 |
| Field project | | 40 |

Required Texts and materials:

Glassman, A. and Cummings, T., <u>Cases in Organizational Development</u>, Homewood, IL: Irwin, 1991.

<u>Readings Package</u> available from the supply kiosk in the basement of the Angus Building.

There will be handouts for which the photocopying cost is estimated to be $4.

## OUTLINE

| Week | Topic | Assignment |
|---|---|---|

1.  **I. INTRODUCTION**
    Wed., Sept. 7
    Fri., Sept. 9
    Readings
    "Toyota keeps getting better and better" (Taylor)
    "Ch. 1: Management and leadership" (Kotter)

2.  **II. FUNDAMENTALS OF MANAGED CHANGE**
    Six Cell model
    Phases of change
    Change agent actions and skills
    Wed., Sept. 14
    Readings
    "Introduction + Part 1: Intro. (pp.1-9) (case text)
    "Evolution and resolution as organizations grow" (Greiner)
    Case #1 (case text)
    Fri., Sept. 16
    Readings
    " Ch. 2: excerpts from clients letter + contracting (Neilson)
    "pp. 25-29: "Overorganized and underorganized situations" (Huse and Cummings)
    Case #2 (case text)

3.  **III. ENTREPRENEURIAL ORGANIZATIONS (CELL 1 SITUATIONS)**
    Wed., Sept. 21
    Readings
    "Methods for finding out what's going on" (Fordyce and Weil)
    "Part II: Intro. (pp. 57-58, case text)
    Cases #4 & 5 (case text)
    Fri., Sept. 23
    Readings
    "Intro + Ch. 2 Growing pains" (Flamholtz)
    Case #9 TEAM WRITTEN ANALYSIS DUE HERE

4.  **IV. FLEXIBLE ORGANIZATIONS (CELL 2 SITUATIONS)**
    Wed., Sept. 28
    Reading
    "IV: Achieving flexibility by empowering people" (Peters)
    Case #6

Fri., Sept. 30
　　Readings
　　　　"Wanted: Leaders who can make a difference" (Main)
　　　　"The causal, intervening, and end-result variables" (Likert)
　　　　"Who needs a boss?" (Dumaine)
　　Case #7

5. Wed., Oct. 5
　　Reading
　　　　"The skills of the OD practitioner" (Neilson)
　　Case #15
　Fri., Oct. 7
　　Reading
　　　　"Positive image, positive action: The affirmative basis of organizing" (Cooperrider)
　　Cases #20 & 21

6. V. EFFICIENT AND HUMANE BUREAUCRACY (CELL 3 SITUATIONS)
　Wed., Oct. 12
　　Reading
　　　　"Rules of thumb for change agents" (Shepard)
　　Case #14
　Fri., Oct. 14
　　Readings
　　　　"1: Kaizen, the concept + 23-27: improvement, east and west" (Imai)
　　　　"What flexible workers can do" (Alster)
　　Case #23

7. Wed., Oct. 19
　　Reading
　　　　"Ch. 20: Doing it with data" (Walton)
　　Case #16
　Fri., Oct. 21
　　Reading
　　　　"Ch 8: Talking with clients" (Neilson)
　　Case #19 INDIVIDUAL WRITTEN ANALYSIS DUE

8. CONSOLIDATION DAY (#1)
　　Wed., Oct. 26
　　　　Review and reflect on previous cases; identify emerging issues.
　　　　Verbal interim reports on field project progress; preliminary assessment of findings

　VI. DEALING WITH INCREASED COMPLEXITY
　　Fri., Oct. 28
　　　　Reading
　　　　　　"Choosing the depth of organizational intervention" (Harrison)
　　　　Case #24

9.   Wed., Nov. 2
         Readings
             "So you want an innovative organization"
                 (Zaloudek)
             "The politics of innovation"  (Dyer)
         Case #25

     Fri., Nov. 4
         Readings
             "Making over middle managers"  (Labich)
             "Two person disputes"  (Rogers)
         Case #32

10.  Wed., Nov. 9
         Reading
             "Ch. 10: Implementing new designs: managing
                     organizational change" (Nadler/Tushman
         Case #33

     Fri., Nov. 11 - NO CLASS - Remembrance Day

11.  Wed. Nov. 16   CONSOLIDATION DAY (#2)
         Reading
             "Human resistance to change (350-362)"
                 (Kotter, Schlesinger & Sathe)
         Review and reflect on complex change projects;
         Pivotal emerging issues.

   VII.  MONITORING AND EVALUATING CHANGE
         Fri. Nov. 18
             Readings
                 "Ch. 7: Monitoring and evaluating change"
                     (Beckhard and Harris)
                 "How to win the Baldridge Award" (Main)
             Case #30 & 31 INDIVIDUAL WRITTEN CASE due--all
             questions for #30 and question 1 for #31

12. VIII. ETHICS
         Wed., Nov. 23
             Reading
                 "Intro to Part IV" (367-8, case text)
             Case #26
         Fri. BEGIN PROJECT REPORTS/PRESENTATIONS

13.  Wed., Nov. 30   PROJECT REPORTS/PRESENTATIONS

     Fri., Dec. 2   INTEGRATIVE ANALYSIS OF FIELD PROJECT
     TEAM WRITTEN PROJECT REPORTS DUE FRIDAY, DEC. 2

Course Outline: ORGANIZATIONS AND SOCIETY -- Charles Perrow, Soc. 156 B, Spring '95, Mondays, 1:30-3:20

This course will be a slimmed down version of a course in organizational behavior that I gave for some years in this School of Organization and Management at Yale. There will be more emphasis on the social science of organizations and less upon how to manage them, but the SOM version was already a social science course since I believe, in any case, that good analysis is more important and more difficult than good management techniques. The course will utilize some of the paraphernalia of management school OB courses, principally Harvard Business Review cases selected to illustrate the various theories we will encounter. The reading will be heavy. Every week students will submit a 2-3 page paper critically discussing the readings for that week, prior to their discussion in class. (If you are accustomed to taking reading notes to prepare for exams, this will be no great burden, and there are no exams in the course.) One student will be assigned to lead off the discussion of the topic each week. A 10-15 page paper expanding on one of the topics will constitute 35% of the grade. The topic should be proposed in writing not later than session 10. The short papers will count for 50%; class discussion for 15%.

The approach is roughly historical. We will start with the large U.S. corporation and the economic theories of organization that explain and justify these rigid, hierarchical, unresponsive systems. Then we will examine the human relations movement, with its psychodynamics and religious roots, and "bounded rationality" or the so called "garbage can model" of organizations, with roots in modern cognitive psychology. Both were developed to account for the failures of rational economic theory and the growing diversity of organizational forms. Then we will examine the emergence of "structural" theory which tried to account for organizational differences, public and private; it drew on the tradition of sociologist Max Weber. Attention will be paid to the political and economic environment that surrounded organizations. Increasingly new models of organizations began to appear as employees gained a bit more power and as markets required more flexibility in production, and as services increased in importance. Finally, we will confront the issue of U.S. competitiveness, Japanese success, and the faint prospects of networks of small firms that promise a reduction in the concentration of wealth and power while swiftly responding to new technologies and changing market demands. **Since this is a seminar, attendance will be limited. Sociology majors will have first priority.**

Key: L: = Lecture topic. D: = Class discussion. These are essential. You will have read the material and written a short memo, so the discussions should be lively. There should be discussions that interrupt the lectures and following them, as well as those listed. A volunteer will introduce the topic each week. **Read** = readings for the next class. Check the "Summary of Major Theories" in the course packet to help you as you go along. **Course packets will be available at 155 Whitney, MIS. Purchase the following at Book Haven (All paperbacks): Charles Perrow, Complex Organizations: A Critical Essay and Michael Best, The New Competition.**

Assignments: in all cases, a 2-3 page typed paper, to be turned in to my box in sociology mailroom by **10:00 a.m. on Monday.** These will be graded by Wednesday a.m. and can be picked up in mail room. An E-mail option will be discussed. *Office Hours: Wednesdays, 11-12 and Thursdays 1:30-2:30, Williams Hall Room 202.*

1/9  1.  INTRODUCTION; MICRO AND MACRO APPROACHES TO ORG. ANALYSIS
Overview of course, discussing short memos, critical paper.
Personal introductions of class members.
D: What would you like from a course like this?
Read Stockwell case, in class (short).
D: Discuss case: what would you do?
L: Micro and macro approaches.
> Read for next class: Charles Perrow, Complex Organizations: A Critical Essay, 3rd ed., Random House, Chpt. 1. and Alfred DuPont Chandler, The Visible Hand, Cambridge University Press, 1977, pps. 1-12 carefully; 258-69 skim; 287-314 skim; 484-500 carefully.
> *Assignment:* 2-3 pages criticizing Chandler. Due 1/16, 10AM

1/16  2. MASS PRODUCTION: THE BASIS FOR INDUSTRIAL POWER
D: Discuss papers.
D: Efficiency for whom?
L: Alternative views of growth of large organizations
> Read for next class: Richard Du Boff and Edward Herman, "Alfred Chandler's New Business History: A Review," Politics and Society 10, no. 1 (1980), pp. 87-110; Michael Best, The New Competition, Harvard, 1990, pp. 29-134
> *Assignment:* Reactions to readings. Due 1/23, 10AM

1/23  3. MASS PRODUCTION: ECONOMIC THEORIES MATTER
D: Discuss papers.
L: Reading Best; a walk through his theories.
D: How might sociological and economic theories of behavior and of organizations differ? When use one or the other? How might the widespread use of one rather than the other affect the economy? Which is best for moving from a command to a market society?
> Read for next class: Perrow, Chpt. 7; "Technotronics Co."; James March, "Bounded Rationality, Ambiguity, and the Engineering of Choice," Bell Journal of Economics 9 (Autumn 1978): 587-608; James G. March and Johan P. Olsen, Ambiguity and Choice in Organizations, Bergen, Norway: Universitetsforlaget, 1976, pp. 10-53.
> *Assignment:* Critique mass prod. and economic theories using Technotronics case as evidence, and at least mention Chpt. 7 and March & Olsen.

1/31  4. LIMITED RATIONALITY THEORIES
D: Discuss papers.

2

L: Three views of behavior: economic rationality, or rational acquisitive view, rooted in stimulus-response psychology; bounded rationality, rooted in cognitive psychology; human relations tradition, rooted in psychodynamic psychology. The cognitive revolution in psychology, and its relevance for today's rapid economic changes. The (past) psychodynamic revolution and its relevance for worker productivity and worker unrest during mass production.

D: Is there a human nature? Do we have "personalities" (psychodynamic) or just "traits" (rat psychology), or "social constructions of reality" (cognitive)?

> Read for next class: "Demystifying Organizations" in The Management of Human Services, R. C. Sarri and Y. Hasenfeld (eds.) NY: Columbia Univ. Press, 1978, 105-120 ; and "Disintegrating Social Sciences," New York Univ. Educational Quarterly 12, no. 2 (Winter 1981); Perrow chpts. 2,3; Perrow, Agency Chart.
> *Assignment: Defend the human relations model against Perrow's attacks.*

2/7    5. HUMAN RELATIONS THEORIES AND ORGANIZATIONAL CULTURE

D: Discuss papers. What is human relations theory good for?

L: Human relations models, economic models and mass production. Human relations in a period of downsizing, part time work, contracting out. Human relations and unions and worker unrest in Germany, Spain, England and the U.S.

L: Organizational culture as a catch word, but important.

> Read: Vroom, "Two Decades of Research ..." Edward Schein, "The Role of the Founder in Creating Organizational Culture," Organizational Dynamics, Summer, 1983, pp. 13-28; Managing the U.S. Supersonic Transport Program (A & B); Perrow, chpt 4; Perrow: "Technology", pp. 75-91 from Organizational Analysis.
> *Assignment: Discuss the Supersonic case as an example of the limited rationality model. Be explicit and detailed.*

2/14    6. STRUCTURAL THEORIES

D: Discuss papers. Does the theory help?
D: Stockwell case revisited.
L: Review of contingency theory, conflict theory.

> Read: Hewlett-Packard: Challenging the Entrepreneurial Culture; Olivetti Purchasing Policy; Resource dependency sections of Davis and Powell.
> *Assignment: Paper on either Hewlett-Packard or Olivetti cases.* The HP case is presented in standard cultural and human relations (HR) terms, and these are certainly relevant and convincing. But make a case for a structural interpretation. Do not review the case (assume I have read it), or the cultural and HR arguments more than is necessary to contrast with a structural one. 3-2 pages.

3

Or, Olivetti case: Break out the structural units and problems (cent/decent; dependent or independent suppliers; production vs. innovation in the allocation of resources; etc.) and write a memo to a top management person of your choice that makes recommendations and illustrates your understanding of organizational structure. 2-3 pages.

2/21 7. POWER THEORIES
D: Discuss papers.
L: Resources dependency as a mild power theory.
L: Macro power theories: William Roy and the railroads; Perrow and the textile mills, steel mills. Contrast with Chandler, economic theories.
  Read: Rosabeth Kanter, Men and Women of the Corporation, NY: Basic Books, 1977, chpts. 6, 7 (pp. 129-205); Henry Mintzberg, "Organizational Power and Goals: A Skeletal Theory," in Dan E. Schendel and Charles W. Hofer, eds, Strategic Management (1979), 64-92.
  *Assignment:* What is the difference between human relations and structural theories in terms of power? Or, discuss the role of power in one of the previous cases, contrasting it to other explanations. Or, what are the problems and limitations of power theories. In all cases, make explicit reference to (including contrasts, if you wish) Kanter and Mintzberg.

2/28 8. ENVIRONMENT AND INSTITUTIONS
D: Discuss papers.
L: The new institutional school: culture, cognition and context. Minimization of power and conflict, emphasis upon imitation and symbols. John Meyer and the world-historical rational convergence.
  Read: Perrow, chpts 5, 6, and 8.
  *Assignment:* What is the weakest spot(s) in Perrow's argument in these chapters. Why and how might he strengthen it or why should he abandon it.
SPRING VACATION! ENJOY!.....................
3/21 9. ENVIRONMENT, INSTITUTIONS AND POWER
D: Discuss papers
L: Davis and Powell on environments. Saxenian and other research.
  Read: Walter Powell, "Neither Market nor Hierarchy," Research in Organizational Behavior, Vol. 12, 1990; Bradach & Eccles, "Price, Authority, and Trust," Annual Review of Sociology, 1989, 15:97-118. Mass High-technology Council, A and B.
  *Assignment* Discuss the Mass. High Tech case as an illustration of environmental theories, and power too if you wish.
  Good time for a memo on proposed topic for paper.

4

3/28 10. **FLEXIBLE PRODUCTION SYSTEMS: JAPAN**
D: Discuss papers.
L: The Japanese miracle: David Friedman's research, Gerlach.
Read: Best, 135 to end; The Misunderstood Miracle, Cornell University Press, pp. 1-36, 126-151; Kamata-Henwood "Japan in the Passing Lane"; Charles Sabel, et. al., "How to Keep Mature Industries Innovative," Technology Review, April, 987, 27-35.
*Assignment:* What struck you most about Best on Japan? Last day to turn in proposed topic.

4/4 11. **FLEXIBLE PRODUCTION SYSTEMS: EUROPE**
D: Discuss papers.
L: U.S. productivity issues; industrial scandals.
Read: Charles Sabel, "Flexible Specialization and the Re-emergence of Regional Economies," P. Hirst and J. Zeitlin (eds) Reversing Industrial Decline, pp. 17-70. Robert Hayes and Ramchandran Jaikumar, "Manufacturing's Crisis: New Technologies, Obsolete Organizations," Harvard Business Review Sept.-Oct. 1988, 77-85; C. Perrow, "Conventional Contrast of Small and Large Firms," 2 pages; Johnson and Johnson Case.
*Assignment:* Discuss J & J as example of flexible production, citing Sabel as evidence.

4/11 12. **SMALL FIRM NETWORKS**
D: Discuss papers.
L: Small Firm Networks and Social Welfare.
Read: Charles Perrow, "Small-Firm Networks," in Nitin Nohria and Robert G. Eccles Networks and Organizations: Structure, Form, and Action, Boston: Harvard Business School Press, 1992; Charles Perrow, Society of Organizations, Theory and Society, 20:725-762, 1991.
*Assignment:* Evaluate the course; which parts did you like best, worst, and give recommendations. This assignment should be brought to class on the last day and held by one student until grades are turned in. -- 2 to 3 pages as usual.

4/18 13. **A SOCIETY OF ORGANIZATIONS**
D: Notion of a society of organizations.
D: Where are we going, economically; where is the world going, economically; what role does organizational theory have to play.

**Social Behavior in Organizations
(#4771)**

**Prof. Robert J. Robinson**
Morgan 443
(617) 495-6068 (W)
(508) 881-7704 (H)

**Secretary: Hilary Gallagher**
Morgan 470D
(617) 495-6430

**Cumnock 330**

**Wednesdays 1-3 PM**

## The Course:

This course will be largely concerned with the "classics" of social psychology. I believe that contemporary organizational behavior research is impossible to understand in context without appreciating the research roots it has grown out of. While we will examine various aspects of contemporary organizational behavior work therefore, we will return again and again to more fundamental research in the area of social psychology. Our task as a class is to develop an understanding for this research, and to discuss how it applies to the world of business and organizations, and our own research interests, today.

For the most part, reading in this course will be from original source articles, which reach back in some cases to the 1940's. Where the original readings are not sufficient, we will use more contemporary summaries.

## Course Requirements & Grading:

This course will not have a final exam: Rather, you will be asked:

i) to produce a memo for each weekly class which synthesizes (rather than summarizes) the reading for the week. Ideally, the important ideas will be briefly summarized, followed by a (preferably creative) exposition on the relevance of these thought for organizational questions today. Length may vary, but as guideline, 2-3 single-spaced typed pages will be the *maximum* acceptable length.

ii) In addition, each week, one student will be assigned primary responsibility for opening the discussion, and will be expected to be able to speak for 10-15 minutes in this context.

iii) Finally, at the end of the course, each student will do a short paper (not to exceed 10 typed pages), the content of which is to be negotiated with me. This piece which will preferably be a research proposal inspired by ideas contained in one or other part of the course, or *may* entail reflection on the conceptual theories underlying the course.

Final grade will therefore be determined in the following way: weekly summaries + formal opening + class participation = 2/3 of grade. Final paper = 1/3 grade. This scheme may be reviewed, depending on the size of the class and the opportunity that everyone has to participate.

## Materials:

It is my sincere desire to provide you with a course pack at some point. Since copyright permissions etc. are still being obtained, I will make available copies of the various articles for the following week at each meeting, until the situation is resolved. The one exception to this is Fisher & Ury's *Getting to Yes*, which we will use in section IV A (People as Influencers). Students will be required to buy this book themselves, since it is a cheap classic available at the Coop, which I would suggest you have regardless of whether or not you actually take this course. Should students be in need of a copy of an article at any time, this may be obtained from my secretary.

## Venue:

We will meet every Wednesday in Cumnock 330, from 1-3pm. On the following pages, the probable dates for each topic are given. These may change as the course progresses, in order to allow us to explore certain topics in greater depth, to allow for a guest teacher, or for a number of other reasons. If there is sufficient interest, we may also schedule additional sessions on certain topics.

## Topics:

**Introduction**: September 7

Introduction to class, course, and one another. There is no reading assignment for this week. However, please make sure that you get the assignment for the following week (September 14).

### I) The Basics

#### A) Some Classics: September 14

Coch, L. & French, J. P. R., Jr., (1948). Overcoming resistance to change. Human Relations, 1, 512-532.
Lewin, K. (1952). Group decision and social change. In G. E. Swanson, T. M. Newcomb, & E. L. Hartley (Eds.), Readings in social psychology. New York: Holt, Reinhart, & Winston, pp. 459-473.
French, J. P. R. & Raven, B. (1968). The bases of social power. In D. Cartwright & A. Zander (Eds.), Group dynamics. New York: Harper & Row, pp. 259-269 (Ch. 20).
Sherif, M. (1979). Superordinate goals in the reduction of intergroup conflict. In W. G. Austin & S. Worchel (Eds.), The social psychology of intergroup relations. California: Brooks/Cole, pp. 257-261 (Ch. 16).
Tajfel, H. & Turner, J. (1979). An integrative theory of intergroup conflict. In W. G. Austin & S. Worchel (Eds.), The social psychology of intergroup relations. California: Brooks/Cole, pp. 33-47 (Ch. 3).

#### B) Traditional I/O Research: September 21

Salancik, G. & Pfeffer, J. (1977). An examination of need-satisfaction models of job attitudes. Administrative Science Quarterly, 22, 427-456.
Hackman, J. R., Oldham, G., Janson, R., & Purdy, K. (1983). A new strategy for job enrichment. In B. M. Shaw (Ed.), Psychological foundations of organizational behavior (2nd ed.). Glenview, IL: Scott, Foresman & Co., pp. 64-79.
Staw, B. (1984). Organizational behavior: A review and reformulation of the field's outcome variables. In M. Rosenzweig & L. Porter (Eds.), Annual review of psychology, Vol. 35, pp. 627-666.

#### C) Groups: September 28

Cartwright, D. & Zander, A. (1968). Groups and group membership: Introduction. In D. Cartwright & A. Zander (Eds.), Group dynamics. New York: Harper & Row, pp. 45-62 (Ch. 3).
Janis, I. L. (1977). Groupthink. In J. R. Hackman, et al. (Eds.), Perspectives on behavior in organizations. New York: McGraw Hill, pp. 378-384 (no. 36).
Manz, C. C. & Sims, H. P. (1982). The potential for 'groupthink' in autonomous work groups. Human Relations, 35, 773-784.
Leavitt, H. J. (1983). Suppose we took groups seriously. In J. R. Hackman, et al. (Eds.), Perspectives on human behavior in organizations. New York: McGraw Hill, pp. 370-377 (no. 35).
Gersick, C. J. G. (1988). Time and transition in work teams: Towards a new model of group development. Academy of Management Journal, 31, 9-41.

**D) Culture:** October 5

Perrow, C. (1981). Normal accident at Three Mile Island. Society, 18, 17-26.
Martin, J. & Siehl, C. (1983). Organizational culture and counterculture: An uneasy symbiosis. Organizational Dynamics, Autumn, 52-64.
Schein, E. H. (1985). How organization founders shape culture. In Organizational culture and leadership. San Francisco, CA: Jossey Bass, pp. 209-222.
Schein, E. H. (1985). How leaders embed and transmit culture. In Organizational culture and leadership. San Francisco, CA: Jossey Bass, pp. 223-243.

## II) People as Thinkers

**A) Judgment and Decision-Making:** October 12

Tversky, A. & Kahneman, D. (1974). Judgment under uncertainties: Heuristics and biases. Science, 185, 1124-1131.
Kahneman, D. & Tversky, A. (1984). Choices, values, and frames. American Psychologist, 39, 341-350.
March, J. (1981). Decisions in organizations and theories of choice. In A. Van de Ven & W. Joyce (Eds.), Perspectives on organization design and behavior. New York: Wiley, pp. 204-244.
Taylor, S. E. (1983). Adjustment to threatening life events: A theory of cognitive adaptation. American Psychologist, 38, 1161-1173.

**B) Attribution, Dissonance, Construal:** October 19 <u>and</u> October 26 (2 weeks on this topic).

Aronson, E. (1969). The theory of cognitive dissonance: A current perspective. In L. Berkowitz (Ed.), Advances in experimental social psychology, Vol. 4, pp. 1-34.
Gerard, H. B. & Mathewson, G. C. (1966). The effects of severity of initiation on liking for a group: A replication. Journal of Experimental Social Psychology, 2, 278-287.
Doob, A. N., Carlsmith, J. M., Freedman, J. L., Landauer, T. K., & Tom, S., Jr. (1969). Effect of initial selling price on subsequent sales. Journal of Personality and Social Psychology, 11, 345-350.
Bem, D. J. (1972). Self-perception theory. In L. Berkowitz (Ed.), Advances in experimental social psychology, Vol. 6, pp. 2-62.
Fiske, T. and Taylor, S. E. (1984). Attribution theory. In Fiske & Taylor, Social cognition (Second edition) New York: McGraw-Hill, pp. 22-56 (Chapter 2).
Ross, L., Bierbrauer, G., & Hoffman, S. (1976). The role of attribution processes in conformity and dissent. American Psychologist, 31, 148-157.
Ross, L. (1987). The problem of construal in social inference and social psychology. In N. E. Grunberg, R. E. Nisbett, J. Rodin, & J. E. Singer (Eds.), A distinctive approach to psychological research: The influence of Stanley Schachter. Hillsdale, NJ: Erlbaum, pp. 118-150.

## C) The Person and the Situation: November 2

Latane, B., & Darley, J. (1969). Bystander 'apathy'. <u>American Scientist, 57,</u> 244-268.
Darley, J. M., & Batson, C. D. (1973). "From Jerusalem to Jericho": A study of situational and dispositional variables in helping behavior. <u>Journal of Personality and Social Psychology, 27,</u> 100-108.
Platt, J. (1973). Social traps. <u>American Psychologist, 28,</u> 641-651.
Jones, E. E. & Nisbett, R. E. (1971). The actor and the observer: Divergent perceptions of the causes of behavior. In E. E. Jones, D. E. Kanouse, H. H. Kelley, R. E. Nisbett, S. Valins, & B. Weiner (Eds.). <u>Attribution: Perceiving the causes of behavior.</u> General Learning Press, pp. 79-94.

## III) People as Objects of Influence

### A) Conformity: November 9

Asch, S. E. (1951). Effects of group pressure upon the modification and distortion of judgments. In H. Guetzkow (Ed.), <u>Groups, leadership, and men.</u>
Milgram, S. (1963). Behavioral study of obedience. <u>Journal of Applied Social Psychology, 67,</u> 371-378.
Milgram, Baumrind, Orne, & Holland exchange (1972). In A. Miller (Ed.), <u>The social psychology of psychological research.</u> New York: Free Press, pp. 82-154.
Schachter, S. (1968). Deviation, rejection, and communication. In D. Cartwright & A. Zander (Eds.), <u>Group dynamics.</u> New York: Harper & Row, pp. 165-181 (Ch. 13).

### B) Influence: November 16 (<u>Note</u>, will also do Motivation this day).

Freedman, J. L. & Fraser, S. C. (1966). Compliance without pressure: The foot-in-the-door technique. <u>Journal of Personality and Social Psychology, 4,</u> 195-202.
Cialdini, R. B., Vincent, J. E., Lewis, S. K., Catalan, J., Wheeler, D., & Darby, B. L. (1975). Reciprocal concessions procedure for inducing compliance: The door-in-the-face technique. <u>Journal of Applied Social Psychology, 31,</u> 206-215.
Jones, E. E. & Pittman, T. S. (1982). Toward a general theory of strategic self-presentation. In J. Suls (Ed.), <u>Psychological perspectives on the self.</u> Hillsdale, NJ: Lawrence Erlbaum, pp. 231-262.

### C) Motivation: November 16

Lepper, M. R., Greene, D., & Nisbett, R. E. (1973). Undermining children's intrinsic interest with extrinsic reward: A test of the 'overjustification' hypothesis. <u>Journal of Personality and Social Psychology, 29,</u> 129-137.
*Wood, R. & Bandura, A. (1988). Self-regulatory mechanisms governing organizational management. Draft document: Stanford University.* (or final published version of this article).

**D) Attitude and Attitude Change**: November 23

Hovland, C. I. & Weiss, W. (1951). The influence of source credibility on communication effectiveness. Public Opinion Quarterly, 15, 635-650.

Aronson, E., Turner, J. A. P., & Carlsmith, J. M. (1963). Communication credibility and communication discrepancy as determinants of opinion change. Journal of Applied Social Psychology, 67, 31-36.

Hovland, C. I. (1959). Reconciling conflicting results derived from experimental and survey studies of attitude change. American Psychologist, 14, 8-17.

Lord, C., Ross, L., & Lepper, M. R. (1979). Biased assimilation and attitude polarization: The effects of prior theories on subsequently considered evidence. Journal of Personality and Social Psychology, 37, 2098-2109.

## IV) People as Influencers

**A) Conflict and Negotiation**: November 30

Fisher, R. & Ury, W.[1] (1981). Getting to Yes: Negotiating agreement without giving in. Boston: Houghton Mifflin.

Ross, L., Ward, A. (in press). Psychological barriers to dispute resolution. To appear in M. P. Zanna (Ed.), Advances in Experimental Social Psychology, 27.

**B) Discrimination & Inequality, Injustice & Action**: December 7

Kanter, R. (1977). Numbers: Minorities and majorities. In Men and women of the corporation. New York: Basic Books, pp. 206-242.

Pettigrew, T. (1979). The ultimate attribution error: Extending Allport's cognitive analysis of prejudice. Personality and Social Psychology Bulletin, 5, 461-476.

Dweck, C. S., Davidson, W., Nelson, S., & Enna, B. (1978). Sex differences in learned helplessness: II. The contingencies of evaluative feedback in the classroom and III. An experimental analysis. Developmental Psychology, 14, 268-276.

Aronson, E. & Osherow, N. (1980). Cooperation, prosocial behavior, and academic performance: Experiments in the desegregated classroom. In L. Bickman (Ed.), Applied Social Psychology Annual, Vol. 1, pp. 163-196.

## V) Conclusions: Where are We? December 14

Greiner, L. E. (1972). Evolution and revolution as organizations grow. Harvard Business Review, 50, 37-46.

Gergen, K. (1978). Toward generative theory. Journal of Personality and Social Psychology, 36, 1344-1360.

Pfeffer, J. (1985). Organizations and organization theory. In G. Lindzey & E. Aronson (Eds.), The handbook of social psychology (3rd. ed.). Reading, MA: Addison-Wesley, pp. 379-440.

---

[1] - *Getting to Yes* is available at the Coop. This book is a classic, and although it has had many detractors, it remains a provocative and useful piece. If you do not own this book, I strongly urge you to buy it.

# Business 478

# CAREER MANAGEMENT

### COURSE OUTLINE

### FALL TERM, 1994

Professor: Mitch Rothstein
Office: 147A
Telephone: 661-3298
Secretary: Carole Kinahan
Room 147
679-2111, ext. 5277

## COURSE OBJECTIVES

This course is designed to assist students to (1) develop their self-assessment skills, specifically to further their understanding and appreciation of themselves and their own unique career goals and aspirations, (2) develop the ability to determine a good "fit" between their unique talents and relevant personal factors, and a satisfying career, and (3) develop the ability to sell themselves effectively in a focused job search, to enhance the "fit" for both themselves and their chosen organizations. A variety of methods and activities are used to achieve these objectives:

a. Regular exercises throughout the course enable students to better understand their skills, abilities, aptitudes, interests, needs, values and beliefs, and to improve their skills in finding a job and developing a career to maximize productivity, satisfaction and personal growth.

b. Class sessions provide students the opportunity to share and compare insights obtained from the exercises, and to examine the implications of these insights for their personal career development strategies.

c. Readings and case studies are provided to increase students' knowledge about themselves, and to stimulate their thinking regarding effective ways of getting jobs and managing their careers.

## REQUIRED TEXTS

1. Self-Assessment and Career Development by J. Clawson, J. Kotter, V. Faux, and C. McArthur, Third Edition, 1992.

2. Casebook.

## FEEDBACK ON CAREER MANAGEMENT SKILLS

You will be asked to write two reports for purposes of evaluation in this course (see below for a full explanation of the requirements and grading). Above and beyond these formal course requirements, you will be asked to do a variety of assignments and exercises designed to develop your career management skills (e.g., self-assessment, environmental scanning, selling yourself). These exercises are not to be handed in, although substantial parts of them will be used for your reports. You will desire (and deserve) feedback on these exercises, as feedback is an essential component of skill development. It is practically and physically impossible for the instructor to provide extensive and detailed feedback to every student on an individual basis on these assignments and exercises, as well as provide feedback on the reports. Therefore, feedback on the assignments and exercises must be primarily your responsibility.

To ensure that you obtain feedback essential to your ongoing skill development, a requirement of the course is that you become a member of a "reality testing and support" (RTS) group for the duration of the course. You are responsible for forming your own RTS group. The objectives of your RTS groups are to share and compare the work you produce in the course (from the skill development assignments and exercises), and provide feedback, support, and encouragement to each other. Openness, trust, and confidentiality are paramount in this process. It will be up to you to develop, honour, and reinforce these norms in your RTS group. You will be working in your RTS groups on various assignments in preparation for class as well as in in-class workshops. In addition, you are strongly encouraged to meet with your groups in informal sessions to provide each other with feedback on your self-assessment and selling skills. These meetings will be very useful as you work your way through the Career Management course so do not let all the other pressures on you perpetually postpone your opportunity to manage your most valuable resource -- yourself!

RTS groups must be formed by the end of the second week of classes (**Sept. 23**). Since the RTS groups are so essential to the objectives of the course, group membership must be a formal course requirement. Please provide a list of your group members to the instructor once you have settled into your groups.

## GRADES

Developing a system for evaluation and grading students' performance in such a course has to reconcile several factors. One factor is that the impact of the course on individuals comes largely through the completion of the daily exercises and subsequent reflection on and discussion of these preparations. Secondly, because of the personal nature of the data, it is important that we minimize the potentially distorting influence of the grading system on the content of the reports. In general it is desirable that an atmosphere be maintained that is conducive to productive and free pursuit of individual career plans and to helpful exchanges among the participants. It is difficult to devise a grading system consistent with these requirements that, at the same time, does not invite student abuse because of the grade-conscious, competitive environment in which the course exists.

The following grading system therefore attempts to reconcile these sometimes opposing factors. Two written reports are required, each worth 40% of the final grade. Class participation will be evaluated by a method of peer assessment (see below for a full description of this) worth 20% of the final grade.

The content of the written reports is described in more detail below. They are to be **TYPED**, double-spaced, with a length of from 10 to 20 pages. All reports are graded by the instructor.

## REPORT I - SELF-ASSESSMENT

This report will be a summary and integration of all the self-assessment assignments and exercises you have completed. Data for this report will come primarily from the Work as Flow exercise, the Values System analysis, the Career and Life Values Card Sort, the Personal Success Inventory, the Personal Failure Inventory, and the Three Year Plan. You may use any other source of data you wish, such as other optional exercises in the Clawson et al. book or anything that you have used to come to understand yourself better, but <u>as a common basis for evaluation everyone must at least use the above mentioned assignments and exercises</u>.

Three criteria will be used to evaluate this report: (1) the degree of insight and self-awareness displayed in discussing the results from your self-assessment exercises, (2) the degree that the self-assessment data is <u>integrated</u> into a coherent, consistent analysis, and (3) the degree that the career implications of the self-assessment have been clearly articulated.

> DUE DATE: OCTOBER 28

## REPORT II - A PERSONAL FOCUSED PORTFOLIO

This report will include your Job Focused Ability Statement, Focused Resumé, and Focused Letter <u>as exhibits</u>. The objective of the report is to convince the reader that you are an excellent fit with your focused job. Your task is to integrate everything you have learned about selling yourself from the various workshops (i.e., Job Focused Ability Statement, Focused Resume, Focused Letter, Interview) and put together the most important sales promotion of your life -- you! From your predecessor interviews, or any other source of data on your focused job, you will need to describe the important requirements and performance demands of this job in detail. How do your skills, typical behaviours, personality traits, values, etc. specifically fit these job requirements? Imagine the reader of this report is the person who can hire you. You are attempting to persuade this person as honestly, sincerely, and convincingly as possible, that you are the right person for the job.

Two criteria will be used to evaluate this report: (1) the degree that the job and organizational characteristics and performance requirements and demands are clearly understood and articulated (this is absolutely essential when you begin to interact with the organization you have targeted for a job), and (2) the degree that you provide an honest, sincere, convincing sales presentation of yourself in which you clearly display a focused job search, the integration of all your skills and attributes toward this focus, and the inescapable conclusion that you are a good fit with the job.

> DUE DATE: DECEMBER 2

## PEER EVALUATION PROCEDURE

Contributions to classroom discussion and to your RTS groups are absolutely essential to this course. Obtaining a full appreciation of the issues involved in career management requires the active involvement of all participants. Sharing ideas, providing feedback and encouragement, and helping to integrate others' data, are some of the essential behaviours required of participants in order to achieve the course objectives. To provide some incentive for active participation, therefore, 20% of the course grade will be determined by classroom and RTS group contributions. However, since the instructor will not be present at RTS group meetings, and since the <u>nature</u> of the participation is of critical importance to the <u>students</u> (as opposed to the evaluation needs of the instructor), peer assessment seems to be the most appropriate method of evaluation.

The method will work as follows. Students will be responsible for evaluating each member of their RTS group (except, of course, themselves). The average of the ratings given to each student by his/her peers will constitute the grade for this part of the course. The following guidelines should be used as a basis for your evaluations:

| 0 | 1 | 2 | 3 | 4 |
|---|---|---|---|---|
| Refuses to cooperate, to take on responsibilities, or tasks. Is not prepared for group discussions or is unwilling to contribute. Is a negative or destructive influence on group cohesion and/or satisfaction. | | Cooperates with group and takes on fair share of responsibilities and tasks if asked. Is prepared for group discussions and is willing and able to contribute. Provides positive constructive comments and feedback and contributes to group cohesion and/or satisfaction. | | Volunteers to take on responsibilities and tasks, and/or takes on leadership role in organizing the group's activities. Is a constant and knowledgeable contributor to group discussion. Demonstrates enthusiasm and commitment to meeting the group's needs. |

Evaluations will be based on participation in class as well as in RTS groups. Note that the use of the term "group", therefore, will sometime refer to RTS group as well as the class as a whole. RTS group members should provide each other with continuous feedback on their participation ratings so that individuals will have the opportunity to change their behaviour and improve their evaluations (i.e., there should be no surprises at the end of the term).

> **DUE DATE:** DECEMBER 9

## DAILY CLASS SCHEDULE

| DATE | SESSION # | TOPIC |
|------|-----------|-------|
| Sept. 13 | 1 | Introduction: The rationale for developing career management skills will be presented and the course objectives, methods, and requirements, will be discussed. |

Sept. 15  2  **THE SELF-ASSESSMENT PROCESS**

    Read:    Clawson et al., Chapters 1, 2, 4, 12, 22
(N.B. Assignment and case in Ch.2 are not required.)
Values System Analysis (casebook)
Personal Success Inventory (casebook)
Personal Failure inventory (casebook)
Three Year Plan (casebook)

    Optional: Clawson et al., Chapters 3, 5-10.
These chapters provide some additional self-assessment exercises. They do not necessarily have to be read for today's class and they are not <u>required</u> as part of the overall self-assessment procedure. Many students find these exercises less useful than those assigned, but <u>some</u> students have found them helpful. As you get into the self-assessment process, your own judgment will be the best guide as to whether or not you want to go through these additional exercises.

    Assignment:    Complete the "Career and Life Values Card Sort" exercise in Chapter 4, but concentrate on interpreting your own results rather than the example given in the text. Be prepared to ask any questions you may have about any of the self-assessment exercises.

    In Class:    The self-assessment exercises will be introduced and discussed.
(N.B. Your self-assessment exercises should be completed by Oct. 11 - <u>not</u> for hand-in, but to provide a basis for discussion in this class.)

Sept. 20  3  **FOCUSED RESUMÉ WORKSHOP I**

    Read:    Clawson et al., Chapter 26

    Assignment:    Update your resumé and bring it to class. Evaluate your resumé against the guidelines and suggestions provided in the text. How does it match up?

|             |   |                                                                                                                                                                 |
|-------------|---|---|

In Class: An introduction to the principles underlying a <u>focused</u> resumé will be presented. Discussion will focus on the <u>value added</u> of a sharply focused resumé and examples will be given to compare with your own.

Sept. 22    4    **FOCUSED LETTER WORKSHOP I**

Read: Clawson et al., Chapter 26

Assignment: Prepare an example of a cover letter that you would send to a prospective employer along with your resumé. How does this letter compare to the example provided on page 301 of the text? (Note: this is <u>not</u> an example of an excellent <u>focused</u> cover letter)? Bring your letter to class.

In Class: An introduction to the principles underlying a <u>focused</u> cover letter will be presented. Discussion will focus on the <u>value added</u> of a sharply focused cover letter and examples will be given to compare with your own.

Sept. 27    5    **FOCUSED INTERVIEW WORKSHOP I**

Read: Clawson et al., Chapter 27
    (N.B. Assignment and case in Ch. 27 are not required for today, but they are worth just reading for additional perspective on the interview.)
The New Job Interview: Show Thyself (casebook)
Interview Workshop (casebook)
    (N.B. The assignment described in this handout is <u>not</u> for today. This assignment will be due for the second interview workshop on <u>Nov. 3</u>. However, read this over for today's class and bring any questions you may have about the exercise.)

Assignment: From Chapter 27 in the text and your own experience, draw up a <u>first draft</u> of a strategic plan of how you will perform successfully in your job interviews (i.e., <u>what</u> do you wish to communicate and <u>how</u> will you do this).

In Class: A simulated job interview will be demonstrated. You will be asked to provide a critical analysis of the interview and comment on the implications for your strategic plan.

| | | |
|---|---|---|
| Sept. 29 | 6 | **OBTAINING CAREER INFORMATION I: THE PREDECESSOR INTERVIEW** |

> Read: The Critical Incident Technique (casebook)
> Clawson et al., Chapters 24 (Appendix: pp 274-289), 28
>
> In Class: An interview procedure will be demonstrated, the "critical incident technique" (CIT), that can be used to great effect in obtaining information about jobs and careers.

| | | |
|---|---|---|
| Oct. 4 | 7 | **OBTAINING CAREER INFORMATION II: ANALYZING CIT DATA** |

> Read: Clawson et al., Chapters 23, 29
> (N.B. Assignments in these chapters are optional.)
>
> Assignment: On the basis of your observations and notes taken from the previous class, develop a profile of the job you heard described. The objective is to obtain a clear, realistic, and vivid picture of the job so that you can ultimately make an informed decision about your interest in having a job like this. Try to break down the information into categories (such as skills required, demands, rewards, culture, lifestyle, etc.) so that when you do your own CIT interviews you can readily make comparisons between jobs you are interested in.
>
> In Class: Be prepared to contribute to the development of composite job profile constructed by all members of the class. Identify any problems you are having with the CIT so that these can be addressed in class and you are prepared to begin your predecessor interviews.

| | | |
|---|---|---|
| Oct. 6 | 8 | **WORK AS FLOW** |

> Read: Work as Flow (casebook)
>
> Assignment: Identify several work related situations in which you have experienced "flow". In a few sentences describe each situation and your experience of "flow". What do these experiences tell you about yourself? I would like you to hand in this assignment, but there is no need to put your name on it.

|  |  |  |  |
|---|---|---|---|
| | | In Class: | Analysis and discussion of flow experiences. |
| Oct. 11 & 13 | 9 & 10 | \multicolumn{2}{l|}{INTEGRATING SELF-ASSESSMENT DATA} |

Oct. 11 & 13    9 & 10    **INTEGRATING SELF-ASSESSMENT DATA**

        Read: Clawson et al., Chapters 14, 16, 20, 21, 33
(N.B. Assignments in these chapters are not required).
Optional: Clawson et al., Chapters 15, 17, 18, 19
(N.B. These chapters are assigned mainly for information purposes only. They provide an additional perspective on how to approach writing up your self-assessment. However, the requirements for your self-assessment report are somewhat different than those given in the text. Therefore the exercises and assignments given in these chapters are strictly optional -- if they help you in your own self-assessment, by all means use them, but they are not required. You should read these chapters, however, because they provide excellent insights into the self-assessment process that you will find useful in preparing Report I.)

        Assignment: Be prepared to discuss the results of your self-assessment (strictly voluntary).

        In Class: In preparation for your first report, a workshop will be conducted in which a process will be demonstrated for integrating self-assessment data.

Oct. 18    11    **JOB HUNTING STRATEGY WORKSHOP**

        Read: Ian Henry's Personal Job Search (casebook)
Clawson et al., Chapters 24, 25
N.B. - The assignments and exercises in Chapters 24 and 25 are useful and are highly recommended, although they will not be directly taken up in class.

        Assignment: Meet in your RTS groups prior to class and map out a strategy for a focused job search. Compare this strategy with Ian Henry's. What did he do right and wrong, and what will you do differently and why?

        In Class: Discussion of Ian Henry case.
Workshop on developing an effective job hunting strategy for you.

| | | |
|---|---|---|
| Oct. 20 | 12 | **IMPLEMENTING YOUR JOB HUNTING STRATEGY: THE IMPACT OF A FOCUSED JOB SEARCH** |

**Assignment:** Meet in your RTS groups prior to class and evaluate the resume of Geoff Fournie (distributed in class). Be prepared to discuss the following questions.
1. Who is Geoff Fournie? What do you know about him?
2. What is the "focus" of this resume? What job would be a good fit with the profile presented here?
3. Given the data you have about Geoff and his job focus, develop a Job Hunting Strategy for him. Be specific.

**In Class:** We will discuss the assignment questions, what happened to Geoff, and, in preparation for the next class, the implications for developing a focused resume and job hunting strategy.

Oct. 25      NO CLASS (Due to OB Module for Juniors)

| | | |
|---|---|---|
| Oct. 27 | 13 | **SHARPENING THE FOCUS AND SELLING TO NEEDS: INTEGRATING SELF-ASSESSMENT DATA WITH THE FOCUSED JOB - THE JOB FOCUSED ABILITY STATEMENT** |

**Read:** The job focused ability statement (casebook)

**Assignment:** Review your predecessor interviews, self-assessment data, focused resumé and letter, and your video interview and feedback. Are you presenting a truly focused picture of yourself to your potential employer? Is the information about yourself integrated effectively to maximize the perception that you are a good fit with the job? What isn't working? What needs to be refined to really sell yourself effectively (i.e., close the sale)? Complete a job focused ability statement for yourself and be prepared to discuss the results of your analysis.

**In Class:** In preparation for your second report, a workshop will be conducted in which a process will be demonstrated for integrating your self-assessment data with the job in focus.

| | | | |
|---|---|---|---|
| Nov. 1<br>(Evening Class) | 14 & 15 | \multicolumn{2}{l|}{FOCUSED RESUMÉ AND LETTER WORKSHOP II} |

Nov. 1 (Evening Class)    14 & 15    **FOCUSED RESUMÉ AND LETTER WORKSHOP II**

Review: Clawson et al., Chapter 26

Assignment: <u>Prior</u> to class, meet in your RTS groups for a peer analysis and feedback seminar concerning your focused resumés and letters. Plan to get together for 2-3 hours (depending on the size of your RTS group). Each person in the group should have the opportunity to receive <u>constructive</u> feedback on his/her resumé and letter from the other group members. A well functioning RTS group will go through this exercise several times in an iterative process that enhances the focus of the resumé and letter with each succeeding feedback session. The substantive basis of the feedback should stem from the principles of a focused resumé and focused letter presented in Workshop I. Each group will choose one example resumé and letter, make an overhead slide, and present it to the class to illustrate and share the <u>learning points</u> from their analysis and feedback(i.e., why it is particularly effective or ineffective, why you would or would not interview this person, what impressions and inferences you draw about this person, etc.).

In Class: Each RTS group will present one resumé and letter from their group and illustrate and share their learning points. You may take the name off the resumé and letter if you wish.

Nov. 3    16    **FOCUSED INTERVIEW WORKSHOP II**

Review: Interview workshop (casebook)
Clawson et al., Chapter 27
The New Job Interview: Show Thyself (casebook)

Assignment: Each RTS group must have completed the videotaping of their interviews, and each individual must have had an opportunity to analyze their own strengths and weaknesses, prior to this workshop.

In Class: The workshop will provide feedback to some (volunteers) on their interview skills, and illustrate an effective process by which RTS groups can meet for further feedback and development of interview skills.

| Nov. 8 | 17 | **DECIDING ON A JOB OFFER** |

Read: Clawson et al., Chapters 30, 31
(N.B. Assignment in Ch. 31 is not required.)

Assignment: Fill out the "Job Characteristics" questionnaire (distributed in class) and do all calculations indicated. Prepare the "Mike Downer" case in Ch. 30 with the assignment questions given.

In Class: Discussion of Mike Downer case. Your data from the questionnaire will be compared with a large sample of practising managers.

| Nov. 10 | 18 | **DEALING WITH "FAILURE" AND DISAPPOINTMENT** |

Assignment: Review your Personal Failure Inventory and select at least two examples of significant failure experiences in your life. Analyze these experiences with the following questions as guidelines.
1. How did the failure make you feel? How did it affect the way you think about yourself?
2. What effect did the experience have on your behaviour, in general and in similar circumstances?
3. How did you get over the experience?

N.B. Be prepared to discuss your answers to <u>these questions</u> in class and in small group discussions. The specifics of the actual failure experiences do not have to be disclosed unless you wish to share them.

In Class: We will discuss the assignment questions and a model for understanding and coping with failure and disappointment.

| Nov. 15 | 19 | **CAREER DEVELOPMENT IN ORGANIZATIONS I** |

Read: Organizational Career Development Systems: The State of the Practise (casebook).

Assignment: Prepare the Human Resource Planning and Management Development at C.U. (A) case with the following questions.
1. How does C.U.'s international operations present unique challenges to human resource planning and the development of career management systems.

2. What are the pros and cons of the highly centralized human resource planning system developed by C.U.? What alternative (if any) would you recommend?
3. Assume that the centralized human resource planning system is here to stay at C.U. As a senior manager in Group Human Resources, what actions would you recommend to address the "challenges ahead" discussed at the end of the case?

**In Class:** Analysis and discussion of case.

Nov. 17   NO CLASS (Due to OB Module for Juniors)

Nov. 22   20   CAREER DEVELOPMENT IN ORGANIZATIONS II

**Review:** Assigned reading from Session 20.

**Assignment:** Prepare the Assessing Managerial Talent at AT&T (A) case (in casebook) with the following questions.
1. What is your reaction to the assessment centre approach to evaluating managerial potential used by AT&T as (a) an employee who must be assessed by this method to be considered for promotion, and (b) a manager who has access to assessment centre reports on all candidates being considered for a promotion?
2. What are the pros and cons of an assessment centre program at AT&T, or any organization as a whole? As a senior executive in such an organization, list the costs and benefits of assessment centres.
3. For organizations concerned about human resource planning and the availability of managerial talent in the future, what are the alternatives to the use of assessment centres?

**In Class:** Analysis and discussion of case.

Nov. 24   21   NETWORKING

**Read:** Clawson et al., Chapter 36 (including the case study — Karen Harper)

| | | | |
|---|---|---|---|
| | | Assignment: | Make a list of the people that provide you with career support and/or advice. This may include immediate and extended family, friends, and past and present business relationships — anyone who at the <u>present</u> time you could count on for some support and/or advice. Beside each name, jot down a few points about the type of specific support and/or advise that each gives. What is the importance of this network to you? How do you use it...or do you? |
| | | In Class: | The role and value of networks in career management will be discussed, and some research will be presented on the characteristics of networks and their importance in managerial careers. |
| Nov. 29 | 22 | **CAREER DERAILMENT: MINIMIZING THE RISK** | |
| | | Read: | Clawson et al., Chapters 34 and 35<br>(N.B. Assignments and cases in these chapters are not required for class, although the cases are worth reading as a companion to the experiences of George Herbert) |
| | | Assignment: | Prepare the case "George Herbert, MBA" (in casebook), with the following questions:<br>1. Identify the factors that you believe contributed to George Herbert being fired. Could these factors have been prevented or managed? How?<br>2. What issues can you identify as being critical to manage effectively to avoid career derailment? |
| | | In Class: | Analysis and discussion of case, and strategies for minimizing the risk of career derailment. |
| Dec. 1 | 23 | **DUAL CAREERS** | |
| | | Read: | Surviving Success: Relationships and the MBA (casebook)<br>Clawson et al., Chapter 32<br>(N.B. Assignment, case, and exercise in this chapter are not required, but the exercise may be useful to those of you involved in dual career decision making at this time.) |
| | | Assignment: | Prepare the Two Careers (A), (B), and (C) case (in casebook) with the following instructions and questions. Individually, read the (A) and (B) parts of |

**187**

the case <u>only</u>, and then answer the following questions.
1. What are Anne's career aspirations, expectations, and current issues? What are Paul's?
2. Given your analysis in (1), should Paul take the job at Harwood? Why? Why not?

Now meet in your RTS groups and read the (C) case (if your group is all the same gender, get together with another group with some "opposites", i.e., it's important to share perspectives in answering the final question.)

3. (C) case provides some additional insight into the lives of Anne and Paul and their relationship. What does your <u>group</u> recommend now regarding Paul's job offer? If your group can't reach a consensus, be prepared to present opposing (or different) sets of recommendations in class.

**In Class:** Analysis and discussion of case and dual career issues in general.

## Dec. 6 — 24 — CAREER STAGES, CHANGES, AND PLATEAUING

**Read:** The Future of Managerial Work: Careers vs. Crafts (casebook)
What is Plateauing and Why is it so Important (casebook)
Clawson et al., Chapters 37, 38

**Assignment:** Prepare the Ben Jerrow case (Ch. 37) using the assignment questions provided in the text.

**In Class:** Analysis and discussion of case. A general discussion will follow concerning issues around career stages, changes, and plateauing.

## Dec. 8 — 25 — WRAP-UP AND COURSE REVIEW

**Assignment:** Take a few minutes to think about what you have learned in this course, what you have really valued and what was of less value, what was missing in this course for you, what you would like more of or less of, or any other observations that might serve to improve the course.

**In Class:** Wrap-up of course.
Course evaluations.

Carlson School of Management
University of Minnesota

## Doctoral Seminar 8303: Sensemaking in Organizations
### Spring 1994, Wednesday, 1:00 - 4:00

Instructor, Kathleen M. Sutcliffe, 819 Mgmt/Econ, 625-3548
Office Hours: 8-10am T/Th or by appointment

### Seminar Overview

The purpose of this elective seminar is to look more closely at sensemaking in organizations. The basic idea of sensemaking is that reality is an ongoing accomplishment which emerges from efforts to create order and make retrospective sense of what occurs. Much organizational research has been dominated by a focus on decision making and a conception of "strategic rationality" in which organizational action is conceptualized as the intentional and rational behavior of individuals and organizations to attain some goal. But, the rational model--attractive both as a normative ideal and as a limiting analytical construct--has two important limitations. First, it rests on simplifying assumptions that ignore the inherent complexity and ambiguity of real-world organizations and their environments. Second, it presumes a causal link between intention and action that is often missing in practice. Consequently, organizational scholars have begun to pay increasing attention to "contextual rationality" or the idea that organizational action is often legitimated retrospectively in order to maintain institutional order and create meaning. Thus, organizations are important because they can provide meaning and order in the face of environments that impose ill-defined, contradictory demands.

In this elective course, we will become immersed in the topic of sensemaking and will learn from one another as we go along. The course will be run as a discussion seminar. Seminar participants will rotate the role of discussion leader. There will be a minimal amount of lecturing by the instructor.

Evaluation will be based on a series of written memos and class participation.

### Course Requirements:

1. **Readings**: A copy of the readings are available (for copying) in a file cabinet in room 837 Mgmt/Econ. You may sign out the readings for copying. Please be aware that others in the class have to make copies too.

2. **Memos**: Students will be required to write a series of 6 memos on topics assigned by the instructor and noted under each class assignment. Write no more than 5 double spaced pages for each assignment. Put a title on each paper. End each paper with a summary paragraph which summarizes the key points you have made. No late papers accepted.

## Schedule of Assignments

Class 1. March 30, 1994: Introduction and sensemaking episodes.

    1. Perrow, Charles. 1984. Marine accidents. In C. Perrow, Normal accidents: 170-231. New York: Basic Books.

    2. Starbuck, W. & Milliken, F. 1988. Challenger: Fine tuning the odds until something breaks. Journal of Management Studies, 25(4): 319-340.

    3. Weick, Karl E. 1993. The collapse of sensemaking in organizations: The Mann Gulch disaster. Administrative Science Quarterly, 38(4): 628-652.

    4. Meyer, A. 1982. Adapting to environmental jolts. Administrative Science Quarterly, 27: 515-537.

**Writing for this class:** None

Class 2. April 6, 1994: Toward a definition of sensemaking.

    5. Huber G. & Daft, R. 1987. The information environment of organizations. In F. Jablin, L. Putnam, K. Roberts, & L. Porter (Eds.), Handbook of organizational communication: 130-164. Newbury Park, CA: Sage.

    6. Starbuck, W., & Milliken, F. 1988. Executives' perceptual filters: What they notice and how they make sense. In D. Hambrick (ed.), The executive effect: Concepts and methods for studying top managers: 35-66. Greenwich, CT: JAI.

    7. Louis, M. 1980. Surprise and sense making: What newcomers experience in entering unfamiliar organizational settings. Administrative Science Quarterly, 25: 226-251.

    8. Thomas, J., Clark, S., & Gioia, D. 1993. Strategic sensemaking and organizational performance: Linkages among scanning, interpretation, action, and outcomes. Academy of Management Journal, 36: 239-270.

    9. Westley, F. 1990. Middle managers and strategy: Microdynamics of inclusion. Strategic Management Journal, 11: 337-351.

**Writing for this class:** Write an abstract for any four of the papers read thus far for the class.

Class 3. April 13, 1994: Toward a clearer definition of sensemaking.

    10. Weick, K. 1993. Sensemaking in organizations: Small structures with large consequences. In J. K. Murnighan (ed.), Social psychology in organizations: Advances in theory and research: 10-37. Englewood Cliffs, NJ: Prentice Hall.

11. Staw, B.M. 1980. Rationality and justification in organizational life. In B.Staw and L.Cummings (Eds.), Research in organizational behavior, 45-80. Greenwich, CT: JAI.

12. Salancik, G. 1977. Commitment and control of organizational behavior and belief. In B. Staw and G. Salancik (Eds.), New directions in organizational behavior: 1-54. Chicago, IL: St. Clair Press.

13. Czarniawska-Joerges, B. 1992. Ethnomethodology: Taking the cover off everyday life. In Czarniawska-Joerges, B. Exploring complex organizations: 117-138. Newbury Park, CA: Sage.

14. Barr, P. 1994. Understanding strategic response to environmental events: Event interpretation, response interpretation, and strategic change. Working paper, Emory Business School, Atlanta, GA.

15. Salancik, G., & Pfeffer, J. 1978. A social information processing approach to job attitudes and task design. Administrative Science Quarterly, 23: 224-253 **(skim if you haven't read this already).**

**Writing for this class:** The terms sensemaking and interpretation are often used interchangeably. Are they synonymous? Specifically, explain the differences and/or similarities between interpretation and sensemaking.

Class 4. April 20, 1994: Articulating the characteristics of sensemaking.

16. Weick, K. 1994. Seven properties of sensemaking. In K. Weick, Sensemaking in organizations: 19-75. Manuscript, The University of Michigan.

17. Porac, J., Thomas, H., & Baden-Fuller, C. 1989. Competitive groups as cognitive communities: The case of Scottish knitwear manufacturers. Journal of Management Studies, 26: 397-416.

18. Weick, K. 1990. The vulnerable system: An analysis of the Tenerife air disaster. Journal of Management, 16: 571-593.

19. Gioia, D., & Chittipeddi, K. 1991. Sensemaking and sensegiving in strategic change initiation. Strategic Management Journal, 12: 433-448..

**Writing for this class:** None

Class 5. April 27, 1994: Sensemaking in organizations.

20. Huff, A., & Schwenk, C. 1990. Bias and sensemaking in good times and bad. In A. Huff (ed.), Mapping strategic thought: 89-

21. Daft, R., & Winginton, J. 1979. Language and organization. Academy of Management Review, 4: 179-191.

22. Barley, S. 1986. Technology as an occasion for structuring: Evidence from observations of CT scanners and the social order of radiology departments. <u>Administrative Science Quarterly</u>, 31: 78-108.

23. Smircich, L., & Stubbart, C. 1985. Strategic management in an enacted world. <u>Academy of Management Review</u>, 10: 724-736.

24. Schall, M. 1983. A communication-rules approach to organizational culture. <u>Administrative Science Quarterly</u>, 28: 557-581.

25. Bougon, M., Weick, K., & Binkhorst, D. 1977. Cognition in organizations: An analysis of the Utrecht jazz orchestra. <u>Administrative Science Quarterly</u>, 22: 606-639.**(skim)**

**Writing for this class:** Link the properties cited in Weick (Chapter 2, reading 15) to either Porac et al. (reading 16), Weick (Tenerife, reading 17), or Weick (Mann Gulch, reading 3).

Class 6.  May 4, 1994: Sensemaking opportunities.

26. Schroeder, R., Van de Ven, A., Scudder, G., & Polley. 1989. The development of innovation ideas. In A. Van de Ven, H. Angle, & M. Poole (Eds.), <u>Research on the management of innovation: The Minnesota studies</u>: 107-134. New York: Ballinger.

27. McCaskey, M. 1982. Chapters 1 & 3 in <u>The executive challenge: Managing change and ambiguity</u>. Marshfield, MA: Pitman.

28. Milliken, F. 1987. Three types of perceived uncertainty about the environment: State, effect, and response uncertainty. <u>Academy of Management Review</u>, 12: 133-143.

29. Daft, R., & Macintosh, N. 1981. A tentative exploration into the amount and equivocality of information processing in organizational work units. <u>Administrative Science Quarterly</u>, 26: 207-224.

30. Louis, M., & Sutton, R. 1991. Switching cognitive gears: From habits of mind to active thinking. <u>Human Relations</u>, 44: 55-76.

**Writing for this class:** Describe your own personal experience with senselessness in such a way that it can be used to generate theory. Describe concretely what facilitated meaning in the experience. What leads to senselessness for you?

Class 7.  May 11, 1994: Raw material for sensemaking.

31. Sproull, L. 1981. Beliefs in organizations. In P. Nystrom & W. Starbuck (Eds.), <u>Handbook of organizational design</u>: 203-224. New York: Oxford University Press.

32. Perrow, C. 1977). The bureaucratic paradox: The efficient organization centralizes in order to decentralize. <u>Organizational Dynamics</u>, Spring:

33. Hedberg, B. 1981. How organizations learn and unlearn. In P. Nystrom & W. Starbuck (Eds.), <u>Handbook of organizational design</u>: 3-27. New York: Oxford University Press.

34. Beyer, J. 1981. Ideologies, values and decision making in organizations. In P. Nystrom & W. Starbuck (Eds.), <u>Handbook of organizational design</u>: 167-202. New York: Oxford University Press.

35. Gioia, D., & Poole, P. 1984. Scripts in organizational behavior. <u>Academy of Management Review</u>, 9: 449-459.

**Writing for this class:** None

Class 8. May 18, 1994: Making sense through cognition

36. Walsh, J. 1994. Managerial and organizational cognition: Notes from a trip down memory lane. <u>Organization Science</u> (in press).

37. Weick, K. 1994. Belief-driven processes of sensemaking. In K. Weick, Sensemaking in organizations: 181-210. Manuscript, University of Michigan.

38. Barr, P., Stimpert, J., & Huff, A. 1992. Cognitive change, strategic action, and organizational renewal. <u>Strategic Management Journal</u>, 13: 15-36.

39. Kiesler, S., & Sproull, L. 1982. Managerial response to changing environments: Perspectives on problem sensing from social cognition. <u>Administrative Science Quarterly</u>, 27: 548-570.

**Writing for this class:** Find and present in your paper, an organizational story about sensemaking. Show how beliefs or actions (or both) facilitated the making of sense.

Class 9. May 25, 1994: Making sense through action.

40. Starbuck, W. 1983. Organizations as action generators. <u>American Sociological Review</u>, 48: 91-102.

41. Starbuck, W. 1985. Acting first and thinking later: They versus reality in strategic change. In J. Pennings & Associates (Eds.), <u>Organizational strategy and change</u>: 336-372. San Francisco: Jossey-Bass.**

42. Starbuck, W. 1982. Congealing oil: Inventing ideologies to justify acting ideologies out. <u>Journal of Management Studies</u>, 19: 3-27.

43. Brunsson, N. 1982. The irrationality of action and action rationality: Decision, ideologies and organizational actions. <u>Journal of Management Studies</u>, 19: 29-44.

44. Weick, K. 1994. Action-driven processes of sensemaking. In K. Weick, Sensemaking in organizations: 211-233. Manuscript, University of Michigan.

45. Sutcliffe, K., Waller, M., & Huber, G. 1994. Accounting for change: Exploring the antecedents of causal attributions. Working paper, University of Minnesota.

**Writing for this class**: What is the best research idea you've found in this course? Be sure to describe it so it is researchable and doable within the next 12 months

Class 10. June 1, 1994: Methodological and research considerations. So what, where next?

46. Thorngate, Warren. 1976. Possible limits on a science of social behavior. In L.H. Strickland, F.E. Aboud, and K.J. Gergen (Eds.), Social Psychology in Transition. New York: Plenum Press.

47. Webb, E., & Weick, K. 1979. Unobtrusive measures in organizational theory: A reminder. In J. Van Maanen (ed.), Qualitative Methodology, 209-224. Beverly Hills, CA: Sage.

48. Jick, T. 1979. Mixing qualitative and quantitative methods: Triangulation in action. In J. Van Maanen (ed.), Qualitative Methodology, 135-148. Beverly Hills, CA: Sage.

49. Czarniawska-Joerges, B. 1992. Toward an anthropology of complex organizations. In Czarniawska-Joerges, B., Exploring complex organizations: 186-225. Newbury Park, CA: Sage.

50. Brief, A., & Dukerich, J. 1991. Theory in organizational behavior: Can it be useful? In L.L. Cummings & B. Staw (Eds.), Research in organizational behavior, 13: 327-352. Greenwich, CT: JAI.

**Writing for this class:** None. But, reflect upon all that you have learned in the course up to this point and be ready to discuss the following: What are the implications of this line of research for your primary research interest area (i.e., strategy, policy, organizational behavior, communication, etc.)?

## ORGANIZATIONS AND THE MANAGEMENT OF CHANGE
## MBA 8325, SPRING 1994

Kathleen M. Sutcliffe
819 Mgmt/Econ
625-3548

Office Hours: T/Th 8am-10am
or by appointment

### COURSE DESCRIPTION AND STRUCTURE

Change is a pervasive feature of organizations. As the management of organizations becomes increasingly complex, the ability to analyze and respond to change is a fundamental part of effective management. This course focuses on fostering an understanding of organizational change processes in order to facilitate students' abilities to effectively influence organizational change situations. It is primarily intended to assist students in applying behavioral science theory to the management of organizations and organizational change.

### LEARNING OBJECTIVES

As a result of this course, students will be able to:

1. Understand the systems view of organizations.

2. Explain and diagnose environmental pressures, organizational pressures, and strategic pressures for change.

3. Understand models of organizational change.

4. Explain and diagnose resistance to change.

5. Understand and apply frameworks for analyzing and managing organizational change.

6. Understand the nature of learning organizations.

### TEXTS AND REQUIRED READING

There is no required textbook for the course. A packet of required readings and cases is available at Copies on Campus, West Bank.

### STUDENT ASSIGNMENTS AND EVALUATION

Each class will involve a combination of lecture, discussion, cases and exercises. Students are expected to have read all assigned readings before they come to class and are expected to participate actively in class discussions, case analyses, and exercises. I have developed the course requirements (i.e., readings and assignments) to allow students sufficient time to deeply think about and reflect on the issues being studied.

Students will be evaluated on the basis of the written case analyses (due in class for each of the cases), class participation, and a final exam. These assignments are explained more fully below, as are the schemes by which final grades will be computed.

Written Case Analyses (50%)

Written case analyses will be required for each case discussed in class. Six cases will be discussed during the quarter and all six will be written as a group. Of the cases to be handed in, the first will be used as a "practice case" for students to get feedback on how to prepare a one-page analysis of a complex case--it will not be graded. Cases are to be turned in at the beginning of the class in which that case will be discussed. Since one of the purposes of the assignment is to insure that everyone is prepared for our case discussion, no late case analyses will be accepted. All cases must be typed, single spaced, and fit on a single page. I have students prepare cases in groups because it is not always easy to know how to recognize, analyze, and respond to difficult organizational problems; therefore it is often beneficial to discuss the case (face-to-face) with other people.

Specific guidelines for how to approach case analysis and how to prepare a written analysis are attached to the syllabus. Although the required format is challenging to learn at first, it has proven to be an extremely effective way for MBA students to learn some very practical lessons: (1) to be able to identify a few key elements to focus on in analyzing complex situations, (2) to express their ideas simply and directly (3) to translate theoretical material into action-oriented terms, and (4) to present a persuasive analysis that will increase the probability of getting a superior to follow through on a recommended course of action. Although it may be difficult at first to provide a sound, substantive analysis of a complex case in a single page, nearly all students have been able to master this in the past.

Cases will be graded as follows: 1 (superficial), 2 (some major problems), 3 (acceptable), 4 (good), 5 (excellent, insightful, these are fairly rare). All group members will receive the same grade for the case analysis.

Class Participation/Contribution (20%)

Each class session will involve some lecture material, but discussion will be a more substantial part of the course. Therefore, student participation is an essential part of the course--both for your own learning and for that of the other students in the class. Particular emphasis will be placed on quality of participation during case discussions. In grading this component, I will look for student participation in our discussion of the cases and in the discussion of the group exercises. The emphasis is on quality participation, not quantity.

Final Exam (30%)

Each student will be required to write and submit a final in-class exam. The exam will be composed of short answer essay questions and an analysis of a short case. The exam will be given on **Friday, April 29.**

COURSE PACKET CONTENTS
MBA 8325, SPRING 1994

## Class 1. Introduction to Change

Borucki, C., & Barnett, C. 1990. Restructuring for self-renewal: Navistar International Corporation, *Academy of Management Executive*, 4: 36-49.

Tichy, Noel. The essentials of strategic change management, *Journal of Business Strategy*, 55-67.

Schein, E.H. 1969. The mechanisms of change. In W. Bennis, K.Benne, & R. Chin (Eds.), *The planning of change* 2nd ed.: 98-107. New York: Holt, Rinehart, & Winston.

Nadler, D. & Tushman, M. 1984. A general diagnostic model for organizational behavior: Applying a congruence perspective. In R. Daft & M. Sharfman (Eds.), *Organization theory: Cases and applications*: xi-xxvi. St. Paul, MN: West.

## Class 2. A Systems View of Organizations and Organizational Effectiveness

Ashmos, D., & Huber, G. 1987. The systems paradigm in organization theory: Correcting the record and suggesting the future, *Academy of Management Review*, : 607-619.

Cameron, K. 1980. Critical questions in assessing organizational effectiveness, *Organizational Dynamics*, Autumn: 66-80.

Cameron, K. 1986. Effectiveness as paradox: Consensus and conflict in conceptions of organizational effectiveness, *Management Science*, 32: 539-553.

## Class 3. Goals, Leadership, and Planned Change

Leavitt, H. 1983. Management and management education in the West: What's right and what's wrong?, London Business School Journal, Summer. Reprinted in M. Tushman, C. O'Reilly, and D. Nadler (Eds.), *The management of organizations*: 33-42. New York: Harper & Row.

Bourgeois, L.J., & Brodwin, D.R. 1983. Putting your strategies in action, *Strategic Management Planning*, March/May: 297-308.

Jemison, D., & Sitkin, S. 1986. Acquisitions: The process can be a problem, *Harvard Business Review*, March-April: 107-116.

Case 1: Cray Research, Harvard Business School Case #9-385-011.

### Class 4. Bottled Change

Kilmann, R. 1985. Principles for organizational success. In *Beyond the quick fix: Managing the five track to organizational success*: 1-29. San Francisco: Jossey-Bass.

Kotter, J. 1990. What leaders really do, *Harvard Business Review*, May-June: 103-111.

Falvey, J. 1988. Before spending #3 million on leadership, read this, *Wall Street Journal*, October 3.

Case 2: Selkirk Associates. From Rhodes, Lucien. 1986. That's easy for you to say, Inc., June. Reprinted in R. Daft & M. Sharfman (Eds.), 1990, *Organization theory: Cases and applications*, 3rd ed.: 297-302. St. Paul, MN: West.

### Class 5. Resistance to Change

Kotter, J. & Schlesinger, L. 1979. Choosing strategies for change, *Harvard Business Review*, March-April: 106-114.

Klein, D. 1969. Some notes on the dynamics of resistance to change: The defender role. In W. Bennis, K. Benne, & R. Chin (Eds.), *The planning of change*, 2nd ed.: 498-507. New York: Holt, Rinehart, & Winston.

Case 3: Mod IV Product Development Team, Harvard Business School Case # 9-491-030.

### Class 6. Cultural Change

Reynolds, P. 1987. Imposing a corporate culture, *Psychology Today*, March: 33-38.

Schein, E. 1985. How culture forms, develops, & changes. In R. Kilmann, M. Saxton, & R. Serpa (Eds.), *Gaining control of the corporate culture*: 17-43. San Francisco: Jossey-Bass.

Silverzweig, S & Allen, R. 1976. Changing the corporate culture, *Sloan Management Review*, Spring: 33-49.

Deal, T. 1988. Cultural change: Opportunity, silent killer, or metamorphosis? In R. Kilmann, M.Saxton, R. Serpa (Eds.), *Gaining control of the corporate culture*: 292-331. San Francisco: Jossey-Bass.

Case 4: Manufacturers Hanover Corporation (A), Harvard Business School Case #9-188-037.

Class 7. Change in new and declining organizations

Martin, J., Sitkin, S., & Boehm, M. 1985. Founders and the elusiveness of a cultural legacy. In P. Frost, L. Moore, M. Louis, C. Lundberg, & J. Martin (Eds.), *Organizational culture*: 99-124. Beverly Hills: Sage.

Gilmore, T., & Hirschorn, L. 1984. Managing human resources in a declining context. In C. Fombrun, N. Tichy, M. Devanna (Eds.), *Strategic human resource management*: 297-318. New York: John Wiley.

Dreyfuss, J. 1988. What do you do for an encore?, *Fortune*, December 19: 111-119.

Case 5: People Express (A), Harvard Business School Case # 9-483-103.

Class 8. Change Agents

Taylor, D. & Singer, E. The change agents. In New Organizations From Old, Institute for Personnel Management: 89-104. THIS ARTICLE IS NOT INCLUDED IN THE PACKET. IT WILL BE HANDED OUT BEFORE CLASS

Schaffer, R. & Ashkenas, R. Anxiety: The change agent's unwelcome companion, *Journal of Management Consulting*, 1: 1-9.

Case 6: DAAG Europe, Harvard Business School Case # 9-374-037.

Class 9. Creating Learning Organizations

Argyris, C. 1991. Teaching smart people how to learn, *Harvard Business Review*, may-June: 99-109.

Hurst, D. 199 . Of boxes, bubbles, and effective management, *Harvard Business Review*: 78-88.

Sitkin, S. 1992. Learning through failure: The strategy of small losses. In L.Cummings & B. Staw (Eds.), *Research in Organizational Behavior*, 14: 231-266. Greenwich, CT:JAI.

Class 10. Organizational Change and Renewal

Kanter, R. 1989. Mastering the art of change: Managing convergence and upheaval, Harvard Business School Note # 9-389-168.

Beatty, R. & Ulrich, D. 1991. Re-energizing the mature organization, *Organizational Dynamics*, Summer: 16-30.

# MGMT 761 THE INDIVIDUAL IN THE ORGANIZATION

Spring 1995   Wednesday 3:00-6:00 pm.

Ross Arkell Webber, Professor of Management
2106 Steinberg Hall-Dietrich Hall: Tel. 898-9368

---

Most of us will spend a major portion of our lives working in organizations. Although from time to time we may yearn for an independent, professional practitioner's, artist's, or even yeoman farmer's autonomous life, economic reality dictates that we take jobs in firms or create our own. The course will examine the uneasy, love-hate relationship that often exists between organizations and their individual members. We shall examine the kinds of problems we confront as we enter an organization and with the passage of time (and outstanding performance) move upward to increased authority and responsibility. Numerous short cases and public incidents will be used to illustrate frequent dilemmas and methods for handling situations. Students will make oral presentations or written reports on their personal experiences

**Readings**:  The text is Ross A. Webber, *BECOMING A COURAGEOUS MANAGER: OVERCOMING CAREER PROBLEMS OF NEW MANAGERS* (Prentice Hall, 1991). Additional readings are contained in a coursepack which should be purchased from Wharton Reprographics. and  (for the exceptionally interested) in a folder of suggested research articles on reserve in Lippincott Library

**Assignments.** Specific oral and written assignments will be made separately.

**WEEK 1: January 18 : INTRODUCTION**
Text: "Introduction: On heroes, optimism, and cynicism"

**WEEK 2: January 26 PERSONAL MATURATION AND CAREER DEVELOPMENT**
Text: Chapter 1: "Growing Up at Work."
Coursepack:
- D. Goleman, "Therapists find last outpost of adolescence in adulthood."
- R. Caro, "One of a Crowd"
- J. Stewart, "Unhappy ending."
- D. J. Levinson, "Growing up with the dream."
- D. Sifford, "How the pursuit of security can stifle personal growth."
- M.S. Kimmel, "What do men want?"
- R.E. Kaplan, "The expansive executive."
- E. Kaye, "The face of power"
- R..J. House & J. Singh, "Power motive"
- W. Kiechel, "The workaholic generation."
- A. Deutschman, "What 25 year olds want."
- P. Leinberger, "The sun sets on the silent generation."
- M. Shechtman, "Teaching young workers to grow up."
- S. Ratan, "Why busters hate boomers."
- W. Kiechel, "How executives think."

Suggested Research Articles (on reserve):
- A.M. Kowaz "Development and Validation of a Measure of Eriksonian Industry."
- M.D. Mumford, et al, "Personality, adaptability and performance."
- W.D. Spangler & R. J. House, "Presidential effectiveness and the leadership motive profile."

Suggested Books:
- J.F. Rychlak, PERSONALITY AND LIFE STYLE OF YOUNG MALE MANAGERS (Academic Press, 1983).
- J.A. Newman & R. Alexander, CLIMBING THE CORPORATE MATTERHORN (Wiley 1985)
- D.T. Hall & Assocs, CAREER DEVELOPMENT IN ORGANIZATIONS (Jossey-Bass 1986)
- C.B. Derr, MANAGING THE NEW CAREERISTS (Jossey-Bass, 1986).
- B.A. Gutek & L. Larwood, eds., WOMEN'S CAREER DEVELOPMENT (Sage 1987).
- H. Levinson, ed., DESIGNING AND MANAGING YOUR CAREER (Harvard Business School Press, 1988).
- J. Calano & J. Salzman, CAREER TRACKING (Simon & Schuster 1988).
- H. Gunz, CAREERS AND CORPORATE CULTURES (Blackwell, 1989)
- J. Parikh, MANAGING YOUR SELF (Blackwell, 1990)
- R. Johnson, FINDING HERSELF-PATHWAYS TO IDENTITY DEVELOPMENT IN WOMEN (Jossey-Bass 1990).
- P. Leinberger and B. Tucker, THE NEW INDIVIDUALISTS: THE GENERATION AFTER THE ORGANIZATION MAN (Harper Collins, 1991).
- L.A. Hill, BECOMING A MANAGER: MASTERY OF A NEW IDENTITY (Harvard Business School, 1992)
- D. Hart, BECOMING MEN: THE DEVELOPMENT OF ASPIRATIONS, VALUES AND ADAPTATION STYLES (1993)

**WEEK 3: February 1: EARLY DISAPPOINTMENT AND DISSATISFACTION**
Text: Chapter 2: "Dealing with Early Disappointment."
**Coursepack:**
- A. Bennett, "New generation asks more than its elders of corporate world."
- C. Hymowitz, "Stable cycles of executive careers shattered by upheaval in business."
- J. Weber, "Farewell fast track."
- C. Hymowitz, "Five main reasons why managers fail."
- A. Scheele, "When you've been passed over."
- M. Rowland, "Sidestepping toward success."
- R. Henkoff, "Winning the new career game."
- K. Labich, "Take control of your career."
- M. Rowland, "The advantages of taking risks."
- R. J. Waterman, et al., "Toward a career-resilient workforce."

**Suggested Research Articles (on reserve)**
- D. C. Feldman & B.A. Weitz, "From the invisible hand to the gladhand: understanding careerist orientation to work,"
- C. A. O'Reilly, et al., "People and organizational culture."
- D. R. Comer, "Organizational newcomers' acquisition of information from peers."
- C. Kirchmeyer, "Nonwork participation and work attitudes."

**Suggested Books:**
- M. London & E.M. Mone, CAREER MANAGEMENT AND SURVIVAL IN THE WORKPLACE (Jossey-Bass, 1987).
- M.T. Mattison & J.M. Ivancevich, CONTROLLING WORK STRESS (Jossey-Bass 1987)
- S. Strasser, WORKING IT OUT: SANITY AND SUCCESS IN THE WORKPLACE (Prentice Hall 1988).
- M. Sinetar, DO WHAT YOU LOVE, THE MONEY WILL FOLLOW (? 1989).
- D.L. Kanter & P.H. Mirvis, THE CYNICAL AMERICANS: LIVING AND WORKING IN AN AGE OF DISCONTENT AND DISILLUSION (Jossey-Bass, 1989).
- S. R. Baumgardner, COLLEGES AND JOBS: CONVERSATIONS WITH RECENT GRADUATES (Plenum, 1989).
- W.F. Roth, WORK AND REWARDS: REDEFINING OUR WORK-LIFE REALITY (Praeger 1989)
- R.M. Bramson, COPING WITH THE FAST TRACK BLUES (Doubleday 1989)
- J.L. Speller, EXECUTIVES IN CRISIS (Jossey-Bass, 1990).
- J.C. Quick et al (eds), CAREER STRESS IN CHANGING TIMES (Haworth Press, 1990)
- N. Yeager, CAREER MAP (Brace-Park, 1990).
- S.R. Covey, THE 7 HABITS OF HIGHLY EFFECTIVE PEOPLE (Simon & Schuster 1990)
- R.S. Weiss, STAYING THE COURSE: THE EMOTIONAL AND SOCIAL LIVES OF MEN WHO DO WELL AT WORK (Fawcett Columbine 1990)
- W. Roberts, STRAIGHT A's NEVER MADE ANYBODY RICH (Harper Collins 1991).
- T. Morris, TRUE SUCCESS (Grosset/Putnam 1994).

**WEEK 4: February 8: ROLE OVERLOAD AND STRESS**
   Text: Chapter 3: "Overcoming Overload and Stress."
   **Coursepack:**
   T. Lewin, "At the bar."
   S. Nasar, "A Wall Street star's agonizing confession."
   N. Gibbs, "How America has run out of time."
   V. Loeb, "Overworked: Japan's way of life, death."
   A. Quindlen, "What makes a workaholic keep working?"
   W. Kiechel, "When executives crack."
   NYT, "Drinking problems rise among young women.
   B.P Noble, "Women pay more for success.""
   B. O'Reilly, "Is your company asking too much?"
   E.T. Smith, "Stress: The test Americans are failing."
   M. D. Glicken, "Executives under fire: the burnout syndrome."
   M. Begun Kane, "When executives should say no."
   W.D. Rees, "A system for assessing work priorities."
   B. P Noble, "Want to survive? learn to negotiate!"
   W. Kiechel, "Now some good news about stress."
   **Suggested Research Articles (on reserve)**
   R.S. Schuler, "Definition and Conceptualization of stress in organizations."
   R. T. Lee & B.E. Ashforth, "A longitudinal study of burnout among supervisors and managers."
   D. Etzion, "The experience of burnout and work/non-work succession in male and female engineers"
   M. Alvesson, "Organizations as rhetoric: knowledge-intensive firms and the struggle with ambiguity."
   **Suggested Books:**
   M. Machlowitz, WORKAHOLICS (New American Library, 1980).
   H.J. Freudenberger, BURN OUT (Doubleday 1980; Bantam, 1981)
   M.H. Shaevitz, THE SUPERWOMAN SYNDROME (Warner 1984)
   J.K. Sprankle & H. Ebel, THE WORKAHOLIC SYNDROME (Walker 1987)
   H.B. Braiker, THE TYPE E WOMAN: HOW TO OVERCOME THE STRESS OF BEING EVERYTHING TO EVERYONE (Dodd Mead 1987)
   A.Pines & E. Aronson, CAREER BURNOUT: CAUSES AND CURES (The Free Press 1988)
   P.A. Wallace, MBA's ON THE FAST TRACK (Ballinger Pubs. 1988)
   R.M. Bramson, COPING WITH THE FAST TRACK BLUES (Doubleday 1989)
   P.G. Hanson, STRESS FOR SUCCESS: HOW TO MAKE STRESS ON THE JOB WORK FOR YOU (Doubleday, 1989).
   B. Gale and L. Gale, STAY OR LEAVE (Harper Collins, 1990).
   W. Rybczynski, WAITING FOR THE WEEKEND (Viking 1991)
   K.B. Matheny & R.J. Riordan, STRESS AND STRATEGIES FOR LIFESTYLE MANAGEMENT (Georgia State Univ., 1992)

**WEEK 5. February 15. TACTICAL TIME MANAGEMENT**
  Text: Chapter 4: "Managing short-term time"
  **Coursepack:**
   P. T. Kilborn, "Tales from the digital dreadmill,"
   M.L. Rozansky, "Americans work too hard."
   B.K. Hunnicutt, "Are we all working too hard?"
   C. Reed, "Be wary of beeper bondage.".
   R. A. Mackenzie, "Myths of time management."
   A.S. Grove, "Manage faster"
   G. Fuchsberg, "Its the Quality, not the quantity of your work hours."
   P. Drucker, "How to manage your time."
   T.W. Firnstahl, "Growing concerns:letting go."
   W. Oncken, "Management time: who's got the monkey?"
   E. Calonius, "How top managers manage their time."
   W. Kiechel, "12 reasons for leaving at five."
   B. Miller, "Got a minute?"
  **Research Articles (on reserve):**
   S. L Kirmeyer & K. Biggers, "Environmental demand and demand engendering behavior: an observational analysis of the type A pattern."
   R. J. Larsen & M. Kasimatis, "Individual differences in entrainment of mood to the weekly calendar"
   R. H Doktor, "Asian and American CEO's: a comparative study."
  **Suggested Books:**
   D. Scott, HOW TO PUT MORE TIME IN YOUR LIFE (Rawson, Wade, 1980).
   R. A. Mackenzie, THE TIME TRAP ( Exec Enterp, 1980)
   M.E. Douglas and D.N. Douglas, MANAGE YOUR TIME, YOUR WORK, YOURSELF (Amacom, 1980).
   J.D. Ferner, SUCCESSFUL TIME MANAGEMENT(John Wiley, 1980)
   L.R. Jannz and S.K. Jones, TIME MANAGEMENT FOR EXECUTIVES (Scribner's, 1981).
   A. Goodloe, J. Bensahel, and J. Kelly, MANAGING YOURSELF(Franklin Watts, 1984).
   J.B. Burka & L.M. Yuen, PROCRASTINATION (Addison-Wesley, 1985).
   S. Schlenger and R. Roesch, HOW TO BE ORGANIZED IN SPITE OF YOURSELF (New American Library, 1989).
   J. J. Mayer, IF YOU HAVEN'T GOT THE TIME TO DO IT RIGHT, WHEN WILL YOU FIND THE TIME TO DO IT OVER? (Simon & Schuster, 1990).
   L.H. Hedrick, FIVE DAYS TO AN ORGANIZED LIFE (Dell 1990)
   R. Moskowitz, HOW TO ORGANIZE YOUR WORK AND YOUR LIFE (Doubleday 1993)
   S.A. Winston, THE ORGANIZED EXECUTIVE: NEW WAYS TO MANAGE TIME, PAPER AND PEOPLE (W.W. Norton, 1994).

**WEEK 6. February 22: : STRATEGIC TIME MANAGEMENT**
  Text: Chapter 5: "Managing Longer-term Time."
  **Coursepack:**
   NYT, "Technology will force a shorter workweek."
   B. P. Noble, "Keep the workplace in its place."
   S.R. Weisman, "Japanese workers demanding shorter hours and less hectic work."
   M. Csikszentmihalyi, "Relax? relax and do what?"
   A. Dacyczyn, "The two income whiners."
   T. Lewin, "Men whose wives work earn less."
   E. Goodman, "Sharing the second shift."
   C. Satulllo, "A call for a truce in the housework wars."
   J. Connelly, "How dual income couples cope."
   B. P. Noble, "Round two on the mommy track."
   D. Jacobs, "Back from the mommy track."
   L. Genasci, "Firms offer flexible schedules, but participation not keeping pace."
   A. Deutschman, "Pioneers of the new balance
   J. Fierman, "Are companies less family friendly?"
   M. Galen, "Work and family."
   D.T. Hall, "Promoting work/family balance."
  **Suggested Research Articles (on reserve):**
   K. J. Williams & G. M. Alliger, "Role stressors, mood spillover, and perceptions of work-family conflict in employed parents."
   H. Presser, "Employment schedules among dual-earner spouses and the division of household work by gender."
   W.T Bielby & D.D. Bielby, "Family Ties: Balancing Commitments to work and family in dual earner households."
   H. M. Rosin, "The effects of dual career participation on men."
  **Suggested Books:**
   U. Sekaran, DUAL-CAREER FAMILIES (Jossey-Bass 1986).
   C. R. Hobbs, TIME POWER (Harper & Row 1987)
   J.L. Pierce at al. ALTERNATIVE WORK SCHEDULES (Allyn & Bacon 1988).
   L.A. Gilbert, SHARING IT ALL: THE REWARDS AND STRUGGLES OF TWO-CAREER FAMILIES (Plenum, 1988).
   A. Hochschild, THE SECOND SHIFT: WORKING PARENTS AND THE REVOLUTION AT HOME (Viking, 1989).
   E.B. Goldsmith, ed., WORK AND FAMILY (Sage, 1989).
   A. Mackenzie, TIME FOR SUCCESS (McGraw Hill 1989)
   R. I Winwood, TIME MANAGEMENT: AN INTRODUCTION TO THE FRANKLIN SYSTEM (Franklin International Institute 1990)
   R. Keyes, TIMELOCK: HOW LIFE GOT SO HECTIC AND WHAT YOU CAN DO ABOUT IT (Harper Collin 1991).
   W. Oncken, Jr., MANAGING MANAGEMENT TIME (Prentice Hall, 1984).
   K. Blanchard, W. Oncken, Jr., and H. Burrows, THE ONE MINUTE MANAGER MEETS THE MONKEY (William Morrow, 1989).
   R.A. Webber, BREAKING YOUR TIME BARRIERS: BECOMING A STRATEGIC TIME MANAGER (Prentice Hall 1992)
   H. R. Smith, THE 10 NATURAL LAWS OF SUCCESSFUL TIME AND LIFE MANAGEMENT (Warner Books 1994)

**WEEK 7: March 1: AMBIGUOUS AUTHORITY**
    **Text:** Chapter 6: "Clarifying Delegation.
    **Coursepack:"**
        H.J. Maihafer, "The rewards and dangers of over delegating authority"
        W. Kiechel, "The importance of visibility."
        T. A. Stewart, "New ways to exercise power."
        J. P. Kotter, "Power, dependence and effective management."
        S. M Davis & P. R. Lawrence, "Problems of matrix organizations."
        A. R. Cohen & D.L. Bradford, "Influence without authority."
        W. L. Gardner, "The art of impression management."
        J. J. Gabarro, "When a new manager takes charge."
    **Suggested Research Articles (on reserve)**
        R. B. de Laat, "Matrix Management of Projects and Power Struggles."
        R. E. Miles & C.C. Snow, "Causes of failure in network organizations
        S. Finkelstein, "Power in Top Management Teams."
    **Suggested Books**
        S.B. Bacharach & E.J. Lawler, POWER AND POLITICS IN ORGANIZATION (Jossey-Bass 1980).
        J.P. Kotter, POWER AND INFLUENCE (Free Press 1985)
        G.R. Funkhouser, THE POWER OF PERSUASION (Times Books 1986)
        P. Block, THE EMPOWERED MANAGER: POSITIVE POLITICAL SKILLS AT WORK (Jossey-Bass 1987)
        J.A. Conger, R.N. Kanungo and associates, CHARISMATIC LEADERSHIP (Jossey-Bass 1988)
        W. Bennis, ON BECOMING A LEADER (Addison-Wesley 1989)
        A.R. Cohen & D.L. Bradford, INFLUENCE WITHOUT AUTHORITY (Wiley, 1990).
        J.E. Emshoff and T.E. Denlinger, THE NEW RULES OF THE GAME: THE FOUR KEY EXPERIENCES MANAGERS MUST HAVE TO THRIVE IN THE NON-HIERARCHICAL 90's AND BEYOND (Harper Business 1991).
        A. L. Frohman & L.W. Johnson, THE MIDDLE MANAGEMENT CHALLENGE (McGraw Hill 1993)
        J. M. Kouzes & B.Z. Posner, CREDIBILITY (Jossey-Bass 1993)
        E. Batof & F. Harwood, JUST PROMOTED: HOW TO SURVIVE AND THRIVE IN YOUR FIRST 12 MONTHS AS A MANAGER (McGraw Hill 1993).
        R. R. Ritti, THE ROPES TO SKIP AND THE ROPES TO KNOW (John Wiley 1994)
        R.L. Dilenschneider, ON POWER (Harper Business 1994).
        G. Egan WORKING THE SHADOW SIDE: A GUIDE TO POSITIVE BEHIND THE SCENES MANAGEMENT (Jossey-Bass 1994)

**WEEK 8: March 15: STAFF ADVISING AND EXTERNAL CONSULTING**
  Text: Chapter 7, "Giving Advice."
  **Coursepack:**
   G. Rifkin, "Andersen Consulting's culture of clones."
   G. Rifkin, "Don't ever judge this consultant by her cover."
   J. Kingley, "It's up or out at A.T. Kearney."
   M. Ciuchta, "Benefits of niche consulting."
   J. Huey, "How McKinsey does it."
   L.R. Gallese, "Counsel for the King."
   L. Berton, "Consulting for audit clients: a conflict of interest?"
   C.B. Deutsch, "Consultant as boss: James B. Farley."
   M. Breecher, "Where you are and how you dress may affect your power of persuasion."
   R.E. Sabath, "Dressing for impact in the 90's"
   J. A. Byrne, "The craze for consultants."
   E. C. Shapiro, "Consulting: has the solution become part of the problem?"
   C.C. Lundberg, "Transactions and games in consultant-client relations."
  **Suggested Research Articles (on reserve)**
   J.B. Miner, "Success in management consulting and the concept of eliteness motivation."
   J.B. Miner, "The management consulting firm as a source of high level managerial talent."
   S. Suryanarayanan, "Trends and outlook for U.S. consulting."
  **Suggested Books**
   P. Block, FLAWLESS CONSULTING: A GUIDE TO GETTING YOUR EXPERTISE USED (University Assoicates, 1981).
   J. Gallessich, THE PROFESSION AND PRACTICE OF CONSULTATION (Jossey-Bass1983)
   L.E. Greiner & R.O. Metzger, CONSULTING TO MANAGEMENT (Prentice Hall 1983).
   M. Kubr, MANAGEMENT CONSULTING: A GUIDE TO THE PROFESSION (ILO 1986).
   W.M. Greenfield, SUCCESSFUL MANAGEMENT CONSULTING (1987)
   R. Tepper, BECOME A TOP CONSULTANT (John Wiley 1987)
   R.E. Kelley, CONSULTING: THE COMPLETE GUIDE TO A PROFITABLE CAREER (1987)
   G. Lippitt & R. Lippitt, THE CONSULTING PROCESS IN ACTION (University Associates, 2nd ed., 1988).
   E. Schein, PROCESS CONSULTATION , vols 1 and 2, (Addison-Wesley, 1987 & 1988).
   R.O. Metzger, PROFITABLE CONSULTING (Addison-Wesley, 1989).
   J. Heron, HELPING THE CLIENT (Sage, 1990).
   G.M. Bellman, THE CONSULTANT'S CALLING (Jossey-Bass 1990).
   H. Shenson, COMPLETE GUIDE TO CONSULTING SUCCESS (Enterprise Pub. 1991).

**WEEK 9: March 22: RELATIONS WITH MENTORS AND SUPERIORS**
   Text: Chapter 8, "Being a Protege."
**Coursepack:**
   L. Maitland, "The Dean files: flattery in the quest for power."
   W. Kiechel, "Breaking bad news to the boss."
   R. McGarvey, "Working with the boss."
   D. Sifford, "Learning to handle a problematic boss."
   J.J. Gabarro & J.P. Kotter, "Managing your boss."
   L. Baird & K. Kram, "Career dynamics: managing the superior/subordinate relationship."
   G. R. Roche, "Much ado about mentors."
   S. Feinstein, "Women and minority workers in business find a mentor can be a rare commodity."
**Suggested Research Articles (on reserve)**
   B. Ashforth, "Petty tyranny in organizations."
   K.E. Kram, "Phases of the mentor relationship."
   N.B. Brown & T. Scandura, "The effect of mentorship and sex-role style on male-female earnings."
   D. A. Thomas, "Racial dynamics in cross-race developmental relationships."
**Suggested Books:**
   R.M. Bramson, COPING WITH DIFFICULT PEOPLE (Doubleday 1981).
   M.G. Zey, THE MENTOR CONNECTION (Dow Jones Irwin 1984).
   M.M. Lombardo & M.W. McCall, Jr., COPING WITH AN INTOLERABLE BOSS (Center for Creative Leadership, 1984).
   M. Grothe and P. Wylie, PROBLEM BOSSES (Fawcett Crest, 1987).
   K. Kramm, MENTORING AT WORK (Univ Press of America, 1988 ).
   C.M. Kelly, THE DESTRUCTIVE ACHIEVER (Addison-Wesley, 1988)
   A. DuBrin, WINNING OFFICE POLITICS (Prentice Hall 1990).
   P.G. Stern and T. Shachtman, STRAIGHT TO THE TOP: BEYOND LOYALTY, GAMESMANSHIP, MENTORS AND OTHER CORPORATE MYTHS (Warner 1990).
   A. Ries and J. Trout, HORSE SENSE: THE KEY TO SUCCESS IS FINDING A HORSE TO RIDE (McGraw Hill 1991).
   C. Carter-Scott, THE CORPORATE NEGAHOLIC: HOW TO DEAL SUCCESSFULLY WITH NEGATIVE COLLEAGUES, MANAGERS, AND CORPORATIONS (Villard, 1991).
   M. Solomon, WORKING WITH DIFFICULT PEOPLE (1991)
   M.F.R. Kets de Vries, LEADERS, FOOLS AND IMPOSTERS (Jossey Bass 1992)
   J. Kottler, BEYOND BLAME: A NEW WAY OF RESOLVING CONFLICTS IN RELATIONSHIPS (Jossey-Bass 1994)

**WEEK 10: March 29: LOYALTY AND WHISTLEBLOWING**
   **Text:** Chapter 9: "Loyalty and Whistleblowing."
   **Coursepack:**
   B. Meier, "Courtroom drama pits GM against a former engineer."
   C. Sims, "GE whistleblower is awarded $13.4 million."
   M. O'Toole, "The whistleblower and the train wreck."
   J.R. Emshwiller, "For Ford engineer life became unbearable ordeal of inquisition."
   N. R. Kleinfield, "The whistle blower's morning after."
   C. Sims, "Trying to mute the whistle-blowers."
   L. Driscoll, "A better way to handle whistle-blowers: let them speak."
   A. Dunkin, "Blowing the whistle without paying the piper."
   R.P. Nielsen, "Changing unethical organizational behavior."
   W. Kiechel, "Resurrecting corporate loyalty."
   F. Swoboda, "A plan for leaves rather than layoffs."
   J. M. Kouzes, "When leadership collides with loyalty"
   C. H. Deutsch, "Passing sentence before trial."
   A. Farnham, "The trust gap."
   F. Bartolome, "Nobody trusts the boss completely - now what?"
   B. O'Reilly, "The new deal: What companies and employees owe each other."
   **Suggested Research Articles (on reserve)**
   F. F. Reichheld, "Loyalty-based management"
   J.C. Haughey, "Does loyalty in the workplace have a future?"
   L. van Dyne et al., "Organizational citizenship"
   M. Withey & W.H.Cooper, "Predicting exit, voice, loyalty and neglect."
   **Suggested Books:**
   A. F. Westin (ed.), WHISTLE-BLOWING: LOYALTY AND DISSENT IN THE CORPORATION (1981).
   M. Pastin, THE HARD PROBLEMS OF MANAGEMENT: GAINING THE ETHICS EDGE (Jossey-Bass 1986).
   B.L. Toffler, TOUGH CHOICES: MANAGERS TALK ETHICS (Wiley, 1987).
   R. Jackall, MORAL MAZES: THE WORLD OF CORPORATE MANAGERS (Oxford 1988)
   D.W. Organ, ORGANIZATIONAL GOOD CITIZENSHIP BEHAVIOR: THE GOOD SOLDIER SYNDROME (Lexington 1988).
   M.P. Glazer and P.M. Glazer, THE WHISTLE BLOWERS: EXPOSING CORRUPTION IN GOVERNMENT AND INDUSTRY (Basic Books, 1989).
   A. Bennett, THE DEATH OF THE ORGANIZATION MAN (W. Morrow, 1990).
   L.L. Nash, GOOD INTENTIONS ASIDE: A MANAGER'S GUIDE TO RESOLVING ETHICAL PROBLEMS (Harvard Business School Press 1990).
   D.P. Westman, WHISTLEBLOWING: THE LAW OF RETALIATORY DISCHARGE (BNA 1990)
   W.J. Morin, TRUST ME (Drake Beam Morin 1990).
   M.P. Miceli & J.P. Near, BLOWING THE WHISTLE: THE ORGANIZATIONAL AND LEGAL IMPLICATIONS FOR COMPANIES AND EMPLOYEES (Lexington Books 1992)

**WEEK 11 April 5: BEING "DIFFERENT" IN THE ORGANIZATION**
  Text: Chapter 10: "Being Different in the Organization."
  **Coursepack:**
     C.E. Cohen, It's lonely near the top."
     K. Foltz, "Women deflate some adland images."
     A. B. Fisher, "Where women are succeeding."
     A. B. Fisher, "When will women get to the top?"
     N. Arnott. "Should you manage like a man?"
     L. Snowden, "My life as a man."
     L. Williams, "Stress of adapting to white society."
     V. Byrd, "The struggle for minority managers."
     S. Mydans, "Black identity vs. success and seeming 'white'"
     C. Leinster, "Black executives: how they're doing."
     F.E. James, "More blacks quitting white run firms."
     C. Deutsch, "Listening to women and blacks"
     P.T. Kilborn, "U.S. workers say Japanese keep them out of top jobs."
     P. Kruger, "Being "out" at the top finds new tolerance."
     C.H. Deutsch, "Gay rights, issue of the 90's."
     B.P. Noble, "The unfolding of gay culture."
     A. Parsons, "Study cites 'paradoxes' of Asian groups."
     V. Louis, "For Asian-Americans, a way to fight a maddening stereotype."
     D. Seligman, "The case for white males."
  **Suggested Research Articles (on reserve)**
     A.S. Tsui, "Being different: relational demography and organizational attachment."
     H. Ibarra, "Homophily and differential returns: sex differences in network structure and access in an advertising firm."
     J. A. Espinoza & R.T. Garza, "Social group salience and interethnic conflict."
  **Suggested Books:**
     F. Dickens. THE BLACK MANAGER: MAKING IT IN THE CORPORATE WORLD (Amacom, 1982).
     A. Jacobson, WOMEN IN CHARGE (Van Nostrand Reinhold, 1985)
     E.D. Irons & G. Moore, BLACK MANAGERS (Praeger 1985)
     S. Hardesty & N. Jacobs, SUCCESS AND BETRAYAL: THE CRISIS OF WOMEN IN CORPORATE AMERICA (Touchstone : Simon & Schuster 1986)
     B.A. Gutek & L. Larwood (eds), WOMEN'S CAREER DEVELOPMENT (Sage 1987)
     A.M. Morrison et al, BREAKING THE GLASS CEILING (Center for Creative Leadership, 1987)
     J. Hearn and W. Perkin, SEX AT WORK: THE POWER AND PARADOX OF ORGANIZATION SEXUALITY (St. Martin's Press 1987)
     G.N. Powell, WOMEN AND MEN IN MANAGEMENT (SAGE 1988)
     D.E. Thompson. ENSURING MINORITY SUCCESS IN CORPORATE AMERICA (Penum, 1988).
     A.K. Korman, THE OUTSIDERS: JEWS IN CORPORATE AMERICA (Lexington 1988)
     J.I. Herbert, BLACK MALE ENTREPRENEURS AND ADULT DEVELOPMENT (Praeger, 1989).
     S. Helgesen, THE FEMALE ADVANTAGE: WOMEN'S WAYS OF LEADERSHIP ( Doubleday 1990).
     S. Freeman, MANAGING LIVES : CORPORATE WOMEN AND SOCIAL CHANGE (Univ. of Mass 1990)
     J. Hearn et al, THE SEXUALITY OF ORGANIZATION (Sage 1990).
     S. L. Carter, REFLECTIONS OF AN AFFIRMATIVE ACTION BABY (Basic Books 1991)
     C. Cockburn, IN THE WAY OF WOMEN: (ILR Press 1992)
     F. Schwartz, BREAKING WITH TRADITION (Warner Books 1992)
     E. Cose, THE RAGE OF A PRIVILEGED CLASS (Harper Collins 1993)
     M.F. Kastre, THE MINORITY CAREER GUIDE (Peterson's 1993)
     C. Shields & L.C. Shields, WORK SISTER WORK: WHY BLACK WOMEN CAN'T GET AHEAD AND WHAT THEY CAN DO ABOUT IT (BirchLane Press 1993)

## WEEK 12: April 12  INTEGRITY AND PRIVACY
**Coursepack:**
- M. Hill, "Couple sue Walmart after being fired because they dated."
- B. Garfield, "Fallout from purple-hair incident for a woman in blue."
- Z. Schiller, "If you light up on Sunday, don't come in on Monday."
- T. Lewin, "Ban on beards by Domino's Pizza is unfair to Blacks, court rules."
- J. Gross, "Navy is urged to root out lesbians."
- T.A.S., "Should your company save your soul?"
- M. Janofsky, "Drug use and workers' rights."
- B.P. Noble, "Testing employees for drugs."
- W. B. Green, "Drug testing becomes corporate mine field."
- A. Sipress, "Private lives becoming employers' business."
- L. Reibstein, "Firms find it tougher to dismiss employees for off-duty conduct."
- M. Geyelin, "Fired managers winning more lawsuits."
- T. L. Leap, "When can you fire for off-duty conduct.?
- M. Galen, "Is your boss spying on you?"
- J. Markoff, "Europe plans to protect privacy worry business."
- G. Rifkin, "Do employees have a right to electronic privavcy?"
- A. S. Grove, "Mind your own business boss!"

**Suggested Research Articles (on reserve)**
- B.Z. Posner & W.H. Schmidt, "Values and the American Manager."
- R. Ladd et al, "Liability-driven ethics: the impact of hiring practices."
- H. Willmont, "Strength is ignorance; slavery is freedom: managing culture in modern organizations."

**Suggested Books**
- P. Hirsch, PACK YOUR OWN PARACHUTE (Addison-Wesley, 1987)
- J. Hunt, THE LAW OF THE WORKPLACE: RIGHTS OF EMPLOYERS AND EMPLOYEES (BNA Books, 1987).
- S. Srivastva & Assocs, EXECUTIVE INTEGRITY: THE SEARCH FOR HIGH HUMAN VALUES IN ORGANIZATIONAL LIFE (Jossey-Bass, 1988).
- J.L. Badaracco & R.R. Ellsworth, LEADERSHIP AND THE QUEST FOR INTEGRITY (Harvard Business School Press, 1988).
- C.C. Walton, THE MORAL MANAGER (Ballinger Pub., 1988).
- A.F. Westin & J.D. Aram, MANAGERIAL DILEMMAS (Ballinger Pub., 1988).
- D. McWhirter, YOUR RIGHTS AT WORK (John Wiley 1988).
- J.D. Rapoport and B.L.P. Zevnik, THE EMPLOYEE STRIKES BACK! (Macmillan, 1989).
- D.W. Ewing, JUSTICE ON THE JOB (Harvard Business School Press, 1990).
- M.E. Guy, ETHICAL DECISION MAKING IN EVERYDAY WORK SITUATIONS (Quorum Books, 1990).
- F. Neil Brady, ETHICAL MANAGING: RULES AND RESULTS (Macmillan 1990).
- J.D. Bible and D.A. McWhirter, PRIVACY IN THE WORKPLACE (Quorum 1990)

## WEEKS 13 & 14: APRIL 19 and 26  TO BE ANNOUNCED

Course Syllabus
Social Psychology of Organizing
OBHRM 700-1
University of Michigan
School of Business Administration
Professor Karl E. Weick
Winter 1995

Content of course

The focus of this course is on the ways people in organizations manage meaning. The central premise is that events in organizations are typically both complex and ambiguous. As a result, those events are subject to different interpretations. For action to take place, the diversity of these interpretations must be reduced. This reduction is where power, culture, expertise, language, commitments, memory, and organizational structure all affect the outcomes. We will examine the role of each of these. The question we will ask over and over is, how do people deal with confusion and what does this imply you should do to manage during times of confusion? If you think of organizations as a mix of financial controls and interpretation controls, this course will focus on the latter.

This course has been designed with several assumptions in mind.

First, I assume that organizations are complicated environments. Given the reality of complication, it follows that only complicated observers and complicated concepts will be sufficient to register accurately the events that occur. Thus, part of our joint responsibility to one another is to increase the complexity of our analyses.

Second, I assume that a "perfect" explanation of behavior is simultaneously general, accurate, and simple. I also assume that there is no such thing as a perfect explanation. Any explanation we discuss will be deficient in one of the three characteristics of generality, accuracy, or simplicity. For example, any explanation that is general and accurate will also be complex. It is impossible to get explanations that will fit all three criteria, so we ought to make our peace with that from the outset.

Third, I assume that when people are under considerable pressure and stress, their attention narrows (they become highly selective in what they notice) and they regress to simple, primitive ideas about what is happening. Both of these tendencies are deadly when you try to analyze problems. You neglect key factors causing the problem, which means the problem worsens, which raises the stress even higher, which degrades the analysis even further, and you make errors you never intended. One way to offset or at least slow this threat to diagnosis is to overlearn relatively sophisticated tools for analyzing behavioral problems. Overlearned tools are less susceptible to deterioration than are tools that are learned more tentatively. People who are confident of their skills to think behaviorally often have stress build at a slower rate than do people who have less confidence. Furthermore, people whose confidence is grounded in thorough familiarity with behavioral tools show less regression when they try to puzzle over problems than do people who have less familiarity with tools.

Finally, I assume that understanding is a joint product of common sense and things people commonly overlook. Common sense sometimes is helpful, sometimes is misleading, and it is not always easy to predict which is more likely at any given moment. While we can't always be sure of the validity of common sense, we can be sure that people often overlook possible explanations when they analyze any particular situation. A valuable function of a behavioral approach to organizations is that it provides reminders of those explanations which people commonly overlook.

Participation

Class meetings are a mixture of discussion and lecture. We will often start with brief discussion of how material covered in class applies to events being discussed in the media. Thorough preparation is assumed, which means a logical place to start is simply for me to say, "Mary, today's topic is 'Structures at a distance', so will you get us started." Class sessions are intended to be reasonably dense with information, concepts, and principles. Discussion is intended to uncover subtle key points that are easy for all of us to miss.

One of the great truths about how to make sense of any confusing situation is found in the question "how can I know what I think, until I see what I say?" Since we're going to be working with complicated material, it's imperative that we try to get our arms around it by talking, so we can discover what we think is in the material. Much of that talk may be fumbling, but that's usually only temporary. We fumble until we finally figure out what we wanted to say, then we say it with more clarity and eloquence, and wind up with clearer thinking than we started with. Talk is the basic raw material we have to work with in this course. The better the talk is, the more we learn. and the more diverse and the more frequent the talk, the better the chances that some of the talk will be good.

Therefore, I expect people to come to class prepared. And I expect them to plunge in when called upon and to help their classmates when they can, to consolidate some good ideas about what all this material about organizations means. People who get lower grades on participation are those who come unprepared, fail to listen to what others say, talk without making an effort to see what they say and improve the saying, criticize without putting something better in place of what was criticized, indulge in unbroken glibness, take no chances, and live in absolute terror that they will utter THE stupid question (there is no such thing).

People have to think on their feet in everyday life. They have to cope with disagreement and be prepared to change their minds or someone else's. Thus, our classroom discussions are merely microcosms of this normal natural trouble. If you make a consistent, informed, thoughtful effort to help all of us build a workable understanding of what we're talking about, then you'll have met your responsibility to everyone in this course.

Diagnostic Memos

Deliverables will be six short papers that encourage linking class discussions with personal experience, current events, and previous classes. The papers are intended to develop your skills in writing compact diagnoses. In addition, they will provide input for class discussions. Every effort will be made to return papers with comments, the next session after they are handed in. These papers are the basis for the final grade. Late papers are not accepted and are recorded as an "F".

Diagnostic memos will be used in a variety of ways. On some occasions, some papers will be reproduced on an overhead transparency and will be the point of departure for class discussion. On other occasions the paper will be exchanged and class members will comment on the analysis of someone else and be graded on their critique. On still other occasions the writer will be given an opportunity, after the class discussion has been completed, to add whatever changes seem appropriate, before the paper is graded.

The purpose of these memos is to improve the articulation and analysis of behavioral issues as they unfold in organizations. In grading these papers I will look for such things as coherence of the discussion, quality of argument, accessibility of main points, plausibility of analysis, relevance of answer to the question that was posed, comparison with other papers you have submitted and with other papers submitted for the same assignment, and evidence that you've given the question some thought.

I will make every effort to return the graded papers

promptly with sufficient feedback so that the next paper is better. It is difficult to communicate clearly when complicated events and analyses are involved, and the purpose of the diagnostic memo is to provide a medium for improving this skill. The memo also forces the student to choose which are the key ideas in readings which may have several seemingly important points.

The topics for the assigned memos will be distributed in class.

Readings

A packet of 40 readings related to the management of meaning will be covered at a rate of roughly 2 readings per class session. The readings are demanding but accessible, and are good resources for whatever position papers you may be called on to write in the future. The readings packet is available at Dollar Bill Copying, 611 Church St.

Final Grade

The final grade in the course will be based largely on the grades assigned to your diagnostic memos. Classroom participation and preparation for class will influence borderline grades. There will be no final exam.

Summary

Let me know how I can be helpful to you. My intention is that we create a non-threatening, upbeat setting where people can review and sort through their theories of how things get done in organizations and revise some portions of those theories while reaffirming other portions. The vehicle to do this is to focus on the topic of meaning and confusion. If all goes well, we should come out of the experience as more complicated and more appreciative citizens. I can't work magic. But I can listen.

If you have any questions, call me at 763-1339, contact me on e-mail which may be more reliable, drop by my office in 5201, or schedule an appointment.

TIMETABLE FOR OBHRM 700; WINTER 1995

1. Thurs. Jan 5: "Introduction to course."
    #(See Session 4 on Jan. 17 for next writing assignment).


2. Tues. Jan. 10: "Teamwork under pressure."

    A. Weick, K.E. (1990). The vulnerable system: An analysis of the Tenerife air disaster. Journal of Management, 16, 571-593.

    B. Pfeiffer, J. (June 1989). The secret of life at the limits: Cogs become big wheels. Smithsonian Magazine.
    #(See Session 4 on Jan. 17 for next writing assignment).


3. Thurs. Jan. 12: "The dynamics of pressure."

    A. Staw, B.M., Sandelands, L.E., and Dutton, J.E. (1981). Threat-rigidity effects in organizational behavior: a multilevel analysis. Administrative Science Quarterly, 26, 501-524.

    B. Weick, K.E. (1985). A stress analysis of future battlefields. In J.G. Hunt and J.D. Blair (Eds.), Leadership on the future battlefield (32-36). New York: Pergamon.
    #(See Session 4 on Jan. 17 for next writing assignment).


4. Tues. Jan 17: "Threats to reliability."

    #WRITING ASSIGNMENT DUE AT BEGINNING OF SESSION 4, Jan. 17.

    The purpose of this exercise is to link concepts with experience. The exercise has two parts. Part A is about hindsight. Part B is about foresight. In Part A, identify and describe briefly a work experience that actually happened to you, involving multiple people, that the Tenerife disaster makes you think of. Be sure to mention the parallels you see between the two events. What do you now understand about that personal event that had previously puzzled you? Explain.

    In Part B, imagine a plausible work event that could happen to you within the next three years that resembles the Tenerife disaster. Clarify the resemblance between the two events. Then describe how you would prepare yourself and

your associates for the possibility that his event might
occur. Use the readings and class discussions as major
inputs in your discussion of preparations you would make.

Use no more than 5 double-spaced pages for your
discussion.
[Note: The underlined words and phrases are things I
will look for in evaluating your paper. I have highlighted
these words in an effort to help you see what I am looking
for in your discussion. For example, I will pay attention
to whether you describe rather than merely name your
experience ("describe"), whether the experience you choose
has multiple actors just as a cockpit does ("multiple
people"), whether you show specifically how the experience
you discuss resembles Tenerife ("parallels"), etc. A good
paper is one that coheres, makes a clear point, and does so
using a rich set of resources].

------------------------
   A. Starbuck, W.H., and Milliken, F.J. (1988).
Challenger: Fine-tuning the odds until something breaks.
Journal of Management, 25, 319-340.

   B. Reason, J. (1990). The contribution of latent
human failures to the breakdown of complex systems.
Philosophical transactions of the Royal Society of London.
Series B, Vol. 327, pp. 475-484.


5.   Thurs. Jan. 19: "Interactive complexity."

   A. Henshel, R.L. (Unpublished manuscript).
Credibility and confidence loops in social prediction.

   B. Weick, K.E. (1979). Interdependence and
organizing. (This is chapter 3 from Weick, The social
psychology of organizing: Second Ed. Reading, Mass.:
Addison-Wesley, pp. 65-88).
   #(See Session 7 on Jan. 26 for next writing
assignment).


6.   Tues. Jan. 24: "A culture of reliability."

   A. Weick, K.E. (Winter 1987). Organizational culture
as a source of high reliability. California Management
Review, 29(2), 112-127.

   B. Husted, B.W. (1993). Reliability and the design
of ethical organizations: A rational systems approach.
Journal of Business Ethics, 12, 761-769.
   #(See Session 7 on Jan. 26 for next writing
assignment).

7.  Thurs. Jan. 26:  "Lessons from high reliability systems."

#WRITING ASSIGNMENT DUE AT BEGINNING OF SESSION 7, Jan. 26.

Assume that there is a thread of high reliability present in the functioning of every corporation. Thus, what we have examined during class sessions 2-7 applies somewhat, somehow to every setting in which you may find yourself and every setting you are asked to analyze. While all of this material about high reliability is still fresh in your mind, you need to articulate its lessons so you can refer back to them when diagnosing problems, designing preventive relationships, and trying to cope.

Choose some article from the Monday, January 23, 1995 issue of the Wall Street Journal and demonstrate your ability to analyze the event as if it had a <u>core set of dynamics similar</u> to those found in high reliability systems. If your analysis is correct, what <u>realistic remedies</u> does it suggest for the future of the company you analyzed? At the conclusion of your analysis <u>list</u> the ideas from our discussions of high reliability systems that you have used. This list is part of your conceptual tool kit for the future. <u>Attach</u> a copy of the WSJ article you analyzed, to your paper. Use no more than 5 double-spaced pages for your analysis.

------------------------

A. Perrow, C. (1981). Normal accident at three mile island. <u>Society</u>, <u>18</u>(5), 17-26.

---

8.  Tues. Jan. 31:  "Filters in sensemaking."

A. Starbuck, W.H., and Milliken, F.J. (1988). Executives' perceptual filters: What they notice and how they make sense. In D.C. Hambrick (Ed.), <u>The executive effect: Concepts and methods for studying top managers</u> (pp. 35-65). Greenwich, Conn.: JAI.

B. Gioia, D.A. (1992). Pinto fires and personal ethics: A script analysis of missed opportunities. <u>Journal of Business Ethics</u>, <u>11</u>, 379-389.

C. The pinto fire case. Unpublished manuscript.
#(See Session 12 on Feb. 14 for next writing assignment).

9.   Thurs. Feb. 2:   "Puzzles for sensemaking."

   A. Eisenberg, E.M. (1984). Ambiguity as strategy in organizational communication. <u>Communication Monographs</u>, <u>51</u>, 227-242.

   B. Daft, R.L., Lengel, R.H., and Trevino, L.K. (September 1987). Message equivocality, media selection, and manager performance: Implications for information systems. <u>MIS Quarterly</u>, 355-366.
   #(See Session 12 on Feb. 14 for next writing assignment.

10.  Tues. Feb. 7:   "Sensemaking as a retrospective process."

   A. Boland, R.J., Jr. (1984). Sense-making of accounting data as a technique of organizational diagnosis. <u>Management Science</u>, <u>30</u>(7), 868-882).
   #(See Session 12 on Feb. 14 for next writing assignment).

11.  Thurs. Feb. 9:   "The importance of managerial language."

   A. Daft, R.L., and Wiginton, J.C. (1979). Language and organization. <u>Academy of Management Review</u>, <u>4</u>(2), 179-191.

   B. Conger, J.A. (1991). Inspiring others: The language of leadership. <u>Academy of Management Executive</u>, <u>5</u>(1), 31-45).
   #(See Session 12 on Feb. 14 for next writing assignment).

12.  Tues. Feb. 14:   "The management of meaning."

   #WRITING ASSIGNMENT DUE AT BEGINNING OF SESSION 12, Feb. 14.

   The article by David Limerick on "Managers of Meaning" (Reading 12A) is a reasonable introduction to the idea that a sizable portion of managerial activity involves the management of meaning. However, there is more to say about the nature of managing meaning than Limerick has suggested. After the last 11 sessions, you are in a good position to suggest of what Limerick has missed. <u>Deepen, extend</u>, and/or <u>add to</u> the Limerick article more <u>significant</u> as well as <u>applicable</u> to a wider <u>range of settings</u> than it now is. Help Limerick make a better argument than he has. Be sure that your additions and extensions to Limerick's arguments are linked to things he said. This assignment is not about creating a new article. It is about improving an existing one. Use no more than 3 double-spaced pages for your extensions.

---------------------------
A. Limerick, D.C. (Spring 1990). Managers of meaning: From Bob Geldof's band aid to Australian CEOs. Organizational Dynamics, 18(4), 22-33.

---

13. Thurs. Feb. 16: "Mental models and meaning."

A. Weick, K.E. (1990). Cartographic myths in organizations. In A.S. Huff (Ed.), Managing strategic thought (pp. 1-9). Chidester: John Wiley.

B. Porac, J.F., Thomas, H., Baden-Fuller, C. (1989). Competitive groups as cognitive communities: The case of Scottish knitwear manufacturers. Journal of Management Studies, 26(4), 397-416.
#(See Session 17 on Mar. 9 for next writing assignment).


---------------------------
SPRING BREAK
---------------------------


14. Tues. Feb. 28: "Maps as mental models."

A. Barr, P.S., Stimpert, J.L., and Huff, A.S. (1992). Cognitive change, strategic action, and organizational renewal. Strategic Management Journal, 13, 15-36.
#(See Session 17 on Mar. 9 for next writing assignment).


15. Thurs. Mar. 2: "Culture and learning."

A. Cook, S.D.N., and Yanow, D. (1993). Culture and organizational learning. Journal of Management Inquiry, 2(4), 373-390.

B. Ulrich, D., Jick, T., and Von Glinow, M.A. (Autumn 1993). High-impact learning: Building and diffusing learning capability. Organizational Dynamics, 22(2), 52-66).
#(See Session 17 on Mar. 9 for next writing assignment).

16. Tues. Mar. 7: "Learning as a career plan."

    A. Bird, A. (1994). Careers as repositories of knowledge: A new perspective on boundaryless careers. <u>Journal of Organizational Behavior</u>, <u>15</u>, 325-344.
    #(See Session 17 on Mar. 9 for next writing assignment).

---

17. Thurs. Mar. 9: "Creating the environment."

    #WRITING ASSIGNMENT DUE AT BEGINNING OF SESSION 17, Mar. 9.

    The purpose of this exercise is to give you a vehicle to apply the ideas of learning and the boundaryless career to your own circumstances. Assume that you are Allan Bird (reading 16A), that you think like Allan Bird, and that Allan Bird has agreed to sit down and talk with you about <u>your own specific career objectives</u> and how your career itself might unfold. Write a <u>question-answer dialogue</u> in which you ask <u>questions</u> that really matter to you about your own career, and then write the <u>comments and answers</u> that Allan Bird would likely give you in each question. After you have asked and heard the answers to the questions that most concern you, discuss two things. First, what did you <u>learn</u> about your career plans that you didn't know before? Second, how do you <u>rate</u> Bird's advice? Where was he <u>helpful</u>? Where was he <u>unhelpful</u>? Use whatever number of pages you need to get some closure on this exercise. My evaluation of your work will NOT be influenced by length. It will however be influenced negatively by unfocused, wordy dialogue.

-------------------------

    A. Weick, K.E. (1977). Enactment processes in organizations. In B. Staw and G. Salancik (Eds.), <u>New directions in organizational behavior</u>. Chicago: St. Clair, pp. 267-300.

    B. Varadarajan, P.J., Clark, T., and Pride, W.M. (Winter 1992). Controlling the uncontrollable: Managing your market environment. <u>Sloan Management Review</u>, 39-47).
    #(See Session 22 on Mar. 28 for next writing assignment).

18. Tues. Mar. 14: "The enactment of strategy."

   A. Smircich, L., and Stubbart, C. (1985). Strategic management in an enacted world. <u>Academy of Management Review</u>, <u>10</u>(4), 724-736.

19. Thurs. Mar. 16: "The enactment of industry."

   A. Abolafia, M.Y., and Kilduff, M. (1988). Enacting market crisis: The social construction of a speculative bubble. <u>Administrative Science Quarterly</u>, <u>33</u>, 177-193.
   #(See Session 22 on Mar. 28 for next writing assignment).

---

20. Tues. Mar. 21: "Sensemaking as commitment."

   A. Weick, K.E. (1993). Sensemaking in organizations: Small structures with large consequences. In K. Murninghan (Ed.), <u>Social psychology in organizations: Advances in theory and research</u> (pp. 10-37). Englewood Cliffs, N.J.: Prentice-Hall.
   #(See Session 22 on Mar. 28 for next writing assignment).

21. Thurs. Mar. 23: "The escalation of commitment."

   A. Ross, J., and Staw, B.M. (1986). Expo 86: An escalation prototype. <u>Administrative Science Quarterly</u>, <u>31</u>, 274-297.
   #(See Session 22 on Mar. 28 for next writing assignment).

---

22. Tues. Mar. 28: "The struggle for alertness."

   #WRITING ASSIGNMENT DUE AT BEGINNING OF SESSION 22, Mar. 28.

   You need to read the analysis of the Mann Gulch disaster (reading 22A) <u>before</u> writing this paper. You have been called in by the Forest Service to advise them on how to improve the design of smokejumper crews. Prepare a set of recommendations for them in which you (1) <u>summarize</u> their <u>current</u> practices, (2) <u>describe</u> what <u>changes</u> you would make, (3) describe the <u>rationale</u> behind each of your recommended changes, and (4) discuss concrete steps the Forest Service should take to <u>begin to implement</u> your recommendations. Use no more than 5 double-spaced pages for your analysis.

------------------------

A. Weick, K.E. (1993). The collapse of sensemaking in organizations: The Mann Gulch Disaster. <u>Administrative Science Quarterly</u>, <u>38</u>, 628-652.

23. Thurs. Mar. 30: "The structure of improvisation."

A. Eisenberg, E.M. (1990). Jamming: Transcendence through organizing. <u>Communication Research</u>, <u>17</u>(2), 139-164.
#(See Session 26 on April 11 for last writing assignment).

24. Tues. April 4: "Improvisation and innovation."

A. Peters, T. (1990, 1991). Get innovative or get dead. Parts 1 and 2. <u>California Management Review</u>, Fall, 1990, pp. 9-26; and Winter, 1991, pp. 9-23.

B. Perry, L.T. (Spring 1991). Strategic improvising: How to formulate and implement competitive strategies in concert. <u>Organizational Dynamics</u>, <u>19</u>(4), 51-64.
#(See Session 26 on April 11 for last writing assignment).

25. Thurs. April 6: "Improvisation and planning."

A. Starbuck, W.H. (1993). Strategizing in the real world. <u>International Journal of Technology Management</u>, <u>8</u>(1/2), 77-85.

B. Brown, J.S., and Duguid, P. (1989). Learning and improvisation: Local sources of global innovation. Unpublished manuscript.
#(See Session 26 on April 11 for last writing assignment).

---

26. Tues. April 11: "Strategies of change."

#WRITING ASSIGNMENT DUE AT BEGINNING OF SESSION 26, April 11.

Describe the <u>10</u> most significant takeaways you have identified in <u>this course</u>. Describe each of the 10 in <u>sufficient detail</u> so that someone who is <u>unfamiliar</u> with this course could understand the <u>point</u> you are making and _why_ you think it is so important. If you work carefully on this paper it can serve as an initial set of guidelines and reminders for how to wade into quite varied problems and get a toehold to solve them. Use as many pages as you feel you need to complete this assignment.

-------------------------

     A. Weick, K.E. (1984). Small wins: Redefining the scale of social problems. _American Psychologist_, _39_(1), 40-49.

     B. Nemeth, C.J., and Staw, B.M. (1989). The tradeoffs of social control and innovation in groups and organizations. _Advances in experimental social psychology_. Vol. 22 (pp. 175-210). New York: Academic Press.

27. Thurs. April 13: "On changing sense and meaning."

     A. Martin, R. (Nov-Dec 1993). Changing the mind of the corporation. _Harvard Business Review_, 81-94.

28. Tues. April 18: TBA

# Renewing Organizations

## 660
### Course Overview
### Spring 1994

Rod White
Mary Crossan
Harry Lane

## Course Intent

This course explores how complex organizations develop then sustain high levels of performance. How do organizations learn to renew? How they maintain the performance of the current business, while enabling the members of that business to learn new behaviours that will be required for future success?   (See Figure 1)

The assumption underlying much of your program of studies to this point has been that this outcome is accomplished through some rational process; analysis precedes and directs action.  While this course does not reject analysis it does challenge the assertion that individual rationality and analysis is at the centre of ongoing renewal.  This course allows us to consider the role of "softer" things like: intuition, vision, emotion, teamwork, trust and  organizational learning processes.

We do not have all the answers to the question of renewal.  In fact we have many more  questions than answers.  Those of you seeking simple explanations and quick fixes should look elsewhere.  This course provides a context for each of us, individually and collectively to explore this phenomenon.  At one level it is philosophical and asks each of us to examine our core assumptions about management, the role of managers and the real function of organizations.  At another level it is experiential.  Several managers and consultants will be sharing their experiences with us.  And through the behavioral simulation we will have a shared experience which will allow us to examine the process of strategic change and renewal.  The simulation and other exercises also provide an opportunity for understanding individual, group and organizational processes and developing our skills in these areas.

The course is organized from the individual "up".  As indicated in the following summary outline, after a brief introduction, individual level phenomenon believed to be related to the process of renewal are considered.  Then we move to the group or team level and finally brief consideration is given to formal organizational mechanisms.  Following on, there is the behaviourial simulation; in order to help pull our thinking together.  And to complete the course there are several overview cases and discussions with managers in these organizations about their experiences.

This course does not train you for a specific job.   Hopefully it will give you insights into yourself and into organizations that will allow you to contribute more effectively to the renewal of those enterprises which you choose to become a member.

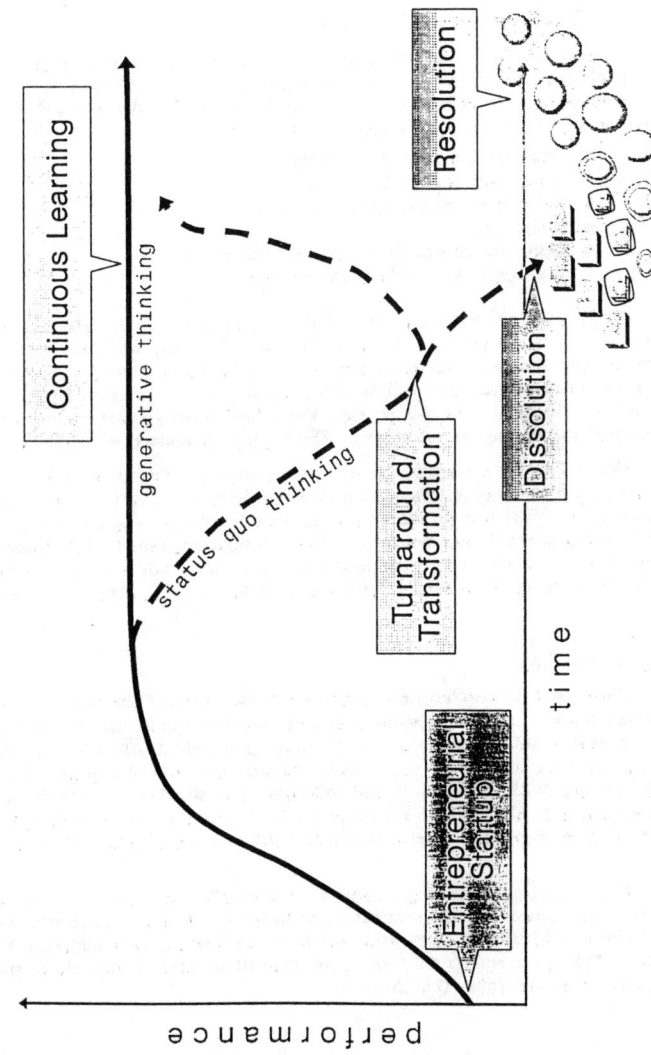

## Learning Method(s) and Philosophy

A basic tenet of the course is that effective learning requires engagement by all those involved in the process. The curriculum provides many opportunities for each of us to engage the process at a variety of different levels. Accordingly the course employs a mixture of learning methods. These include:

- cases (although relatively few),
- dialogue/lectures with readings,
- individual and group exercises,
- reflection,
- behavioural simulation and debrief, and
- managers sharing their experiences.

As part of the course you are required to keep a daily learning journal. A journal is sort of a diary with meaning attached. Not only what happened but what it meant to you. Really an aid in helping you to reflect and develop your understanding. At the end of the course you will be requested to write a synopsis of your learning experiences associated with this course. What (and how) you learned, and how you contributed to the learning of others. Having kept a journal will help in this activity.

When keeping a learning journal it is natural to address what you have learnt. But you may also want to think about how you learn best. What seems to motivate you to learn? What role do others play in your learning?; You in their learning? etc. Your learning journal need not be restricted to what happens in and around this course. You are encouraged to expand your "net" to include other interactions, even beyond the walls of the b-school. It is intended to be a broadly-based exercise in self-reflection.

## Grading Scheme

There isn't a predetermined grading scheme. One of our first tasks is to devise one based upon what is happening in and around the course. (Basic course activities are described in this document.) In the first class students are asked to come with a proposed grading scheme for the course. Assume our overall objective is to get as much learning (both individually and collectively) as possible. (If you feel there is a more appropriate objective please propose it.) A performance evaluation/formal reward system, a grading scheme that will assist in accomplishing this objective is needed.

Please develop a grading scheme for the course. As part of this assignment try to surface and consider what motivates *you* to learn. In addition to whatever scheme you devise also identify the key assumptions about learning that underpin your grading scheme. Whatever results from this process must be administratively feasible --keep that in mind as you think this through.

# RENEWING ORGANIZATIONS
## COURSE OVERVIEW

Spring 1994                                                                 Rod White

INTRODUCTION
1. Introduce Course and Develop a Grading Scheme
2. Honda (A) & (B) [384-049, 384-050] with readings
3. Duplitrace Gmbh [GM-366/IMD], with readings
4. Dialogue/Presentation Lecture: Hunters and Herders by D. Hurst with readings

IMPROVISATION & INTUITION
5. Improvisation Workshop by Second City
6. Individual Learning Styles and Human Dynamics with Susan Booth
7. Susan Booth -cont'd
8. Intuiting/Visioning by Bryan Smith, Innovation Associates with readings
   Dialogue/Lecture with "Visionary" Larry Morden, V-P Human Resources, Ault Foods
9. Reflection and Dialogue
10. Systems Thinking with Bryan Walton

INTERPRETATION & INTEGRATION
12. Cognitive Map Exercise -MBA1
13. Developing a Shared Map: People Express Simulation
14. People Express Simulation -cont'd
15. Lecture/Discussion: Management Teams and Organizational Renewal with readings

INSTITUTIONALIZATION
16. Nike (B) & (E4) case
17. GE Workout Experience -Jeff Gandz with readings
18. Dialogue on Institutionalization with readings
    Setup for behavioural simulation

PUTTING IT ALL TOGETHER
18. BEHAVIOURAL SIMULATION -FoodCorp
    March 17   4 - 9 p.m.
    March 18   8:30 a.m. - 4 p.m.
    March 19   9 a.m. - 4 p.m.
19. Reflect on Behavioural Simulation and dialogue
20. Teamwork and Kaizen: Bill Easdale -SVP Totota Motor Manufacturing Canada
21. Learning - Producing Tension with Jim Rush & Corey Jack IFL, BMo
23. General Feedback/Dialogue; Self-Renewal Reading

## Organizing Framework & Conceptual Underpinnings

The conceptual framework we are developing to help us come to grips with the phenomenon of learning and renewal in organizations is presented in Figure 2. Of course this framework is an abstraction of an exceedingly complex and complicated reality. It is a map of the territory; not the territory itself. To the extent it helps us to navigate the territory we use it. With this proviso we have employed it to aid in structuring the basic flow and development of the course. Could it be enhanced? Definitely! Will it be changed? Yes. Are your ideas welcomed? Certainly.

### Figure 2
### Learning/Renewal in Organizations
### Four Processes through Three Levels

| LEVEL | PROCESS | INPUTS/OUTCOMES |
|---|---|---|
| INDIVIDUAL | *INTUITING/ IMPROVISING* | Experiences/Expertise<br>Imagination/Lateral Thinking<br>Metaphors/Vision |
| | *INTERPRETING* | Language/Dialogue<br>Conversation/Storytelling<br>Shared Understandings/Mission |
| GROUP | *INTEGRATING* | Mutual Adjustment/Teamwork<br>Interactive Systems/Systems Thinking<br>Plans/Strategy |
| ORGANIZATION | *INSTITUTIONALIZING* | Routines<br>Diagnostic System<br>Rules & Procedures |

Source: White, R.E.; Rush, J.C.; Crossan, M.; Lane, H.; Western Business School, 1991/revised 1993.

The concepts developed center around the multi-level framework presented in Figure 2. The model recognizes that learning can be viewed as occurring at three levels: individual, group, and organization. The key learning processes at each level are: a) individual - *intuiting and interpreting*; b) group - *interpreting and integrating*; and c) organization - *integrating and institutionalizing*. The relationship between each of the levels and processes can be illustrated by example.

Take the story of Apple Computer[1]. By all accounts Steve Jobs (along with Stephen Wozniak) had the intuitive insights upon which Apple was founded. Based upon his own experiences and his perceptions of the myriad of events occurring in his "environment" Jobs perceived patterns and evolved certain images (e.g.; the personal computer as an appliance; one in every home) that guided Apple during its early years. He provided the insight and energy that were the genesis of Apple. But these insights were necessarily vague when it came to specific actions. As is often the case with intuitive visions there was necessarily considerable improvisation, "making it up as you go along", early in the process.

As insightful as Jobs was, he could not accomplish his vision alone. He needed to involve others. It was necessary to share this individual vision/image. Jobs could not specifically direct all the actions of his subordinates. The task quickly became too complex for that. He could not even know specifically what needed to be done. Indeed much of what was done was "improvised" by the players directly involved. And Jobs could not be involved in everything.

But how does one communicate something for which words do not (yet) exist. By using images and metaphors in a conversational or narrative way a visionary, like Jobs, can begin to communicate (and negotiate) their insight with others. Interestingly the development of words to describe the vision may sharpen it for the visionary as well. Shared experiences also help in the development of a shared understanding. Through this type of rich interactive, interpretive process a common language evolves. By way of this process one individual's intuitive insights can be shared with, and affected by others.

As a common language evolves people can have productive conversations. They can, through conversation (usually prior to action) identify areas of conflict and agreement. Through this process the work groups evolve a shared understanding or interpretation of their task domain. And thus interpreting flows into integrating. As work groups evolve a common language and a shared understanding of their task domain they quite naturally, as a part of this process, negotiate actions. Since the actions of each individual are based upon a shared understanding of the situation there should be a certain coherence, or pattern to the set of actions (i.e., the strategy) taken by the group.

But what is the context within which shared understandings and negotiated actions occur. Early in an organizations life, as was the case with Apple, these processes are largely informal and spontaneous. But as organizations get larger, as more people are involved informal interactions do not suffice. What had happened more or less spontaneously must now be arranged. What had been an informal discussion over coffee about the future of the company becomes a formal strategic planning system. Simons [1990] calls these types of formal systems "interactive systems".

---

[1] This description is not represented to be an accurate case history. It is a "story" used to help illustrate the conceptual model and is not being employed as empirical support for the model.

The organization as a collection of individuals naturally outgrows its ability to interpret, integrate and take concerted action, given the informal interactions in place. Other organizational needs also emerge; the need to produce and perform, to manage the day-to-day routine. Many systems that were originally interactive become diagnostic; they are used to exploit the current understanding of the business rather than to evolve new and different understandings.

In the Apple situation John Scully was brought in to provide the needed structure, systems and other formal mechanisms. Individual and collective learning became institutionalized (some might say fossilized) and could be more systematically exploited. The institutionalization contributed to more efficient operations, enabling Apple to better deliver on Jobs' original vision. It also may have hindered the organization's ability to renew itself by intuiting, interpreting and integrating new experiences and events. Unable to realize his next vision within Apple, Steve Jobs left to start a new organization, appropriately called NeXT.

Essentially, the process of institutionalization embeds past learning into the organization. It also creates a context through which subsequent events are interpreted. This context may facilitate and/or impede the organization's ability to interpret and respond to the rapidly changing environment. In entrepreneurial start-up situations, like Apple, there is originally little or no learning embedded in the formal organization, indeed there is little formal organization. No unlearning needs to occur. Established organization do have past learning embedded within them. As such learning and renewal in these situations must deal with this difference and as such confronts some different challenges.

From a more theoretical perspective the rationale for viewing organizational renewal and learning as involving three levels is based on the notion that at some basic plane organizations learn through their individual members. Individuals are, of course imbedded in a social and institutional context. But we have to tap into this process somewhere. By explicitly recognizing the role of individuals in this process, we avoid reifying organizations; ascribing to an abstraction powers of thought and behavior that reside with its members. Therefore, individual learning is a fundamental building block for understanding learning within organizations.

But as already recognized, individuals do not learn in isolation. They learn within a context. In organizations an important part of this context is the other members or group of individuals in the organizational community. Learning is necessarily a social or community phenomenon [Seely Brown and Duguid, 1991]. Understanding the process through which groups learn, how individual schema are integrated into shared understandings, and guide negotiated actions, the role of narratives and stories in this process are important. Individuals within groups can through an integrating process, evolve shared understandings that through conversation and negotiations guide the members in taking coherent and sophisticated actions.

Established, complex organizations are more than ad hoc communities, or collections of individuals. Relationships are structured. Individual learning and shared understandings developed by groups become, over time, institutionalized as organization artifacts: formal relationships; structure and systems; and often unstated cultural assumptions. Once established, these artifacts become part of the context that affects learning within the organization.

This view suggests that learning is an individual phenomenon, and at its most basic we believe it is. But all learning occurs within a context, and the group and "organizational" contexts can affect and be affected by what is learnt. When the concept of learning is extended into an organizational setting it is helpful to conceive of learning within organizations occurring over (at least) three levels. Returning to Figure 2, this conception gives rise to four associated processes: intuiting, interpreting, integrating and institutionalizing. Intuiting and interpreting occur at the individual level; interpreting and integrating at the group level; and integrating and institutionalizing are organizational aspects. Although the framework is depicted in a hierarchical fashion, there are many feedback loops amongst the levels emphasizing the recursive and embedded nature of the phenomenon.

## Extra-Cirricular Reading List

One objective of this course is to encourage you to think broadly about management and organizations, to become reflective practitioners. In trying to make sense of our world books can provide a wonderful stimulus. However, books, even the best, do not deliver answers. You, the reader, must map the ideas presented onto your own experience and understanding. But books can be very efficient thought provokers; at least you do not need to re-invent the idea from "scratch".

From the following list of books please read at least one during the course of the term. Write a brief report on what insights it provided you, what new understanding did it help to create. If you would like to read a book not on the list please do so. (That's one way we add to the list.) Just talk over your choice with a faculty person beforehand.

Schön, D.; <u>Organizational Learning -a theory of action perspective</u>. Reading, MA: Addison-Wesley Publishing Co., 1978.

Argyris, C.; <u>Knowledge for Action -a guide for overcoming barriers to organizational change</u>. San Francisco: Jossey-Bass Publishers, 1993.

Beer, M.; Eisenstat, R.A.; Spector, B.; <u>The Critical Path to Corporate Renewal</u>. Boston: Harvard Business School Press, 1990.

Blake, R.R.; Mouton, J.S.; Allen, R.L.; <u>Spectacular Teamwork -how to develop the leadership skill for team success</u>. New York: John Wiley & Sons, 1987.

Briggs, J.; Peat, F.D.; Turbulent Mirror -an illustrated guide to chaos theory and the science of wholeness. New York: Harper & Row, Publishers, 1990.

Brookfield, S.D.; <u>Developing Critical Thinkers</u>. San Francisco: Jossey-Bass Publishers, 1988.

Buzan, T.; <u>The Mind Map Book</u>. London: BBC Books, 1993.

Cohen, M.D.; March, J.G.; <u>Leadership and Ambiguity</u>. Boston: Harvard Business School Press, 1974, 1986.

Conger; J.A. <u>Learning to Lead -the art of transforming managers into leaders</u>. San Francisco: Jossey-Bass Publishers, 1992.

Frank, R. H.; <u>Passions within Reason -the strategic role of the emotions</u>. New York: Norton, 1988.

Gardner, J.; <u>Leadership</u>

Gardner, H.; <u>Creating Minds: An anatomy of creativity seen through the lives of Freud, Einstein, Picasso, Stravinsky, Eliot, Graham and Gandhi</u>. New York: Basic Books, 1993.

Hampden-Turner, C.; <u>Maps of the Mind</u>. New York: Collier Books, 1981.

Hampden-Turner, C.; <u>Charting the Corporate Mind -graphic solutions to business conflict</u>. New York: The Free Press, 1990.

Hofstader, D.R.; <u>Metamagical Thema -questing for the essence of mind and pattern</u>. New York: Basic Books, 1985.

Handy, C.; <u>The Age of Unreason</u>. Boston: Harvard Business School Press, 1989.

Kuhn, R.L.; <u>Handbook for Creative and Innovative Managers</u>. New York: McGraw-Hill Book Company, 1988.

Kotter, J.P.; Heskett, J.L.; <u>Corporate Culture and Performance</u>. New York: The Free Press, 1992.

Lightman, A.; <u>Einstein's Dreams</u>. New York: Warner Books, 1993.

Miller, D.; <u>The Icarus Paradox -how exceptional companies bring about their downfall</u>. Harper Business, 1990.

Morgan, G.; <u>Riding the Waves of Change -developing managerial competences for a turbulent world</u>. San Francisco: Jossey-Bass Publishers, 1988.

Morgan, G.; <u>Imaginization --the art of creative management</u>. Newbury Park, CA.: Sage Publications, 1993.

Peters, T. J.; <u>Thriving on Chaos -handbook for a management revolution</u>. New York: Random House, 1987.

Quinn, J.B.; <u>Intelligent Enterprise -a new paradigm for a new era</u>. New York: The Free Press, 1992.

Quinn, R.E.; <u>Beyond Rational Management -mastering the paradoxes of competing demands of high performance</u>. San Francisco: Jossey-Bass Publishers, 1988.

Pascale, R.T.; <u>Managing on the Edge -how the smartest companies use conflict to stay ahead</u>. New York: Simon and Schuster, 1990.

Senge, P. M.; <u>The Fifth Discipline: the art & practice of the learning organization</u>. New York: Doubleday/Currency, 1990.

Schön, D.; The Reflective Practitioner -how professionals think in action. New York: Basic Books, 1983.

Schön, D.; <u>Educating the Reflective Practitioner -toward a new design for teaching and learning in the professions</u>. San Francisco: Jossey-Bass, 1987.

Sculley, J.; <u>Odyssey: Pepsi to Apple --a journey of adventure, ideas and the future</u>. New York: Harper & Row, Inc., 1987.

Smith, D.K.; <u>Fumbling the Future: how Xerox invented then ignored, the first personal computer</u>. New York: W. Morrow, 1988.

Stacey, R.; <u>Managing the Unknowable: strategic boundaries between order and chaos in organizations</u>. San Francisco: Jossey-Bass Publishers, 1992.

Strasser, J.B.; Becklund, L.; <u>SWOOSH --the unauthorized story of Nike and the men who played there</u>. New York: Harper Business, 1991, 1993.

Steward, I.; <u>Does God Play Dice -the mathematics of chaos</u>. London: Penguin Books, 1990.

Tichy, N.; Sherman, S.; <u>Control Your Destiny or Someone Else Will -how Jack Welch is making General Electric the world's most competitive corporation</u>. New York: Currency, Doubleday, 1993

Tjosvold, D.W.; Tjosvold, M.M.; <u>Leading the Team Organization -how to create an enduring competitive advantage</u>. New York: Lexington Books, 1991.

If doing a book interpretation does not appeal to you and you are computer capable (Macintosh) you might want to do a small project on system mapping/thinking. This could be tied into your policy report company, or any other real world organization you wish to better understand from a systems perspective.

February 28, 1995

THE UNIVERSITY OF CHICAGO

GRADUATE SCHOOL OF BUSINESS

Business 468-81   THEORIES OF LEADERSHIP                Spring 1995

Marvin Zonis - Rosenwald 201C                T.A. David Holt
for appointments:  call Marda Gross              493-8651
                   2-8753

WEEK I.    LEADERS AND LEADERSHIP

           ARE THEY NECESSARY?
           HOW WOULD YOU KNOW?

SONJA M. HUNT
Title: THE ROLE OF LEADERSHIP IN THE CONSTRUCTION OF REALTY (CHAPTER 8)
From: LEADERSHIP: MULTIDISCIPLINARY PERSPECTIVES, B. Kellerman (ed.)
PRENTICE-HALL INCORPORATED
Edition: 1984
Pages: 157-178   (#10014)

JAMES R. MEINDL, SANFORD B. EHRLICH
Title:    THE ROMANCE OF LEADERSHIP AND THE EVALUATION OF ORGANIZATIONAL
PERFORMANCE
ACADEMY OF MANAGEMENT JOURNAL
Vol. (MARCH) 1987
Pages 91-107

H. EDWARD WRAPP
Title: GOOD MANAGERS DON'T MAKE POLICY DECISIONS
HARVARD BUSINESS REVIEW
Vol. (SEP) 1967
Pages: 91-99    (#34)

STANLEY LIEBERSON, JAMES F. O'CONNOR
Title: LEADERSHIP AND ORGANIZATIONAL PERFORMANCE: A STUDY OF LARGE
CORPORATIONS
AMERICAN SOCIOLOGICAL REVIEW Vol. 37(2) 1972
Pages: 117-129   (#1808)

WEEK II. TRANSACTIONS AND TRANSFORMATIONS

MARTIN M. CHEMERS
Title: THE SOCIAL, ORGANIZATIONAL, AND CULTURAL CONTEXT OF EFFECTIVE LEADERSHIP (CHAPTER 5)
From: LEADERSHIP: MULTIDISCIPLINARY PERSPECTIVES, B. Kellerman (ed.)
PRENTICE-HALL INCORPORATED
Edition: 1984
Pages: 91-112   (#10011)

KARL W. KUHNERT AND PHILIP LEWIS
Title: TRANSACTIONAL AND TRANSFORMATIONAL LEADERSHIP: A CONTRUCTIVE/DEVELOPMENTAL ANALYSIS
ACADEMY OF MANAGEMENT REVIEW, 1987, Vol. 12, No. 4
Pages: 648-656   (#1930)

BERNARD M. BASS
Title: FROM TRANSACTIONAL TO TRANSFORMATIONAL LEADERSHIP: LEARNING TO SHARE THE VISION
ORGANIZATIONAL DYNAMICS
Pages: 19-31   (#1931)

MICHAEL L. TUSHMAN, WILLIAM H. NEWMAN, ELAINE ROMANELLI
Title: CONVERGENCE AND UPHEAVAL: MANAGING THE UNSTEADY PACE OF ORGANIZATIONAL EVOLUTION
CALIFORNIA MANAGEMENT REVIEW, Vol. XXIX, No. 1, Fall 1986
THE REGENTS OF THE UNIVERSITY OF CALIFORNIA
Pages: 29-44   (#1932)

DAVID A. NADLER, MICHAEL L. TUSHMAN
Title: ORGANIZATIONAL FRAME BENDING: PRINCIPLES FOR MANAGING REORIENTATION
THE ACADEMY OF MANAGEMENT EXECUTIVE, 1989, Vol. III, No. 3
Pages: 194-204   (#1933)

WEEK III. THE ORGANIZATION AND THE INDIVIDUAL

OTTO F. KERNBERG
Title: LEADERSHIP AND ORGANIZATIONAL FUNCTIONING: ORGANIZATIONAL REGRESSION
from: INTERNATIONAL JOURNAL OF GROUP PSYCHOTHERAPY, Vol. 28 No. 1
Heldref Publications, 1975.
Pages: 3-25   (#10005)

JEROME A. WINER, M.D. WITH THOMAS JOBE, M.D. AND CARLTON FERRONO
Title: TOWARD A PSYCHOANALYTIC THEORY OF THE CHARISMATIC RELATIONSHIP
From: THE ANNUAL OF PSYCHOANALYSIS, vol. XII/XIII, January 1984.
INTERNATIONAL UNIVERSITIES PRESS, INC.

Pages: 155-175  (#1799)

CHARLES CAMIC
Title: CHARISMA: IT'S VARIETIES, PRECONDITIONS AND CONSEQUENCES
JOURNAL OF SOCIOLOGICAL INQUIRY, Vol. 50, 1980
Pages: 5-23  (#1935)

ABRAHAM ZALEZNIK
Title: CHARISMATIC AND CONSENSUS LEADERS: A PSYCHOLOGICAL COMPARISON
Edition: 1974
Pages: 222-238  Total Pages: 7
Notes: File copy from Manfred Kets de Vries (ed.), THE IRRATIONAL
EXECUTIVE, International Universities Press, pp. 112-131.  (#1297)


WEEK IV.  NARCISSISM AND SELF OBJECTS

HEINZ KOHUT
Title: ON LEADERSHIP (1969-70) (CHAPTER 2)
From: SELF PSYCHOLOGY AND THE HUMANITIES
W.W. NORTON & COMPANY, INCORPORATED
Edition: 1985
Pages: 51-72  (#914)

RONALD R. LEE AND J. COLBY MARTIN
From: PSYCHOTHERAPY AFTER KOHUT: A TEXTBOOK OF SELF PSYCHOLOGY
THE ANALYTIC PRESS, HILLSDALE, N.J., 1991
Chapters 9-13
Pages: 105-166  (#3926, #5604, #4538, #7001, #4110)


WEEK V.    BUSINESS LEADERSHIP:   CHARISMA AND NON-CHARISMA IN ACTION


GARRY WILLS
Title: CERTAIN TRUMPETS THE CALL OF LEADERS
SIMON & SCHUSTER
Edition: 1994
Pages: 11-22, 117-131

NICOLE WOOLSAY BIGGART
Title: CHARISMATIC CAPITALISM. DIRECT SELLING ORGANIZATIONS IN AMERICA
From: ADMINISTRATIVE SCIENCE QUARTERLY
Vol. (DECEMBER) 1990
Pages: 729-731

RICHARD E. HATTWICK
Title: MARY KAY ASH
From: JOURNAL OF BEHAVIORAL ECONOMICS
Vol. (WINTER) 1987
Pages: 61-70

JOHN P. KOTTER, JOHN STENGREVICS
Title: MARY KAY COSMETICS, INC.
HARVARD BUSINESS SCHOOL
1981
Pages: 1-13
Notes: HBS Case 9-481-126


WEEK VI.   POLITICAL LEADERSHIP: CHAIRMAN MAO


LI ZHISUI
Title:   THE DEATH OF MAO
THE PRIVATE LIFE OF CHAIRMAN MAO
RANDOM HOUSE, INC.
Edition: 1994
Pages: 2-30, 425-429, 440-443, 452-463, 464-477, 482-487, 499-503, 528-532


WEEK VII.   MILITARY-POLITICAL LEADERSHIP: ADOLF HITLER


WALTER C. LANGER
THE MIND OF ADOLF HITLER
BASIC BOOKS, INC.
Edition: 1972
Pages: iv.-306
        (#2253, #2274, #2300, #2750, #2874, #2984, #3088, #3527)


WEEK VIII.   ILLNESS AND LEADERSHIP


JERROLD M. POST AND ROBERT S. ROBINS
Title: WHEN ILLNESS STRIKES THE LEADER
YALE UNIVERSITY PRESS
Edition: 1993
Chapters:   1,2,3,6,7


WEEK IX.   FEMINIST PERSPECTIVES


SUSAN J. CARROLL
Title: FEMINIST SCHOLARSHIP ON POLITICAL LEADERSHIP (CHAPTER 7)
From: LEADERSHIP: MULTIDISCIPLINARY PERSPECTIVES, B. Kellerman, (ed.)

4

PRENTICE-HALL INCORPORATED
Edition: 1984
Pages: 139-156   (#10013)

JUDY B. ROSENER
Title: WAYS WOMEN LEAD
HARVARD BUSINESS REVIEW
Vol. (N/D) 1990
Pages: 119-125
Notes: HBR #90608   (#912)

JOHN HOLUSHA
Title: GRACE PASTIAK'S 'WEB OF INCLUSION'
From: THE NEW YORK TIMES, SUNDAY MAY 5, 1991   (#1800)


WEEK X. LEADERSHIP: THE CHALLENGES


JOHN P. KOTTER
Title: LEADERS IN PROFILE: THE PERSONAL REQUIREMENTS NEEDED TO PROVIDE
EFFECTIVE LEADERSHIP TODAY (CHAPTER 3)
From:  THE LEADERSHIP FACTOR
FREE PRESS
Edition: 1988
Pages: 28-40   (#10018)

ABRAM T. COLLIER
Title: BUSINESS LEADERSHIP AND A CREATIVE SOCIETY
HARVARD BUSINESS REVIEW
Vol. (J/F) 1968
Pages: 418-435   (#913)

GARRY WILLS
Title: REVOLUTION IN STYLE
From: LINCOLN AT GETTSYSBURG: THE WORDS THAT REMADE AMERICA
Pages: 148-175   (#800)